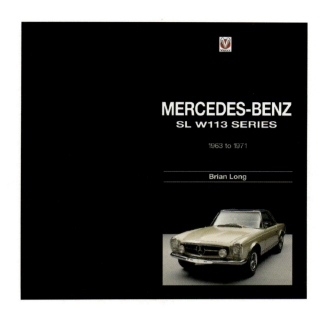

Also from Veloce –

Speedpro Series
4-cylinder Engine – How to Blueprint & Build a Short Block For High Performance (Hammill)
Alfa Romeo DOHC High-performance Manual (Kartalamakis)
Alfa Romeo V6 Engine High-performance Manual (Kartalamakis)
BMC 998cc A-series Engine – How to Power Tune (Hammill)
1275cc A-series High-performance Manual (Hammill)
Camshafts – How to Choose & Time Them For Maximum Power (Hammill)
Competition Car Datalogging Manual, The (Templeman)
Cylinder Heads – How to Build, Modify & Power Tune Updated & Revised Edition (Burgess & Gollan)
Distributor-type Ignition Systems – How to Build & Power Tune New 3rd Edition (Hammill)
Fast Road Car – How to Plan and Build Revised & Updated Colour New Edition (Stapleton)
Ford SOHC 'Pinto' & Sierra Cosworth DOHC Engines – How to Power Tune Updated & Enlarged Edition (Hammill)
Ford V8 – How to Power Tune Small Block Engines (Hammill)
Harley-Davidson Evolution Engines – How to Build & Power Tune (Hammill)
Holley Carburetors – How to Build & Power Tune Revised & Updated Edition (Hammill)
Honda Civic Type R, The – High-Performance Manual (Cowland & Clifford)
Jaguar XK Engines – How to Power Tune Revised & Updated Colour Edition (Hammill)
Land Rover Discovery, Defender & Range Rover – How to Modify Coil Sprung Models for High Performance & Off-Road Action (Hosier)
MG Midget & Austin-Healey Sprite – How to Power Tune New 3rd Edition (Stapleton)
MGB 4-cylinder Engine – How to Power Tune (Burgess)
MGB V8 Power – How to Give Your, Third Colour Edition (Williams)
MGB, MGC & MGB V8 – How to Improve New 2nd Edition (Williams)
Mini Engines – How to Power Tune On a Small Budget Colour Edition (Hammill)
Motorcycle-engined Racing Car – How to Build (Pashley)
Motorsport – Getting Started in (Collins)
Nissan GT-R High-performance Manual, The (Gorodji)
Nitrous Oxide High-performance Manual, The (Langfield)
Race & Trackday Driving Techniques (Hornsey)
Rover V8 Engines – How to Power Tune (Hammill)
Secrets of Speed – Today's techniques for 4-stroke engine blueprinting & tuning (Swager)
Sportscar & Kitcar Suspension & Brakes – How to Build & Modify Revised 3rd Edition (Hammill)
SU Carburettor High-performance Manual (Hammill)
Successful Low-Cost Rally Car, How to Build a (Young)
Suzuki 4x4 – How to Modify For Serious Off-road Action (Richardson)
Tiger Avon Sportscar – How to Build Your Own Updated & Revised 2nd Edition (Dudley)
TR2, 3 & TR4 – How to Improve (Williams)
TR5, 250 & TR6 – How to Improve (Williams)
TR7 & TR8 – How to Improve (Williams)
V8 Engine – How to Build a Short Block For High Performance (Hammill)
Volkswagen Beetle Suspension, Brakes & Chassis – How to Modify For High Performance – Updated & Enlarged New Edition (Hale)
Weber DCOE, & Dellorto DHLA Carburetors – How to Build & Power Tune 3rd Edition (Hammill)

Those Were The Days ... Series
Alpine Trials & Rallies 1910-1973 (Pfundner)
American 'Independent' Automakers – AMC to Willys 1945 to 1960 (Mort)
American Station Wagons – The Golden Era 1950-1975 (Mort)
American Trucks of the 1950s (Mort)
American Trucks of the 1960s (Mort)
American Woodies 1928-1953 (Mort)
Anglo-American Cars from the 1930s to the 1970s (Mort)
Austerity Motoring (Bobbitt)
Austins, The last real (Peck)
Brighton National Speed Trials (Gardiner)
British Drag Racing – The Early Years (Pettitt)
British Lorries of the 1950s (Bobbitt)
British Lorries of the 1960s (Bobbitt)
British Touring Car Racing (Collins)
British Police Cars (Walker)
British Woodies (Peck)
Café Racer Phenomenon, The (Walker)
Drag Bike Racing in Britain – From the mid '60s to the mid '80s (Lee)
Dune Buggy Phenomenon, The (Hale)
Dune Buggy Phenomenon Volume 2, The (Hale)
Endurance Racing at Silverstone in the 1970s & 1980s (Parker)
Hot Rod & Stock Car Racing in Britain in the 1980s (Neil)
Last Real Austins 1946-1959, The (Peck)
MG's Abingdon Factory (Moylan)
Motor Racing at Brands Hatch in the Seventies (Parker)
Motor Racing at Brands Hatch in the Eighties (Parker)
Motor Racing at Crystal Palace (Collins)
Motor Racing at Goodwood in the Sixties (Gardiner)
Motor Racing at Nassau in the 1950s & 1960s (O'Neil)
Motor Racing at Oulton Park in the 1960s (McFadyen)
Motor Racing at Oulton Park in the 1970s (McFadyen)
Superprix – The Story of Birmingham Motor Race (Page & Collins)
Three Wheelers (Bobbitt)

Truckmakers
DAF Trucks since 1949 (Peck)

Enthusiast's Restoration Manual Series
Citroën 2CV, How to Restore (Porter)
Classic Car Bodywork, How to Restore (Thaddeus)
Classic British Car Electrical Systems (Astley)
Classic Car Electrics (Thaddeus)
Classic Cars, How to Paint (Thaddeus)
Jaguar E-type (Crespin)
Reliant Regal, How to Restore (Payne)
Triumph TR2, 3, 3A, 4 & 4A, How to Restore (Williams)
Triumph TR5/250 & 6, How to Restore (Williams)
Triumph TR7/8, How to Restore (Williams)
Volkswagen Beetle, How to Restore (Tyler)
VW Bay Window Bus (Paxton)
Yamaha FS1-E, How to Restore (Watts)

Essential Buyer's Guide Series
Alfa GT (Booker)
Alfa Romeo Spider Giulia (Booker & Talbott)
Austin Seven (Barker)
BMW GS (Henshaw)
BSA Bantam (Henshaw)
BSA 500 & 650 Twins (Henshaw)
Citroën 2CV (Paxton)
Citroën ID & DS (Heilig)
Corvette C2 1963-1967 (Falconer)
Fiat 500 & 600 (Bobbitt)
Ford Capri (Paxton)
Harley-Davidson Big Twins (Henshaw)
Hinckley Triumph triples & fours 750, 900, 955, 1000, 1050, 1200 – 1991-2009 (Henshaw)
Honda CBR600 (Henshaw)
Honda FireBlade (Henshaw)
Honda SOHC fours 1969-1984 (Henshaw)
Jaguar E-type 3.8 & 4.2-litre (Crespin)
Jaguar E-type V12 5.3-litre (Crespin)
Jaguar XJ 1995-2003 (Crespin)
Jaguar XK8 (1996-2005) (Thorley)
Jaguar/Daimler XJ6, XJ12 & Sovereign (Crespin)
Jaguar/Daimler XJ40 (Crespin)
Jaguar Mk2 (1955 to 1969) (Thorley)
Jaguar XJ-S (Crespin)
Land Rover Series I, II & IIA (Thurman)
MGB & MGB GT (Williams)
Mercedes-Benz 280SL-560DSL Roadsters (Bass)
Mercedes-Benz 'Pagoda' 230SL, 250SL & 280SL Roadsters & Coupés (Bass)
MG Midget & A-H Sprite (Horler)
MG TD, TF & TF1500 (Jones)
Mini (Paxton)
Morris Minor & 1000 (Newell)
Norton Commando (Henshaw)
Peugeot 205 GTi (Blackburn)
Porsche 911 (964) (Streather)
Porsche 911 (993) (Streather)
Porsche 911 (996) (Streather)
Porsche 911 SC (Streather)
Porsche 928 (Hemmings)
Rolls-Royce Silver Shadow & Bentley T-Series (Bobbitt)
Subaru Impreza (Hobbs)
Triumph Bonneville (Henshaw)
Triumph Spitfire & GT6
Triumph Stag (Mort & Fox)
Triumph TR6 (Williams)
Triumph TR7 & TR8 (Williams)
Vespa Scooters – Classic 2-stroke models 1960-2008 (Paxton)
VW Beetle (Cservenka & Copping)
VW Bus (Cservenka & Copping)
VW Golf GTI (Cservenka & Copping)

Auto-Graphics Series
Fiat-based Abarths (Sparrow)
Jaguar MKI & II Saloons (Sparrow)
Lambretta Li Series Scooters (Sparrow)

Rally Giants Series
Audi Quattro (Robson)
Austin Healey 100-6 & 3000 (Robson)
Fiat 131 Abarth (Robson)
Ford Escort MkI (Robson)
Ford Escort RS Cosworth & World Rally Car (Robson)
Ford Escort RS1800 (Robson)
Lancia Delta 4WD/Integrale (Robson)
Lancia Stratos (Robson)
Mini Cooper/Mini Cooper S (Robson)
Peugeot 205 T16 (Robson)
Saab 96 & V4 (Robson)
Subaru Impreza (Robson)
Toyota Celica GT4 (Robson)

WSC Giants
Ferrari 312P & 312PB (Collins & McDonough)
Gulf-Mirage 1967 to 1982 (McDonough)
Matra Sports Cars – MS620, 630, 650, 660 & 670 – 1966 to 1974 (McDonough)

Biographies
André Lefebvre, and the cars he created at Voisin and Citroën (Beck)
Cliff Allison, The Official Biography of – From the Fells to Ferrari (Gauld)
Edward Turner: The Man Behind the Motorcycles (Clew)
Jack Sears, The Official Biography of – Gentleman Jack (Gauld)
Jim Redman – 6 Times World Motorcycle Champion: The Autobiography (Redman)
John Chatham – 'Mr Big Healey' – The Official Biography (Burr)
Pat Moss Carlsson Story, The – Harnessing Horsepower (Turner)
Virgil Exner – Visioneer: The Official Biography of Virgil M Exner Designer Extraordinaire (Grist)

General
1½-litre GP Racing 1961-1965 (Whitelock)
AC Two-litre Saloons & Buckland Sportscars (Archibald)
Alfa Romeo Giulia Coupé GT & GTA (Tipler)
Alfa Romeo Montreal – The dream car that came true (Taylor)
Alfa Romeo Montreal – The Essential Companion (Taylor)
Alfa Tipo 33 (McDonough & Collins)
Alpine & Renault – The Development of the Revolutionary Turbo F1 Car 1968 to 1979 (Smith)
Alpine & Renault – The Sports Prototypes 1963 to 1969 (Smith)
Alpine & Renault – The Sports Prototypes 1973 to 1978 (Smith)
Anatomy of the Works Minis (Moylan)
Armstrong-Siddeley (Smith)
Art Deco and British Car Design (Down)
Autodrome (Collins & Ireland)
Autodrome 2 (Collins & Ireland)
Automotive A-Z, Lane's Dictionary of Automotive Terms (Lane)
Automotive Mascots (Kay & Springate)
Bahamas Speed Weeks, The (O'Neil)
Bentley Continental, Corniche and Azure (Bennett)
Bentley MkVI, Rolls-Royce Silver Wraith, Dawn & Cloud/Bentley R & S-Series (Nutland)
Bluebird CN7 (Stevens)
BMC Competitions Department Secrets (Turner, Chambers & Browning)
BMW 5-Series (Cranswick)
BMW Z-Cars (Taylor)
BMW Boxer Twins 1970-1995 Bible, The (Falloon)
BMW Custom Motorcycles – Choppers, Cruisers, Bobbers, Trikes & Quads (Cloesen)
Britains Farm Model Balers & Combines 1967-2007, Pocket Guide to (Pullen)
Britains Farm Model & Toy Tractors 1998-2008, Pocket Guide to (Pullen)
Britains Toy Models Catalogues 1970-1979 (Pullen)
British 250cc Racing Motorcycles (Pereira)
British at Indianapolis, The (Wagstaff)
British Cars, The Complete Catalogue of, 1895-1975 (Culshaw & Horrobin)
BRM – A Mechanic's Tale (Salmon)
BRM V16 (Ludvigsen)
BSA Bantam Bible, The (Henshaw)
Bugatti Type 40 (Price)
Bugatti 46/50 Updated Edition (Price & Arbey)
Bugatti T44 & T49 (Price & Arbey)
Bugatti 57 2nd Edition (Price)
Caravans, The Illustrated History 1919-1959 (Jenkinson)
Caravans, The Illustrated History From 1960 (Jenkinson)
Caring for your 50cc Scooter – Your guide to maintenance & safety checks (Fry)
Carrera Panamericana, La (Tipler)
Chrysler 300 – America's Most Powerful Car 2nd Edition (Ackerson)
Chrysler PT Cruiser (Ackerson)
Citroën DS (Bobbitt)
Classic British Car Electrical Systems (Astley)
Cobra – The Real Thing! (Legate)
Concept Cars, How to illustrate and design (Dewey)
Cortina – Ford's Bestseller (Robson)
Coventry Climax Racing Engines (Hammill)
Daily Mirror 1970 World Cup Rally 40, The (Robson)
Daimler SP250 New Edition (Long)
Datsun Fairlady Roadster to 280ZX – The Z-Car Story (Long)
Diecast Toy Cars of the 1950s & 1960s (Ralston)
Dino – The V6 Ferrari (Long)
Dodge Challenger & Plymouth Barracuda (Grist)
Dodge Charger – Enduring Thunder (Ackerson)
Dodge Dynamite! (Grist)
Draw & Paint Cars – How to (Gardiner)
Drive on the Wild Side, A – 20 Extreme Driving Adventures From Around the World (Weaver)
Ducati 750 Bible, The (Falloon)
Ducati 750 SS 'round-case' 1974, The Book of the (Falloon)
Ducati 860, 900 and Mille Bible, The (Falloon)
Ducati Monster Bible, The (Falloon)
Dune Buggy, Building A – The Essential Manual (Shakespeare)
Dune Buggy Files (Hale)
Dune Buggy Handbook (Hale)
East German Motor Vehicles in Pictures (Suhr/Weinreich)
Efficient Driver's Handbook, The (Moss)
Electric Cars – The Future is Now! (Linde)
Fast Ladies – Female Racing Drivers 1888 to 1970 (Bouzanquet)
Fate of the Sleeping Beauties, The (op de Weegh/Hottendorff/op de Weegh)
Ferrari 288 GTO, The Book of the (Sackey)
Fiat & Abarth 124 Spider & Coupé (Tipler)
Fiat & Abarth 500 & 600 2nd Edition (Bobbitt)
Fiats, Great Small (Ward)
Fine Art of the Motorcycle Engine, The (Peirce)
Ford F100/F150 Pick-up 1948-1996 (Ackerson)
Ford F150 Pick-up 1997-2005 (Ackerson)
Ford GT – Then, and Now (Streather)
Ford GT40 (Legate)
Ford In Miniature (Olson)
Ford Model Y (Roberts)
Ford Thunderbird From 1954, The Book of the (Long)
Formula 5000 Motor Racing, Back then ... and back now (Lawson)
Forza Minardi! (Vigar)
Funky Mopeds (Skelton)
GM In Miniature (Olson)
GT – The World's Best GT Cars 1953-73 (Dawson)
Hillclimbing & Sprinting – The Essential Manual (Short & Wilkinson)
Honda NSX (Long)
Intermeccanica – The Story of the Prancing Bull (McCredie & Reisner)
Jaguar, The Rise of (Price)
Jaguar XJ 220 – The Inside Story (Moreton)
Jaguar XJ-S (Long)
Jeep CJ (Ackerson)
Jeep Wrangler (Ackerson)
Karmann-Ghia Coupé & Convertible (Bobbitt)
Kawasaki Triples Bible, The (Walker)
Kris Meeke – Intercontinental Rally Challenge Champion (McBride)
Lamborghini Miura Bible, The (Sackey)
Lamborghini Urraco, The book of the (Landsem)
Lambretta Bible, The (Davies)
Lancia 037 (Collins)
Lancia Delta HF Integrale (Blaettel & Wagner)
Land Rover Series III Reborn (Porter)
Land Rover, The Half-ton Military (Cook)
Laverda Twins & Triples Bible 1968-1986 (Falloon)
Lea-Francis Story, The (Price)
Lexus Story, The (Long)
little book of smart, the New Edition (Jackson)
little book of microcars, the (Quellin)
Lola – The Illustrated History (1957-1977) (Starkey)
Lola – All the Sports Racing & Single-seater Racing Cars 1978-1997 (Starkey)
Lola T70 – The Racing History & Individual Chassis Record 4th Edition (Starkey)
Lotus 49 (Oliver)
Marketingmobiles, The Wonderful Wacky World of (Hale)
Mazda MX-5/Miata 1.6 Enthusiast's Workshop Manual (Grainger & Shoemark)
Mazda MX-5/Miata 1.8 Enthusiast's Workshop Manual (Grainger & Shoemark)
Mazda MX-5 Miata: The Book of the World's Favourite Sportscar (Long)
Mazda MX-5 Miata Roadster (Long)
Maximum Mini (Booij)
Mercedes-Benz SL – 113-series 1963-1971 (Long)
Mercedes-Benz SL & SLC – 107-series 1971-1989 (Long)
MGA (Price Williams)
MGB & MGB GT– Expert Guide (Auto-doc Series) (Williams)
MGB Electrical Systems Updated & Revised Edition (Astley)
Micro Caravans (Jenkinson)
Micro Trucks (Mort)
Microcars at Large! (Quellin)
Mini Cooper – The Real Thing! (Tipler)
Mitsubishi Lancer Evo, The Road Car & WRC Story (Long)
Montlhéry, The Story of the Paris Autodrome (Boddy)
Morgan Maverick (Lawrence)
Morris Minor, 60 Years on the Road (Newell)
Moto Guzzi Sport & Le Mans Bible, The (Falloon)
Motor Movies – The Posters! (Veysey)
Motor Racing – Reflections of a Lost Era (Carter)
Motorcycle Apprentice (Cakebread)
Motorcycle Road & Racing Chassis Designs (Noakes)
Motorhomes, The Illustrated History (Jenkinson)
Motorsport In colour, 1950s (Wainwright)
MV Agusta Fours, The book of the (Falloon)
Nissan 300ZX & 350Z – The Z-Car Story (Long)
Nissan GT-R Supercar: Born to race (Gorodji)
Northeast American Sports Car Races 1950-1959 (O'Neil)
Nothing Runs – Misadventures in the Classic, Collectable & Exotic Car Biz (Slutsky)
Off-Road Giants! (Volume 1) – Heroes of 1960s Motorcycle Sport (Westlake)
Off-Road Giants! (Volume 2) – Heroes of 1960s Motorcycle Sport (Westlake)
Pass the Theory and Practical Driving Tests (Gibson & Hoole)
Peking to Paris 2007 (Young)
Plastic Toy Cars of the 1950s & 1960s (Ralston)
Pontiac Firebird (Cranswick)
Porsche Boxster (Long)
Porsche 356 (2nd Edition) (Long)
Porsche 908 (Födisch, Neßhöver, Roßbach, Schwarz & Roßbach)
Porsche 911 Carrera – The Last of the Evolution (Corlett)
Porsche 911R, RS & RSR, 4th Edition (Starkey)
Porsche 911, The Book of the (Long)
Porsche 911SC 'Super Carrera' – The Essential Companion (Streather)
Porsche 914 & 914-6: The Definitive History of the Road & Competition Cars (Long)
Porsche 924 (Long)
Porsche 928 (Long)
Porsche 944 (Long)
Porsche 964, 993 & 996 Data Plate Code Breaker (Streather)
Porsche 993 'King Of Porsche' – The Essential Companion (Streather)
Porsche 996 'Supreme Porsche' – The Essential Companion (Streather)
Porsche Racing Cars – 1953 to 1975 (Long)
Porsche Racing Cars – 1976 to 2005 (Long)
Porsche – The Rally Story (Meredith)
Porsche: Three Generations of Genius (Meredith)
Preston Tucker & Others (Linde)
RAC Rally Action! (Gardiner)
Rallye Sport Fords: The Inside Story (Moreton)
Roads with a View – England's greatest views and how to find them by road (Corfield)
Roads With a View – Wales' greatest views and how to find them by road (Corfield)
Rolls-Royce Silver Shadow/Bentley T Series Corniche & Camargue Revised & Enlarged Edition (Bobbitt)
Rolls-Royce Silver Spirit, Silver Spur & Bentley Mulsanne 2nd Edition (Bobbitt)
Runways & Racers (O'Neil)
Russian Motor Vehicles – Soviet Limousines 1930-2003 (Kelly)
Russian Motor Vehicles – The Czarist Period 1784 to 1917 (Kelly)
RX-7 – Mazda's Rotary Engine Sportscar (Updated & Revised New Edition) (Long)
Scooters & Microcars, The A-Z of Popular (Dan)
Scooter Lifestyle (Grainger)
Singer Story: Cars, Commercial Vehicles, Bicycles & Motorcycle (Atkinson)
Sleeping Beauties USA – abandoned classic cars & trucks (Marek)
SM – Citroën's Maserati-engined Supercar (Long & Claverol)
Speedway – Auto racing's ghost tracks (Collins & Ireland)
Standard Motor Company, The Book of the (Robson)
Subaru Impreza: The Road Car And WRC Story (Long)
Supercar, How to Build your own (Thompson)
Tales from the Toolbox (Oliver)
Taxi! The Story of the 'London' Taxicab (Bobbitt)
Tinplate Toy Cars of the 1950s & 1960s (Ralston)
Toleman Story, The (Hilton)
Toyota Celica & Supra, The Book of Toyota's Sports Coupés (Long)
Toyota MR2 Coupés & Spyders (Long)
Triumph Bonneville!, Save the – The inside story of the Meriden Workers' Co-op (Rosamond)
Triumph Motorcycles & the Meriden Factory (Hancox)
Triumph Speed Twin & Thunderbird Bible (Woolridge)
Triumph Tiger Cub Bible (Estall)
Triumph Trophy Bible (Woolridge)
Triumph TR6 (Kimberley)
TWR Story, The – Group A (Hughes & Scott)
Unraced (Collins)
Velocette Motorcycles – MSS to Thruxton New Third Edition (Burris)
Volkswagen Bus Book, The (Bobbitt)
Volkswagen Bus or Van to Camper, How to Convert (Porter)
Volkswagens of the World (Glen)
VW Beetle Cabriolet (Bobbitt)
VW Beetle – The Car of the 20th Century (Copping)
VW Bus – 40 Years of Splitties, Bays & Wedges (Copping)
VW Bus Book, The (Bobbitt)
VW Golf: Five Generations of Fun (Copping & Cservenka)
VW – The Air-cooled Era (Copping)
VW T5 Camper Conversion Manual (Porter)
VW Campers (Copping)
Which Oil? – Choosing the right oils & greases for your antique, vintage, veteran, classic or collector car (Michell)
Works Minis, The Last (Purves & Brenchley)
Works Rally Mechanic (Moylan)

From Veloce Publishing's new imprints:

Battle Cry!
Soviet General & field rank officer uniforms: 1955 to 1991 (Streather)
Red & Soviet military & paramilitary services: female uniforms 1941-1991 (Streather)

Hubble & Hattie
Animal Grief – How animals mourn for each other (Alderton)
Clever Dog! (O'Meara)
Complete Dog Massage Manual, The – Gentle Dog Care (Robertson)
Dinner with Rover (Paton-Ayre)
Dog Cookies (Schops)
Dog Games – Stimulating play to entertain your dog and you (Blenski)
Dogs on wheels (Mort)
Dog Relax – Relaxed dogs, relaxed owners (Pilguj)
Exercising your puppy: a gentle & natural approach – Gentle Dog Care (Robertson)
Fun and games for cats (Seidl)
Know Your Dog – The guide to a beautiful relationship (Birmelin)
Living with an Older Dog – Gentle Dog Care (Alderton & Hall)
My dog has cruciate ligament injury – but lives life to the full! (Häusler)
My dog has hip dysplasia – but lives life to the full! (Häusler)
My dog is blind – but lives life to the full! (Horsky)
My dog is deaf – but lives life to the full! (Willms)
Smellorama – nose games for dogs (Theby)
Swim to Recovery: Canine hydrotherapy healing (Wong)
Waggy Tails & Wheelchairs (Epp)
Walking the dog – motorway walks for drivers and dogs (Rees)
Winston ... the dog who changed my life (Klute)
You and Your Border Terrier – The Essential Guide (Alderton)
You and Your Cockapoo – The Essential Guide (Alderton)

www.veloce.co.uk

First published in August 2011 by Veloce Publishing Limited, Veloce House, Parkway Farm Business Park, Middle Farm Way, Poundbury, Dorchester, Dorset, DT1 3AR, England.
Fax 01305 250479/e-mail info@veloce.co.uk/web www.veloce.co.uk or www.velocebooks.com.
ISBN: 978-1-845843-04-5 UPC: 6-36847-04304-9

© Brian Long and Veloce Publishing 2011. All rights reserved. With the exception of quoting brief passages for the purpose of review, no part of this publication may be recorded, reproduced or transmitted by any means, including photocopying, without the written permission of Veloce Publishing Ltd. Throughout this book logos, model names and designations, etc, have been used for the purposes of identification, illustration and decoration. Such names are the property of the trademark holder as this is not an official publication.

Readers with ideas for automotive books, or books on other transport or related hobby subjects, are invited to write to the editorial director of Veloce Publishing at the above address.
British Library Cataloguing in Publication Data – A catalogue record for this book is available from the British Library. Typesetting, design and page make-up all by Veloce Publishing Ltd on Apple Mac. Printed in India by Replika Press.

MERCEDES-BENZ
SL W113 SERIES

1963 to 1971

Brian Long

Contents

Introduction 5
Acknowledgements 7
1: The three-pointed star 8
2: The SL – born on the track 21
3: The 300SL & 190SL 34
4: Birth of the W113 'Pagoda' series 64
5: The 230SL evolves 95
6: The 250SL 135
7: End of the line 155
8: An SL for the Seventies 183
Appendix I: Year-by-year range details 193
Appendix II: Engine specifications 194
Appendix III: Colour & trim summary 196
Appendix IV: Option codes 199
Appendix V: Chassis numbers & production figures 202
Index 207

Introduction

The Mercedes-Benz SL made its debut on the race track in the spring of 1952. Two years later, at a time when the Silver Arrows returned to the Grand Prix scene, overnight, the gullwing 300SL production model redefined the GT car.

Whilst the smaller-engined 190SL made the sporting Mercedes a little more accessible to the enthusiastic driver, the 300SL Roadster took the place of the gullwing coupé in 1957, confirming the SL to be one of the most glamorous cars to ever carry the three-pointed star.

With something of a reputation to live up to, the second generation SLs made their debut at the 1963 Geneva Show. The 230SL was a mainstream vehicle using off-the-shelf components, blending a strong sporting image with everyday practicality and the added bonus of a fuel-injected six to endow the new car with a technological spirit inherited from the 300s.

As *Road & Track* pointed out at the time of the W113 series' debut: "The 230SL is a median between the 300SL and 190SL in almost all respects. The 170bhp injection engine of the 230SL offers performance between that of the 120bhp 190SL engine and the 250bhp 300SL powerplant. As a 'sports touring car,' it has good roadability with sedan smoothness. The interior is smart rather than luxurious, reflecting the functionalism associated with sports cars, although it is not quite as austere as that of true competition cars."

In effect, Daimler-Benz brought the two extremes of SL motoring together in one reasonably priced machine, ideal for road use, but less suited to serious competition duty – at least on the track, for the 230SL would later prove itself to be a fine rally car.

Although a very different-looking machine to its immediate predecessors, it perfectly captured the changing mood of the Swinging Sixties. The distinctive removable hardtop – the famous 'Pagoda' roof – gave three body configurations (open, closed via the soft-top hood, or as a comfortable coupé with the hardtop in place), while the option of a manual or automatic transmission broadened its appeal still further, especially in the United States.

The 'Pagoda Roof SL' nomenclature was carried over to the short-lived 250SL and the larger-engined 280SL variants that followed in quick succession during the late-1960s. Production finally came to an end in 1971 after a total of almost 50,000 W113-series cars had been built.

This book tells the full production history of the Mercedes-Benz W113-series SL – one of the most desirable machines ever to emerge from Stuttgart. It covers all major markets, year by year, to give a definitive overview of the road cars, as well as a detailed look at the model in competition. To complete the story, there's also a brief overview of the vehicle's replacement in the final chapter.

Contemporary photography sourced from the factory and augmented by other material gathered from around the world ensures an excellent guide for those looking for originality. Extensive appendices are included, covering engine specifications, chassis numbers, build numbers, option codes, and so on.

By the way, this title can be read as a single volume or in conjunction with the 107-series SL/SLC published by Veloce a few months earlier, as all the photography is completely different from book to book.

Stuttgart horsepower at rest with equine horsepower.

Acknowledgements

In this day and age of commerce coming a long way ahead of enthusiasm, not just in the car world, but in the vast majority of hobby activities and life in general, it is truly refreshing to work with Daimler AG – a company, like Porsche (its neighbour in Stuttgart), that values its heritage, and treats owners of older vehicles of the marque with the same respect as an owner of a brand new car.

As with the 107-series book, help came from many quarters during this project. I would particularly like to record my sincere appreciation for the services of Dr Hans Spross, Gerhard Heidbrink, Maria Feifel, Florijan Hadzic and Gerald Mack at Daimler AG in Stuttgart, as well as their colleagues from many years earlier – Max Gerrit von Pein and Dr Harry Niemann. Thanks also to Elif Yilmaz at EVO Eitel & Volland GmbH, who look after older technical publications for the Mercedes-Benz Classic Collection, Bob Geco, Kenichi Kobayashi at Miki Press, Yoshihiro Inomoto, Rob Halloway at Mercedes-Benz UK, and Peter Patrone, Robert Moran, Diane Vatchev and Benjamin Benson at the company's head office in the States.

BRIAN LONG
Chiba City, Japan

Whilst looking for something totally unrelated in some old photo albums, I happened to come across this – a shot of Miho, my wife, and was reminded that she had eyes for just one car on her first visit to the works museum in Stuttgart, well over a decade ago …

1
The three-pointed star

There can be few trademarks so readily recognizable in all corners of the world as the Mercedes-Benz three-pointed star. The three arms signify the land, sea and air, and the Stuttgart company the star has come to represent has indeed conquered each in its own inimitable way over the years. The story behind the star, though, is a long and complicated one, so this chapter will briefly outline the brand's history to set the scene before the arrival of the first SL models.

The story begins with two men – two pioneers in the motor industry – Gottlieb Daimler, and Carl Benz. Amazingly, given the pre-eminence of the pair in a fledgling trade, not to mention their closeness geographically, the two never actually met, but the coming together of their names is the important thing here.

In 1882, Gottlieb Daimler established a small workshop at the back of his villa in Cannstatt, on the outskirts of Stuttgart, about

The Benz family with a 3.5hp Benz Comfortable in the mid-1890s. From left to right, we can see Carl Benz's son Richard, daughters Thilde, Ellen, and Clara huddled around their father, and eldest son Eugen. Bertha Benz, Carl's wife, was a pioneering motorist.

The diverse range of uses for engines made by the Daimler Motoren Gesellschaft, circa 1897. Already, the reference to Daimler products being seen on land, sea, and in the air was quite apt.

12 miles (20km) west of his birthplace, with Maybach working alongside him. A number of single-cylinder, air-cooled petrol engines were duly developed, and used to power the world's first motorcycle in 1885, along with a four-wheeled horseless carriage, which made its initial runs during the autumn of 1886. Within a short space of time, the engines were finding various applications on land, on water, and even in the air. By 1890, the products emanating from the Daimler Motoren Gesellschaft had caught the imagination of the engineering world.

Meanwhile, about 55 miles (90km) north in Mannheim, Carl Benz was busy working on his two-stroke petrol engines, as patents covering four-stroke power-units had already been

FOUNDING FATHERS OF THE BRAND

Gottlieb Daimler

Daimler was born in Schorndorf in March 1834, and after serving an apprenticeship as a gunsmith, promptly moved into the field of engineering, gaining experience in France and Britain before returning to his homeland.

He was appointed Technical Manager of the Deutz Gas Engine Works (founded by Nikolaus August Otto, credited as the father of the four-stroke, or 'Otto-cycle' engine) in 1872, with Wilhelm Maybach as his right-hand man. However, Daimler's overwhelming interest in faster-running, more powerful petrol engines created a rift in the Cologne-based firm, and ultimately a decision was made to form an independent company dealing with this new technology.

After building a second car, this time powered by a water-cooled V-twin, in 1889, it was obvious that Daimler and Maybach were on the right track. The Daimler Motoren Gesellschaft (DMG) was registered in November 1890 to manufacture and market these 2-cylinder units, which were a revelation at the time. As such, Daimler was successful in selling patents to many concerns. One of the first to sign up was Panhard & Levassor in France, which duly provided engines for a number of makers, and became a highly successful car manufacturer in its own right.

Daimler and Maybach remained close friends, even after the latter was forced to leave the Cannstatt company due to a clash of policy with its new investors. Meanwhile, Daimler's health was failing. Internal conflict with members of the Board probably didn't help, and he ultimately resigned from the company he'd founded in 1894.

Daimler and Maybach joined forces again, this time with Daimler's son, Paul, and between them they designed a 4-cylinder engine equipped with Maybach's innovative spray-nozzle carburettor. Known as the 'Phönix,' it signified the rebirth of a fine team in both name and nature, and, following some political manoeuvring from Frederick Simms in England, the pair was asked to return to the DMG on new, far more favourable terms.

Gottlieb Daimler died in March 1900, although Maybach continued his work before ultimately making aero-engines for the famous Zeppelin airships. After the Great War, Maybach built a series of luxury cars until the Second World War put an end to production. Recently, the name was revived for a Mercedes-Benz flagship saloon.

Gottlieb Daimler.

FOUNDING FATHERS OF THE BRAND

Carl Benz

The son of a train driver, Carl Benz was born in November 1844. After moving around a number of concerns, some involved in the building of iron structures, such as bridges, Benz finally established his own engineering shop in Mannheim in 1871. However, with his business failing, Benz turned his attention to two-stroke engines in 1877, with the first unit running successfully only two years later.

By 1882, the Benz engine had attracted investors, and Gasmotorenfabrik Mannheim was established, although Benz left the company soon after when the shareholders tried to influence designs. Notwithstanding, in October 1883, 'Benz & Co Rheinische Gasmotorenfabrik, Mannheim' was formed with the help of two local businessmen, and by 1886 the world's first, purpose-built vehicle to be powered by a petrol engine – the three-wheeled Benz Patent Motorwagon – had made its debut.

Four-wheeled cars were produced in 1891, and Benz continued to innovate, designing steering systems and (amongst other things) developing the horizontally-opposed (boxer) engine. The commercial success of the company can be gauged by the fact that Benz & Cie AG was registered in May 1899. However, by early 1903, Benz became disillusioned with the people running the firm and resigned, although he did retain a position on the Supervisory Board until his death.

Meanwhile, Benz formed a new company with his son Eugen in 1906, called C Benz Söhne, which turned to car production after a spell in the field of gas engines. This business, based in Ladenburg, to the east of Mannheim, was duly handed over to Eugen and his younger brother Richard in 1912. This particular firm officially stopped building cars in 1923.

Incidentally, for many years it was assumed and accepted that Benz's forename was Karl, in the German tradition, but the correct spelling is in fact Carl. He died in April 1929, but at least he was able to witness motoring evolve from a sport for the well-heeled into an essential part of daily life.

Carl Benz.

filed by the Deutz concern, the company Daimler worked for. Eventually, Benz also opted for 'Otto-cycle' engines, putting a single-cylinder unit in a purpose-built frame to produce the world's first petrol-driven car, patented in January 1886. By 1890, Benz & Co was Germany's second largest engine manufacturer, and as the century drew to a close, one of the world's most prolific automobile makers, with almost 600 cars built in 1899 alone.

A HEALTHY RIVALRY

At the end of the day, Daimler and Benz were rival inventors, while the companies bearing their names fought in the showrooms and on the race tracks of Europe. The battle for the hearts of the rich and famous, and the silverware that comes with victory in competition, was never as fierce as it was in the years leading up to the First World War.

A small section of the Daimler works in 1905. Incidentally, the Daimler Motor Co Limited was not linked to the Stuttgart company; only in as much as the German firm granted FR Simms' English company a licence to build Daimler engines in the 1890s.

At Daimler, rapid expansion led to the purchase of a large site in Untertürkheim on the eastern edge of Stuttgart in August 1900, which would duly become the spiritual home of Mercedes-Benz.

The Mercedes moniker was first adopted by Emil Jellinek, an Austrian who, amongst other things, sold Daimlers to wealthy clients in the south of France. Jellinek was a clever businessman, and he proposed a number of changes that he knew would appeal to his customers and his own sporting nature, such as a lower body and longer wheelbase in order to cope with the greater power outputs he outlined.

Jellinek promised to take a large number of these vehicles (at least by the standards of the day) in return for distribution rights

The Daimler Motoren Gesellschaft factory at Untertürkheim, pictured just before the First World War.

in France, Belgium, the Austro-Hungarian Empire and America, but also requested that they carry the 'Mercédès' badge – the name of his daughter, and the pseudonym he used during his various racing exploits.

A deal was struck, and Wilhelm Maybach (1846-1929) set about designing the first Mercédès in conjunction with Paul Daimler. The end result, a racing car which appeared at the end of 1900, provided the foundation stone for the modern automobile, with a low, pressed steel chassis frame playing host to a 5.9-litre, 35hp engine (cooled by a honeycomb radiator), and a gate for the gearchange.

The Mercédès was raced with a great deal of success, and many variations were produced for regular use, from an 8/11hp version all the way up to a 9.2-litre 60hp model. The Mercédès set the standard for the day in the high-class car market, and was built under licence – or often simply copied – by numerous manufacturers.

Count Giulio Masetti on his way to a Targa Florio victory in 1922.

The Mercédès stand at the 1924 Berlin Motor Show.

6-cylinder engines followed in 1906, and there was a limited run of Knight sleeve-valve models just before the First World War. A few years after the conflict, when technology, metallurgy and production techniques made great strides, the first supercharged Mercédès made its debut, and in April 1923, Ferdinand Porsche was drafted from Austro-Daimler to become Chief Engineer, bringing overhead camshafts and front-wheel brakes to the marque in a series of exceptionally elegant supercharged models.

Meanwhile, Benz & Cie also made giant steps forward at the turn of the century, albeit against the wishes of Carl Benz, modernizing the range with conventional 2- and 4-cylinder cars designed by a Frenchman, Marius Barbarou. Internal conflict ultimately led to Benz giving up his post as Chief Engineer, although he remained on the Board until his death, and also formed another company with his sons to allow himself more freedom on design policy. The latter business was short-lived, however, building cars from 1906 to 1923.

The 20hp Benz of Fritz Erle seen at the start of a stage during the Prince Henry Trials of June 1909 – a long-distance epic that took nine days to complete, taking in Germany, Poland, Slovakia, Hungary, and Austria before returning to Germany.

The amazing teardrop Benz RH that made its debut at the 1923 European Grand Prix at Monza. The 2-litre, rear-engined car had originally come off the drawing board of Dr Edmund Rumpler, and incorporated a number of advanced features.

Benz & Cie continued to follow a safe path with its vehicles thereafter, with Hans Nibel in charge of design from 1910. However, Nibel's love of racing spawned a number of interesting competition cars (he had even been involved with the machine that formed the basis for the streamlined 'Blitzen Benz' record breaker), and the Benz marque duly found favour with a wealthy clientele. One of the most ardent supporters of the brand was Prince Henry of Prussia – the brother of Kaiser Wilhelm II.

Benz introduced its first 6-cylinder engine in 1914, and stuck almost exclusively to straight-sixes following the conflict. By this time, the company had produced some magnificent aero-engines, including a supercharged V12, and was also a leading light in the field of diesel technology.

In the background, however, the wheels of finance were turning, and, for a number of reasons, a huge amount of shares in both firms came to be held by the Deutsche Bank. An agreement of mutual interest was signed on 1 May 1924, with a syndicate being formed in order to save production costs in an era of high inflation, and then, on 28 June 1926, a full merger took place, giving birth to Daimler-Benz AG.

Benz advertising from the Great War era.

A NEW STAR IS BORN

Although the company was known as Daimler-Benz, the cars were marketed using the Mercedes-Benz name, with Mercedes officially losing the accents along the way. Only two Benz models made it into the Mercedes-Benz passenger car programme, and both were gone by 1927.

Contemporary poster proclaiming the historic coming together of the Daimler and Benz brands.

EVOLUTION OF THE THREE-POINTED STAR

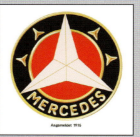

There were straight-eights from October 1928, and the marque went into the mid-1930s with some magnificent creations, with the SS and SSK giving way to the 500K and 540K. By this time, the company was producing a range of vehicles that went from modest 1.3-litre saloons, with its NA (naturally-aspirated) four at the rear, all the way up to 7.7-litre supercharged eights with their glamorous coachbuilt bodies.

Meanwhile, 1934 had witnessed the debut of the first of the Silver Arrows – the W25 Grand Prix car. This was followed by a string of successful models that put Germany at the forefront of the motorsport scene until the outbreak of the Second World War. Record breakers were also built, based on the GP (Grand Prix) cars, and brought the new autobahn network into use in a rather unexpected fashion – the straight, level roads being perfect for the challenge to find the fastest man on Earth.

A scene from the 1927 German GP for Sportscars at the Nürburgring. This Mercedes-Benz Type S won the 3-litre category. Ferdinand Porsche can be seen next to the co-driver in a light suit and dark hat.

A 1936 Mercedes-Benz 500K Special Roadster.

One of the fabled 'Silver Arrows' at the 1938 German Grand Prix, silver rather than Germany's traditional white after Alfred Neubauer (the legendary Mercedes-Benz racing team manager, seen here second from the left) ordered that even paint should be removed to save weight! This shot shows Manfred von Brauchitsch, Richard Seaman, Hermann Lang, and Rudolf Caracciola with the 470bhp W154 model.

Then, of course, 1939 brought with it conflict, first in Europe, and then on a global scale. Virtually all the historic Untertürkheim factory was destroyed during an Allied bombing run in September 1944, so it was difficult for Daimler-Benz to bounce back once the hostilities ended in 1945.

Like so many manufacturers, Daimler-Benz warmed over some of its pre-war designs as part of the rebuilding process, releasing its first post-war car (ignoring utilitarian versions and commercial vehicles) in July 1947 – the 1.7-litre 170V four-door sedan. Two new 170-series variants joined it in May 1949, and production continued until 1955, by which time the 180 had been introduced as a stablemate.

Production at the huge Sindelfingen plant in 1949, with pre-war cars brought back to life after the conflict.

1951 saw the revival of 6-cylinder engines with the launch of the 2.2-litre 220 series (W187) and the 3-litre 300 (W186 II) models in April that year. The sporting two-door 300S made its debut at the 1951 Paris Salon, and shortly after a deal was signed with Max Hoffman, securing a good sales outlet in America. Incidentally, Hoffman also handled Porsche imports for the United States.

Many companies talk of pedigree. However, few can match the bloodlines behind the Mercedes-Benz brand ...

Advertising from 1950 for the elegant Mercedes-Benz Type 170S Cabriolet A. Styling was still influenced by pre-war design concepts until the arrival of the thoroughly modern 'Ponton' line.

2

The SL – born on the track

The Mercedes-Benz racing team had attained legendary status in the 1930s, with its silver cars hitting the headlines in virtually every country they appeared in. But war had broken up the equipe, and it wasn't until March 1952 that Mercedes returned to the racing world with a purpose-built, factory-backed car. This development marked the birth of the SL ...

With the cessation of hostilities and a gradual return to normality in the industrial nations of the world, Alfred Neubauer wanted to return to Grand Prix racing as quickly as possible with new versions of the pre-war W165 voiturettes, but almost as soon as the production order was granted, it was withdrawn again. A meeting of the hierarchy in Stuttgart concluded that if Neubauer wanted to go racing in 1952, it would have to be with sports cars representing the marque, and any plans to enter a GP machine should be delayed until 1954, when a new formula was set to be introduced.

With classic events like Le Mans, the Mille Miglia, and Targa Florio revived, sports car racing was extremely popular following the war, as it was a perfect way of promoting a brand in a manner that allowed enthusiasts to readily associate a victorious machine with a showroom model they could buy, or at least dream about. The need for Europe to export led to an explosion of LWS (lightweight sports) models, with England leading the way, supplying an American market that was taking as many cars as the ships crossing the Atlantic could carry.

Sports car racing also appealed to those looking after company finances, as road vehicle technology could be developed and tested within the competition department budget – 'killing two birds with one stone,' so to speak. For instance, the C-type Jaguar that had won Le Mans in 1951 was based on XK120 components, and lessons learnt during the 24 hours could then be applied to produce a better road car. In the case of the Mercedes-Benz team, the 3-litre W186 II chassis was deemed to provide a suitable starting point for a new kind of sports-racer.

W194: THE FIRST SL

The W194 concept was much the same as that of the Jaguar C-type, using as many proven XK120 parts as possible in a custom-made, lightweight frame, and enhancing power output largely via modifications to the cylinder head and carburetion. The model selected as the donor car by Daimler-Benz was the

One of the first press pictures of the new 300SL (or 300SS as it was nearly called), with the shut line on the 'gullwing' doors finishing on the top of the vehicle's waistline. Note also the bolt-on wheels, finished with hubcaps – remarkable detailing for a racing car!

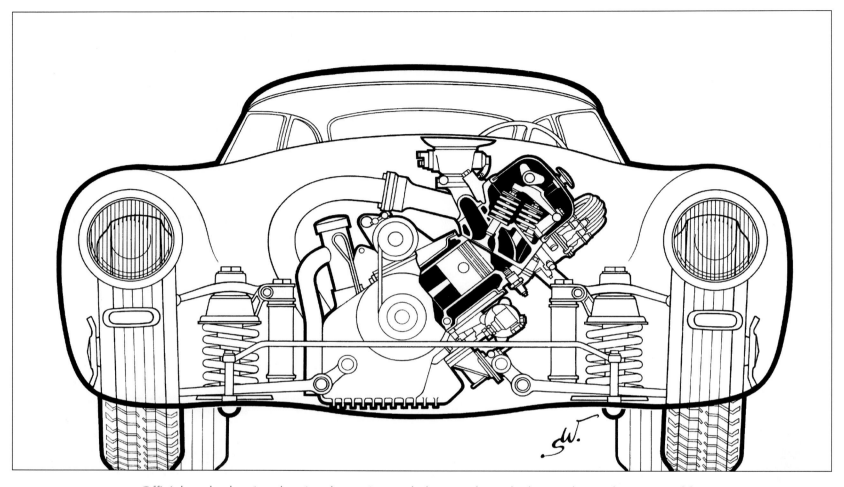

Official works drawing showing the engine angled over to keep the bonnet line as low as possible.

new, upmarket Type 300. It may seem an unlikely vehicle, but it was the powertrain that appealed, and one has to remember that the XK engine also powered limousines, not just sports cars, so the parallel between the Coventry and Stuttgart companies is still valid.

The 3-litre engine – considered the main component to work around – and the Mercedes-Benz 300 model it powered were introduced at the 1951 Frankfurt Show, which opened on 19 April. The short-wheelbase 300S coupés and convertibles made their debut at the Paris Salon six months later, but already plans were at an advanced stage for a sports-racer built around the luxury saloon's straight-six – the engineers in the racing shop, under the direction of Rudy Uhlenhaut, didn't have to wait for the more sporting variant (which came with a tuned powerplant delivering 35bhp more than the regular unit) before embarking on their project.

The sohc (single overhead camshaft) M186 base six had a 2996cc displacement (85 x 88mm bore and stroke), and with a pair of Solex carburettors and a modest 6.4:1 compression ratio (c/r), produced a lazy 115bhp at 4600rpm. Endowing the unit with three downdraught Solexes, a freer exhaust system and a hotter camshaft, then hiking the c/r up to 8.0:1 (via special heads and pistons), released an extra 60 horses according to official data, while maximum torque stood at 188lbft.

Rather than sitting atop a backbone chassis, as used on the 300 saloons, the straight-six and its modified, all-synchromesh

4-speed transmission was placed within a purpose-built tubular spaceframe, produced in steel and designed using the most up-to-date racing car practices. For the 300SL project, the power-unit was tilted over at a steep angle in order to allow a low body-line, despite the height of the engine.

A dry-sump lubrication system was added at an early stage after testing proved the regular system inadequate for the rigours of competition work, and the spark plugs were moved to a new location to allow quicker changes to be carried out. As such, a different block was produced for the W194 project, although it was still made in cast-iron. With all of the modifications in place, the racing unit was given the M194 moniker.

As for the chassis components, steering came courtesy of the familiar Daimler-Benz recirculating-ball system found on the other 300-series models, while the all-round independent suspension was also similar to that of the 300 road car, with double-wishbones and hydraulic dampers placed inside coil springs at the front, and a swing-axle arrangement at the rear, which employed separate springs and telescopic tube shocks.

The first pictures released showed bolt-on wheels (complete with hubcaps!), although knock-off hubs were later adopted to allow for quicker wheel changes. A 15-inch wheel and tyre combination was specified, with alloy rims playing host to Continental racing rubber. Beyond the wheels, there were drum brakes on all four corners, finned for enhanced cooling, while those fitted at the front of the car had a greater friction material area than the 300 saloon's brakes due to their extra width.

As for the body, in addition to the obvious aerodynamic concerns, assuming there was adequate ventilation, a closed coupé configuration also improved driver comfort and concentration, as sports car races tended to be long, and were often held in awful weather – buffeting from an open car at high speeds can be tiring, and no driver could be expected to give his best performance whilst cold and soaked through either.

Rudolf Uhlenhaut.

RUDOLF UHLENHAUT

A key figure in the birth of the 300SL was Rudolf Uhlenhaut, born in July 1906 to a German father and an English mother. Uhlenhaut was put in charge of the new racing shop at Daimler-Benz, established in 1936 to bridge the gap between Neubauer's arm of the experimental department and the central design office. It was a huge responsibility for the young man. However, Uhlenhaut quickly proved he had the technical knowledge and enough skill behind the wheel to make him the perfect man for the job. He was able to lap a Grand Prix car on a par with the best of the Mercedes-Benz team members, and his logical mind, combined with his exceptional level of mechanical sympathy and feel, enabled many problems to be ironed out quickly and efficiently.

As Stirling Moss once said: "He could drive any of the cars nearly as fast as we could. In the 1930s, his performances merited a regular place in the team, but he was too valuable as an engineer to be risked in a possible accident. Apart from his great influence on the design of the cars, it was he who would do everything to see that the driver had the sort of car he wanted ..."

Uhlenhaut was responsible for making the Silver Arrows into winning machines in pre-war days, and also for breathing life into the SL series, taking the notes and drawings made in numerous meetings involving management, engineers, designers and drivers, and transforming them into a car that would form the foundation stone for a new generation of Mercedes-Benz legends ...

Novel 'Gullwing' doors were introduced to keep the spaceframe as stiff as possible, as regular doors require a large cut-out in an area that is critical in retaining chassis strength. It was an ingenious idea, typical of the Daimler-Benz competitions department, with the original doors being no more than windows that tilted upward to allow the driver access to the well-trimmed and beautifully prepared cockpit. However, the design was modified in time for the Le Mans race, with slightly deeper doors that pleased the folk at the Automobile Club de l'Ouest (ACO), but lost little in the way of structural rigidity.

The wheelbase was set at 2400mm (94.5in), as opposed to 2900mm (114.2in) for a production 300S, while the height, at 1265mm (49.8in), was some 245mm (9.6in) lower, helping reduce the car's centre of gravity by a large amount. The front track was narrow to keep as much of the front wheels underneath the aluminium bodywork as possible, aiding aerodynamics, while the rear track was wider to allow the swing-axle to work efficiently at high cornering speeds.

The two spare wheels and fuel tank were placed in the tail of the car to provide better traction, and provide counterbalance for at least some of the weight of the powerplant up front. The aluminium-bodied 300SL was hardly lightweight by absolute standards, but, at 870kg (1914lb), it was half the bulk of a regular 300S coupé.

The first prototype was ready for testing in November 1951. Neubauer wasn't happy, demanding more power, a 5-speed transmission, and bigger brakes behind a 16-inch wheel and tyre combination. However, budget and time restrictions ruled out any further changes.

March 1952 witnessed the press presentation of the new car, with motoring scribes leaving Neubauer out in the cold. As an enthusiastic John Whitten wrote in *Road & Track*: "The 3-litre

THE SILVER ARROWS

Even today, mention of the Silver Arrows immediately conjures up an image of a golden age in the 1930s when Mercedes-Benz and Auto Union dominated the Grand Prix scene with their highly advanced, but technically quite different machines. Like Daimler and Benz in the veteran era, there was a healthy rivalry between Mercedes-Benz and Auto Union, with the two forever inextricably linked.

The Silver Arrows legend was born when the W25 was designed to compete in the new 750kg formula devised for the 1934 Grand Prix season. The cars began life in German racing white, but were stripped of their paint to save enough weight to qualify for their first race, and became silver by default! Silver then became synonymous with the Mercedes 'Works' team, as well as that of the rival Auto Union camp.

Rudy Uhlenhaut was responsible for refining the highly-successful W125 that followed, a car that won many of the big races of 1937. When the formula changed again, Mercedes-Benz replied with the W154, powered by a 3-litre supercharged V12, and with the contemporary Auto Unions, German domination of the race tracks unfolded. Even the Italians changing the rules for the 1939 Tripoli Grand Prix couldn't stop Mercedes winning with a 1.5-litre W165 model, built from scratch in an unbelievably short space of time.

As well as the cars and their heroic drivers, the name of Alfred Neubauer came to the fore as the perfectionist manager of the Mercedes-Benz team. Neubauer had been a racing driver himself, competing in the Porsche-designed Mercédès models of yore. As a matter of interest, there was another link between these Stuttgart neighbours (Porsche and Mercedes, that is), as Daimler-Benz had built some of the early Volkswagen prototypes – the VW (Volkswagen) Beetle being one of Professor Porsche's most acclaimed designs.

After the war, the Silver Arrows returned to the track, first via the Mercedes-Benz 300SL, and then more specialized versions of the model. By 1954, Neubauer's dream of a return to Grand Prix racing had materialized, and another era of domination began ...

Three works cars were entered for the 1952 Mille Miglia. This is the 300SL of Caracciola and Kurrle finding its way through the murky conditions. In weather like this, the drivers must have been happy to be racing coupés rather than open cars.

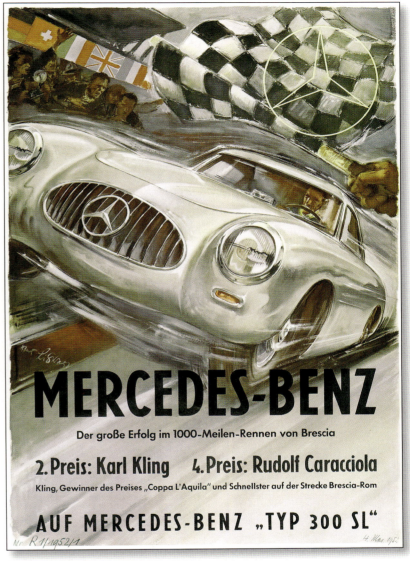

Poster released after the Italian classic.

car, according to its specifications alone, should be a winner; but when you couple it with the name of the team, which is to drive it in competition, it sounds like an unbeatable combination: Rudolf Carraciola! Hermann Lang! Karl Kling!"

Whitten obviously still had lucid memories of the men that handled the Silver Arrows in the heyday of pre-war racing. But there's little doubt that the Mercedes-Benz team had strength in depth, and the advantage of Alfred Neubauer running things from the pits. Neubauer may not have given the 300SL project his full support, but he was not a man to let personal reservations dampen his determination to win.

The first race for the 300SL was the Mille Miglia, held in the first week of May, and taking in almost 1000 miles (1564km, as it happens) of Italian roads on a return trip to Brescia via Rome. Naturally, the three Works cars were painted silver! The Lang/Grupp machine was forced into early retirement, but the Kling/Klenk pairing was second, less than five minutes down on the winning Ferrari, whilst the Caracciola/Kurrle SL came home in fourth.

Start of the sports car race held in Berne, Switzerland, on 18 May 1952. The SLs of Kling and Caracciola can be seen on the front row, alongside the Ferrari of Daetwyler. Victory ultimately went to Karl Kling.

The next event, the sports car race before the Grand Prix in Switzerland, was basically a shakedown for Le Mans, and a chance to try a new door arrangement on the fourth Works entry. Sadly, Caracciola had an accident that brought his career to an end, but the remaining cars all finished on the podium, much to the chagrin of the Ferrari contingent, and the deeper doors were approved for the 24-hour race at the same time.

The modified car used in Berne (chassis 006/52) was rolled out as a spare at Le Mans, joined by three brand new cars with the deeper 'Gullwing' doors. The spare car was used in practice to try an experimental, roof-mounted air brake, and, whilst it wasn't used in the race (more work was definitely needed on the design), the concept was good, and it would be seen again on later Mercedes-Benz sports-racers.

The Kling/Klenk 300SL in action at the Sarthe. Coloured bands around the air intake quickly identified the drivers.

Three brand new 300SLs were built for the 1952 Le Mans 24-hour Race, each incorporating an extended door, and a new fuel filler arrangement. This is the car used by Kling and Klenk for the event.

The Mercedes-Benz of Hermann Lang and Fritz Riess making its way through the Esses at Le Mans, en route to a fine victory in the 24-hour classic.

Although the Kling/Klenk SL dropped out with electrical problems, the Jaguar threat soon disappeared when the new streamlined bodies presented unforeseen cooling difficulties, and the Ferraris buckled under the fast early pace. The engine in Pierre Levegh's Talbot-Lago gave way whilst he was in the lead, leaving Neubauer's team to take the spoils, with the Lang/Riess car taking the flag, and the Helfrich/Niedermayr machine coming second, 14 laps ahead of its nearest rival. In the process, the 300SL duly became the first closed car to win Le Mans.

Mercedes-Benz leading the field at the Nürburgring in August 1952. The works 300SLs filled the first four places in this German Grand Prix support race.

28

An interesting rear three-quarter view of the roadster version of the 300SL, this particular car being chassis 006/52. Several windscreen variations were made, this one being for events like the Carrera, when a co-driver was required. With no passenger to carry, a tonneau cover was fitted, along with a small aero-screen of some sort for the driver.

The Mercedes stand at the 1952 Paris Salon, with a 300SL racer displayed alongside more traditional Stuttgart fare.

Next up was a German Grand Prix support race at the Nürburgring, and naturally, it was important for Daimler-Benz to put on a good show in front of a home crowd. As a short-distance sprint event, running the cars as light and powerful as possible was the key to success, acknowledgement of which came with the birth of the 300SL roadster.

Due to the spaceframe chassis, it was fairly simple to convert the W194 from a coupé into an open car, and thus reduce weight effectively as additional bracing was hardly necessary to retain rigidity. A one-off shortened version (chassis 010/52) was built, powered by a supercharged M197 engine, but traction (and early reliability) was a real problem, and the four Works spiders all ran with normally-aspirated units. Lang won in 007/52 (the Le Mans winner with its new body configuration), followed home by his three team-mates.

A last minute decision was taken to enter the SL in the Mexican road race called the Carrera Panamericana, with two coupés and a roadster handled by top class drivers. The engines

Calm before the storm – the works team pictured prior to the start of the Carrera Panamericana. From left to right: Hermann Lang, Erwin Grupp, Hans Klenk, Karl Kling, John Fitch, and Eugen Geiger.

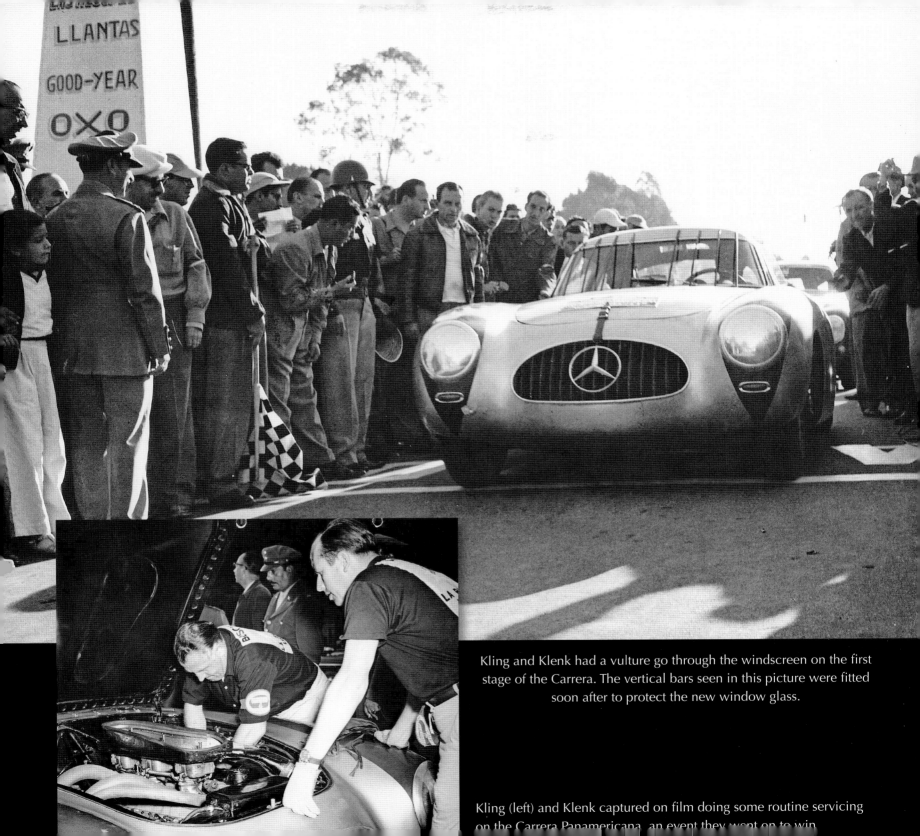

Kling and Klenk had a vulture go through the windscreen on the first stage of the Carrera. The vertical bars seen in this picture were fitted soon after to protect the new window glass.

Kling (left) and Klenk captured on film doing some routine servicing on the Carrera Panamericana, an event they went on to win.

The roadster of Fitch/Geiger was running well in Mexico, but was disqualified for accepting assistance outside an authorised service area.

A summary of Mercedes-Benz racing activity for 1952.

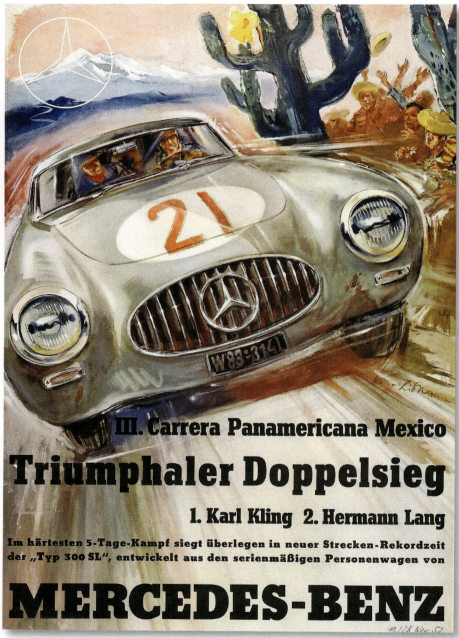

Poster released following the success of the Mercedes-Benz team on the Carrera Panamericana. There is obviously a certain amount of artistic licence in the car's numbering.

were bored out to give a 3105cc displacement, thus releasing a few extra horses, as this was indeed an event in which power was king. Ultimately, John Fitch was disqualified in the open car, but the coupés overcame early tyre problems to finish one-two in a convincing display of German efficiency.

Unfortunately, the 300SL programme was cancelled long before the 1953 season started, but it was certainly a useful exercise, both from a publicity and an engineering point of view. Even the supercharged roadster debacle led to the development of the low-pivot swing-axle, which would later become a signature feature on Mercedes-Benz road cars. As the old saying goes, racing improves the breed ...

Plans were drawn up for a lighter, narrower car for 1953, complete with a fuel-injected engine, a transaxle at the rear, a modified rear suspension incorporating a low-pivot swing-axle, and a 16-inch wheel and tyre combination. However, the project was cancelled in favour of putting greater effort into the 1954 Grand Prix car, and the 300SLR allowed to be based on it. Only one prototype (chassis number 11) was built as a result.

3

The 300SL & 190SL

In the vintage years, enthusiasts were able to buy touring car versions of the Mercedes-Benz racers – the SSK was as awesome on the highways and byways as it was on the track, and no-one will ever forget the lightened SSKL version built strictly for competition use. Now, shaking off the ill-effects of war once and for all, Daimler-Benz was able to modernize its passenger car range, and once again offer connoisseurs of motoring what was essentially a race car for the road ...

The summer of 1953 marked the arrival of the slab-sided 'Ponton' series, giving the styling cue for a whole new generation of Mercedes-Benz models. It was launched in 1.8-litre 4-cylinder guise (W120), but a 2.2-litre 6-cylinder version (W180) had joined the line-up by the following spring.

Meanwhile, the announcement of two new sports cars at the 1954 International Motor Sports Show in New York had enthusiasts in raptures – the 3-litre, fuel-injected 300SL, with styling inspired by the 1953 SL prototype, and the much simpler, smaller-engined 190SL. Although it would be some time before either SL made it into the showrooms (the second Type W198 300SL, for instance, wasn't built until six weeks after the New York exhibition had ended, and even that was still a pre-production prototype), it was no coincidence that they were announced just as the latest W196 F1 car was about to hit the Grand Prix scene.

With the 190SL being an unexpected bonus in New York, it's not surprising that the 300SL was the first to appear in dealerships, with series production of the Type W198 model having started in August 1954. As it happens, Fritz Nallinger, the firm's Technical Director, was bitterly opposed to the idea of a road car, but when Max Hoffman in the States placed an advance order for 500 units to kick-start the project, commercial concerns took precedence, and its birth was almost guaranteed. In many ways, it was a repeat of 1900, with a thinly disguised sports-racer acting as a technological showcase for the German brand.

The first all-new post-war Mercedes-Benz was the Type 180 (W120), often referred to as the 'Ponton' model. This had a unit-construction body (adopted for the first time by the marque) and modern styling that would influence the passenger car line for many years after its public debut in September 1953.

Part of the Mercedes-Benz stand at the 1953 Frankfurt Show, where an older, 1952 SL racer was rolled out for PR duty, seen here in amongst the 170s and 300s.

MERCEDES-BENZ DESIGNATIONS

For many years, Mercedes-Benz models have been identified by a vehicle class letter (or series of letters) and a number, which usually relates to an engine size. It's a system that has continued to this day, with C 350 being a C-Class saloon with a 3.5-litre power-unit, although the engine displacements don't always tie-up precisely in the way they used to.

The designation that interests us the most at this stage in the story, however, is 300SL. The '300' denotes a 3-litre powerplant, while 'SL' is short for 'Sport' and 'Licht' – in English, this would translate into a description of a lightweight sports (LWS) model.

For reference, the addition of an 'R' suffix (to make SLR) distinguished a pure racing model from the later production road cars, while a 'C' (to make SLC) denotes a coupé version of the SL. One will also come across a 'K' quite often in Mercedes circles, which used to refer to short chassis models pre-war (as in 'Kurz'), but nowadays is taken to mean 'Kompressor,' the German for supercharger.

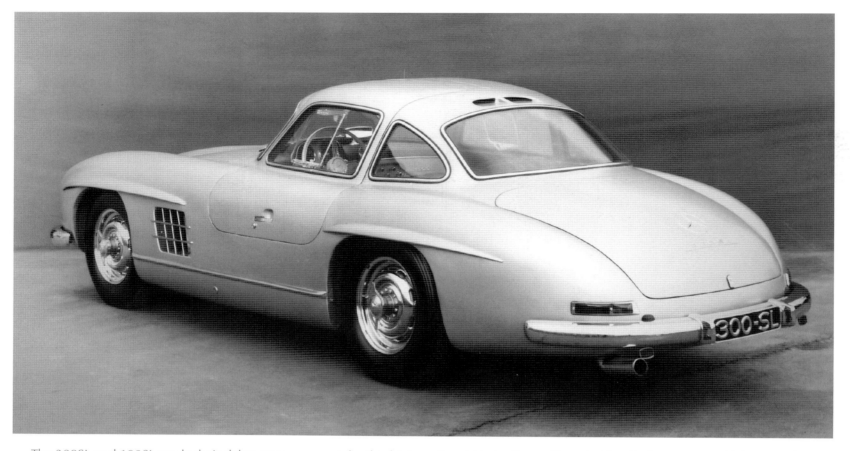

The 300SL and 190SL made their debut appearance at the third International Motor Sports Show in New York, an event which opened on 6 February 1954. Although not quite production specification, they were nonetheless very close to the final design. This is the 300SL that was exhibited on the Mercedes-Benz stand.

Two views of the 190SL shown in 1954. Compared with the 300SL, more significant changes would be applied to the four-cylinder car before it was declared ready for production.

The 300SL, as drawn by the Cutaway King, aka Yoshihiro Inomoto. This shows component locations perfectly, as well as the spaceframe chassis. The 'gullwing' model was built at a rate of around 25 cars per month initially, moving up to 50 soon after. (Courtesy Yoshihiro Inomoto)

THE TYPE W198 300SL

The regular 300 series had been styled by the master, Hermann Ahrens, who had previously conceived the classic lines of the 500 and 540K Roadsters, but the thoroughly modern lines of the SL were the work of Walter Häcker and his team.

Compared with the 1952 racers, the W198 had crisper styling, with a new grille incorporating a large three-pointed star on the lower front-end, parallel power bulges in the bonnet to clear the engine, and headlights that sat more upright than before. The heavy bumpers were classed as a necessity for a road car, and the air vents on the trailing edge of the front wings had been introduced on the 1953 prototype (built on chassis number 11) to reduce aerodynamic drag and allow better cooling of the engine bay.

The side-exit exhaust, introduced midway through the 1952 racing season and carried over to the 1953 model, was not suitable for road use, so a normal silencer arrangement was used with a pipe poking out of the tail on the nearside, and the fussy-looking rear vents were deleted, whilst many of the other details, such as the wheelarch blisters and chrome trim on the sills, were purely cosmetic – items added in a bid to make the car more visually appealing.

Interestingly, although a spaceframe was still employed (very similar to that of the racer, with the same 2400mm/94.5in wheelbase, albeit with a certain amount of additional bracing), most of the body panels were steel for the production models, with only the front and rear lids and door skins crafted in aluminium. On saying that, a handful of all-alloy cars were built for competition work (a total of 58), and there was even a single glassfibre prototype.

The dry-sump straight-six power-unit (Type M198) was a leading edge piece of technology, and, although already proven on the 1953 prototype, the 300SL became the first series-production road car to sport fuel-injection.

With experience relating to fuel-injection gained during the war via aero-engine development, and knowledgeable engineers like Hans Scherenberg (then in charge of the central design office) assigned to the M198 project, the Bosch system was quickly releasing copious amounts of reliable power and

Compared to the New York show car, the production 'gullwing' model had different door handles and side windows, along with numerous detail changes to the interior. All 'gullwing' coupés were sprayed silver unless the customer specifically requested another colour.

While the 1953 car had looked every bit a prototype in appearance, or a functional tool at best, the W198 was a very accomplished piece of design, with an almost timeless quality to its lines.

The actress Sophia Loren with her 300SL. As well as having a glamorous image that attracted the rich and famous, Grand Prix supremo Rob Walker once described the 300SL as "... what must be the greatest road car ever built."

Close-up view of the 300SL, seen here with its steering wheel tilted over to allow easier access to the cockpit – a novel feature for a road car

torque, and any lingering thoughts about moving over to Weber carburettors were duly dismissed.

The configuration of the injection system was very clever, with the injector nozzles placed in the original spark plug holes in the upper part of the 6-cylinder block (a throwback to the days before the plugs were moved to a new head for the SL) to give direct injection. Air, meanwhile, was pulled in through a beautifully crafted plenum chamber and ram pipe casting that became a signature part of the 300SL's design.

With a standard 8.5:1 compression ratio, the 2996cc (85 x 88mm) unit ultimately developed 200bhp DIN at 5800rpm – a figure higher than that quoted for the original SL racing cars. Specifying the 'sports camshaft' released another 15bhp,

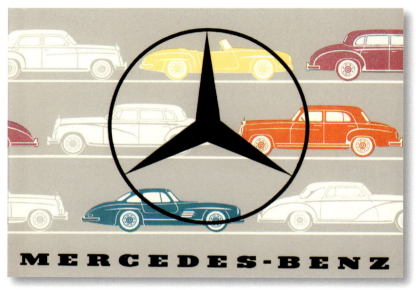

(Right, and p41-42) Catalogue pages relating to the SL from 1955.

Engine of the 300SL road car.

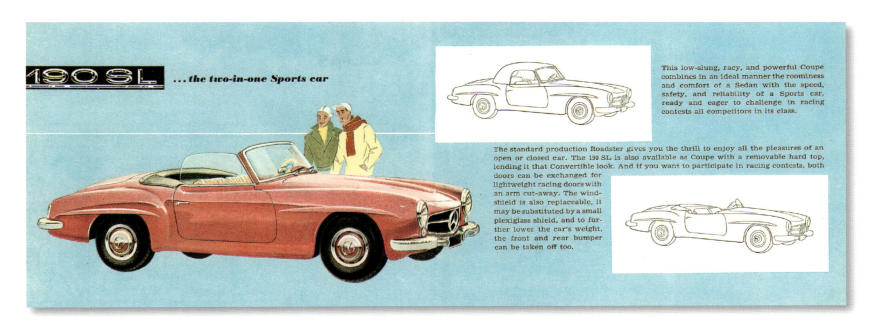

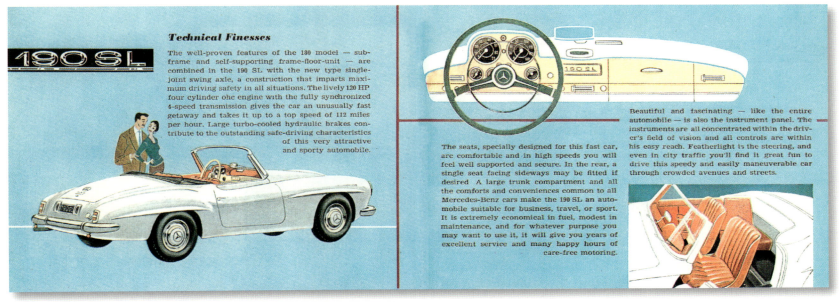

and cars were often supplied with higher compression ratios as well; a 9.5:1 c/r gave ten more horses.

The all-synchromesh 4-speed transmission was carried over from the 1952 racer, and likewise, various axle ratios were available, the highest allowing an observed top speed of 154mph (246kph) – remarkable for the time. At this stage, the steering, suspension and braking set-up was pretty much carried over, too, albeit with softer springs and dampers than the 1952 racers (those intending to use the car in competition could specify the stiffer set-up as an option), and the addition of trailing links at the back. Even the 15-inch wheel and tyre combination was retained rather than taking up the 16-inch

The Sports Car with the Speedway Look

In the 300 SL engineering ingenuity and highest technical skill have produced a true masterpiece. The result — a unique sports car of exceptional beauty with an engine of tremendous output, which makes you master over power and speed with a degree of safety, ease, and comfort which must be experienced to be believed.

With easy-to-read instruments, neatly grouped in line of vision, and with controls conveniently placed, you have full command over this power-packed beauty on wheels.

The operational insensitiveness and the comfort of the 300 SL make it also very well suitable for city driving and cross country touring.

...safe at 160 miles per hour

Also the extremely effective, powerful, servo-assisted hydraulic brakes with turbo-cooled bimetal brake drums and self-adjusting, wide brake shoes assure utmost safety, and impart in every situation the feeling to have the car well under control.

In every speed you become fully aware of the typical Mercedes-Benz characteristics — driving smoothness and road adhesion. The essential prerequisites for the unique roadability of this car lie in the construction of a new type, torsionally rigid, tubular frame, the pyramid design of which allows its individual members to be stressed only longitudinally. The aerodynamic body of very low air drag is a lightweight construction of especially high rigidity which offers safe protection to the occupants.

Wide counterbalanced doors opening upwards and a tilting steering wheel allow you to enter the car easily and without bending down below its roof level. Deep, comfortable bucket seats give full support even when cornering at high speed. The dual heater, which is standard equipment in all Mercedes-Benz cars, draft-free window ventilation, effective heat and noise insulation, a windshield washer, and many little luxuries right down to a cigar lighter are provided for your comfort and convenience. There is ample luggage room behind the seats with a rail to fasten the custom made suitcases, and additional space for baggage is under the rear deck which holds the spare tire.

The extremely flexible 240 HP six cylinder ohc engine with direct gasoline injection will take you in top gear from 15.5 to 165 miles per hour without "bucking". The well-chosen ratios of the fully synchronized 4-speed transmission give the car a fabulous acceleration, taking you from standing still to 60 m/h in a little less than 7 seconds.

Special equipment and the choice of color permit you to give your 300 SL that extra personal touch.

The results of all victories are placed by Daimler-Benz into the hands of every Mercedes-Benz owner.

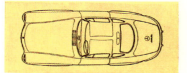

rims selected for the 1953 prototype, although a brake servo was added to the specification list for 1954 to make the car more civilized.

With a more comfortable interior, a hinged steering wheel to aid entry and egress, and greater attention paid to heating and ventilation (the grille in the front bulkhead and two slots in the trailing edge of the roof were added for this reason), the 300SL was an ideal road car, albeit much heavier than the vehicle that spawned it, being catalogued at 1260kg (2772lb). At DM 29,000 (deutsche marks), it was around DM 5000 cheaper than the hand-built 300S line, but still twice the price of a 1.5-litre Porsche Speedster.

GP RACING & THE 300SLR

Mercedes-Benz made its long-awaited return to Grand Prix racing in 1954 with the 2.5-litre normally-aspirated W196 model, fielded with both streamlined and open-wheeled bodies. Having made their debut at Rheims in July, the straight-eight machines went on to dominate the GP scene in 1954 and 1955 in much the same way as the pre-war Silver Arrows had.

Regulations at the time allowed sports-racers to be developed from GP cars, and Daimler-Benz responded with the 300SLR for use in the 1955 World Sports Car Championship. Being based on the Grand Prix car of the time, the 300SLR (W196S) had nothing in common with the regular 300SL, although the 2.5-litre engine was bored out to give a 3-litre capacity, hence the similarity in its designation. The body enclosed the wheels, in much the same way as the streamlined GP cars used on faster circuits.

The 300SLR gave a stunning performance on the Mille Miglia, but at Le Mans, one of the cars was involved in an horrific accident on the pit straight. This prompted the decision for the Mercedes-Benz team to stop racing, although some inside the company say it was largely down to the concerns of Professor Nallinger, who felt that road car development was suffering as a result of all the firm's top designers and engineers being far too busy in motorsport-related activities. Whatever, it was certainly a sad occasion on 24 October 1955, when Alfred Neubauer dropped covers over his beloved racing cars in full view of the press. He wept openly at the event. Enthusiasts everywhere felt his sorrow ...

Poster showing the 1955 W196R monoposto Grand Prix car.

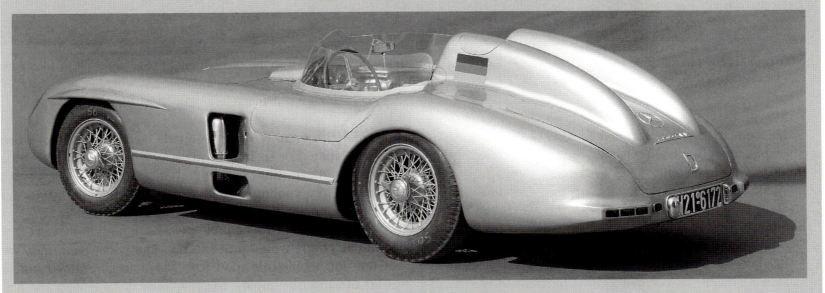

The magnificent 300SLR.

The GT race attached to the 1955 Swedish Grand Prix saw an all-star cast. Karl Kling (right) won the event in this 300SL, while fellow Mercedes driver Stirling Moss (left) followed Juan-Manuel Fangio (centre) home in the F1 race. The Fangio-Moss combination brought Mercedes-Benz an incredible run of race victories before the team was disbanded.

The company's victory in the 1955 Mille Miglia was memorable, and has been recalled in motoring publications literally hundreds of times since, although winning in such a convincing manner has always tended to overshadow the GT Class win by John Fitch's regular 300SL, which finished the Italian event in fifth; Olivier Gendebien was second in the GT category (seventh overall) in a similar machine.

Fitch later recalled that while Italian exotica had an advantage in top speed, the SL "... was tough, and that's why it won races." It also won the hearts of the press and public alike, on both sides of the Atlantic.

America's *Road & Track* reported: "Few cars have been so long anticipated or so long-awaited as the first genuine sports car from Mercedes-Benz in over 20 years. Oftentimes a long wait also serves as a cooling-off period, and the initial trial turns out to be anti-climatic, if not completely disillusioning.

"In this case, just when we were beginning to suspect that the 300SL coupé would prove to be a mediocre performer, we got one for a full-scale road test. The new car turned out to be far beyond our boldest expectations. In fact, we can state unequivocally that, in our opinion, the 300SL coupé is the ultimate in an all-round sports car. It combines more desirable

Paul O'Shea being congratulated on winning the 1955 SCCA Class title with his 'gullwing' 300SL.

Scene from the 1956 Liège-Rome-Liège Rally, which Mercedes won.

A 300SL being chased down by a Ferrari during the 1956 Tour de France Automobile, held at the end of September that year.

Willy Mairesse in action at Spa in 1957.

features in one streamlined package than we ever imagined or hoped would be possible."

It's fair to say that Britain's *Autocar* was equally impressed: "A satisfying movement of the gearlever and one is into top, when the engine gives the impression of being able to propel the car all day at over 100mph. Press the accelerator well down, even at this speed in top gear, and again there is a feeling of being on the end of a rope which is being pulled hard from in front of the car. The way the 300SL does it all with so little fuss is almost uncanny.

"Normally with road tests it is customary to quote cruising speeds, but the 300SL's cruising speed is limited, not by mechanical factors, but by the road and traffic conditions …"

The venerable John Bolster of *Autosport* fame concluded his January 1955 road test with the following prose: "The Mercedes-Benz 300SL is a car of beautiful appearance and almost incredible performance. Its construction and finish are of the very highest class, and its whole design represents a technical tour de force. It has perfect traffic manners, and the sheer joy of handling it on the open road has to be experienced to be believed. There are other cars which are kinder to the less experienced driver, but for the man who is competent to exploit its full performance, this is one of the world's greatest cars."

Coupé production ended in 1956, with the last few of the breed sold in the following year. 1400 had been built in total, with four out of every five cars ultimately shipped to the States (the 300SL was listed at close to $7000 on arrival in the US,

Castrol advertising from early 1957, featuring the Walter Schock 300SL that captured the European Touring Championship (better known as the European Rally Championship) in 1956. Schock was partnered by Rolf Moll during the season.

although prices quickly rose to $8905). Incidentally, in 1994, a 'gullwing' 300SL came to light that was bought piece by piece by an enthusiast in America some two years after production of the model ended. When Bob Doehler, a Studebaker designer, acquired the final parts in 1961, sadly he was unable to complete the project, and the car sat in a half-finished state until he died in 1993. Would this add another unit onto the production total?

THE TYPE W121 190SL

Series production of the 190SL convertible started in May 1955, about six months behind schedule. This was rather ironic, given that the 190SL was always going to provide Daimler-Benz with better volume sales in the United States than the 300SL, so one would have thought it would have been more prudent to get the cheaper machine out first. However, people had an image of the 'Gullwing' body whenever the SL moniker was mooted, hence the model release order, and the smaller-engined car could then ride on its fame using the same 'Sport Licht' badge.

While it's fair to say the 300SL was built using many production parts sourced from the regular road car line, the ratio was much higher in the 190SL. Even the chassis was based on a shortened Type 180 pressed-steel floorpan rather than a dedicated tubular spaceframe, whilst most of the running gear and chassis components were simply lifted straight out of the Type 180 parts bins. This reduced cost and development time, with advantages far outweighing the disadvantages for the manufacturer.

Styled under the watchful gaze of Walter Häcker, the final prototype was exhibited at the Geneva Show in the spring of

The pressed steel floorpan and running gear of the 190SL, introduced to the US market at $3998. At home, it cost DM 16,500.

The Mercedes stand at the 1955 Geneva Show.

1955. Compared with the 1954 show car, the bonnet, bumpers and lights were revised, and the grille and rear wings brought more into line with the 300SL, although the 'Ponton' styling influence was still very much in evidence on the latter.

A hardtop was available from the off, giving the buyer the choice of a convertible roadster (with soft-top only), or a car with a hardtop, supplied with or without a hood. Interestingly, the hardtop model was called a coupé in official paperwork, and came with additional chrome trim on the sills and wheelarch blisters. Early hardtops were crafted from aluminium, but were made from pressed steel from the spring of 1956.

The body itself was largely all-steel on the 190SL, although the front and rear lids and door skins were aluminium. Even lighter doors were announced in the New York press material and appeared in several catalogues thereafter. These, along

Contemporary colour shot of an early 190SL.

The 3000th 190SL, pictured on the line in March 1956.

with the fitment of a lightweight aero-screen and removal of the bumpers helped reduce weight for those wishing to go racing at weekends.

On a more practical note, while the 300SL had next to nothing in the way of trunk space due to its oversized fuel tank, with a parcel shelf behind the seats providing the main luggage area, the 190SL had a good-sized boot. Fitted luggage was available from the maker for both cars. In addition, a third transverse jump-seat was listed for the 190SL, fitting in behind the two front ones, and a bench-style front seat was another option.

The engine was a high output 1897cc sohc four, with the same bore as the 300SL, but a shorter 83.6mm stroke. This bore/stroke combination was quite different to that of the original

A 190SL with hardtop in place, the smaller rear lights indicating that the car was made before June 1956.

The 190SL may not have been quite as glamorous as the 300SL, but it was an accomplished sporting tourer that was infinitely more affordable to buy and run.

The Mercedes stand at the 1957 Frankfurt Show.

Type 180, adding 130cc to the cubic capacity, which had started out at 1767cc for the sedans, but it was duly adopted for the 1956 190 series, as well as the Type 180a of 1957 vintage. In the 190SL, a pair of twin-choke Solex carburettors and an 8.5:1 compression ratio gave 105bhp DIN at 5700rpm, with power taken to the rear wheels through a 4-speed manual transmission.

Production in February 1958. Whilst always fitted to US cars, rear bumper guards had become standard for all markets a year earlier, in July 1957, when they were modified to carry the number plate lights. Note the US reflectors on the tail, introduced at about this time, on the car nearest the camera, and the ROW version on the darker SL in front of it.

British advertising from the autumn of 1958.

A 190SL featured in a brochure produced for members of the US forces serving in Europe, released in late 1959.

Using the Type 180 floorpan allowed the Daimler-Benz engineers to employ the sedan's front subframe arrangement for the SL, with the engine, gearbox and front suspension system carried on an independent pressed-steel cradle that was then attached to the body via rubber mounts to isolate NVH (short for noise, vibration and harshness) – an incredibly advanced feature for the time. The concept was further refined in January 1956 thanks to an improvement in the way the engine was mounted in the subframe.

The suspension itself was quite conventional, with fabricated upper and lower arms at the front, coil springs around damper units, and an anti-roll bar. The back end featured a low-pivot swing axle with the addition of revised, fairly hefty trailing links to give superior roadholding, and the handling was further improved by the adoption of 13-inch wheels and tyres, which, although an unusually small diameter for the day, had the effect of reducing the roll centre height.

A rare Australian 190SL receiving the attention of a Mercedes-Benz Mobile Service technician in 1959, although the rhd car is of slightly earlier

The 190SL dashboard in close to its final form. Only the vent knobs were changed after this, the 1961 models moving over to plastic rather than chrome ends.

The hardtop introduced in October 1959 gave far better rearward visibility. The only significant change applied to the 190SL that helped with identification after this was to the bootlid lock, which was separated from the lift handle in 1960.

Braking was via drums all-round, but with the drums themselves made from cast-iron rather than the expensive Al-Fin bimetal (ribbed alloy sleeves over cast drums) items used on the 3-litre car. They were still finned, at least, for enhanced heat dissipation, while a servo was initially offered as an option before becoming standard shortly after production began. Steering, meanwhile, was via the familiar recirculating-ball system for so long championed by the men in Stuttgart; lhd (left-hand drive) or rhd (right-hand drive) was available, unlike the 300SL coupé, which was officially sold with lhd only.

Walt Woron of *Motor Trend* observed: "Quality is one of the outstanding features. You get the feeling that craftsmen were hard at work, that the artisans who assembled this car are proud of their handiwork … You're certainly hard put to find any faults with the workmanship. It's about as good as you'll see."

BRINGING TOGETHER THE SILVER ARROWS

Bitter rivals in pre-war racing, it is ironic that Daimler-Benz acquired a majority interest in Auto Union in 1958. Auto Union had brought together Horch, Wanderer, Audi and DKW in 1932 – four car companies with expertise in quite different market sectors. With the end of the war, most of the Auto Union factories were placed in what became known as East Germany, so a new company was established in Ingolstadt not long after hostilities ceased. Initially, only the DKW brand rose from the ashes, however.

Complete control of Auto Union was secured in December 1959, when Daimler-Benz was also showing an interest in owning a chunk of BMW. The latter deal fell through, but the Stuttgart firm nurtured the revived Auto Union name before selling the business to Volkswagen in 1964. VW duly brought back the Audi name once it took control of its new subsidiary, later merging it with NSU, which held the rights to the Wankel rotary engine – a power-unit that set the motoring world alight, with Daimler-Benz also falling for its appeal.

Today, Auto Union is ably represented by Audi AG, its cars carrying the same four rings on their noses as the pre-war racers designed by Professor Ferdinand Porsche. Audi is still owned by the Volkswagen group, which has since merged with Porsche. It's a small world in the German car industry!

British advertising for the 190SL from 1961.

Woron's thoughts were echoed by John Bolster in England, who said the 190SL was "... built like a watch, and the finish is superb. Such things as the way the doors close, the fit of the hood, and all the detail work, put this machine in the top quality bracket."

For those who realized the 190SL was not a 300SL – a racer in disguise – it was pleasant to drive, too. *Sports Cars Illustrated* (the forerunner of *Car & Driver*) declared: "Delightful as the car is at low speeds, the upper reaches of the speed range become sheer sensual pleasure. Everything lightens up and the whole car seems to live. The steering becomes seemingly lighter and more positive if such a thing is possible; throttle response gets a pin-point accuracy and, strangely enough, wind-blast lessens in the cockpit."

The 190SL was subjected to a number of detail changes over the years. By far the most important were carried out in time for the 1960 model year, when the engine's compression ratio was upped to 8.8:1 to maintain power output at 105bhp (120bhp SAE), and a new hardtop was introduced to give better visibility. A total of 25,881 190SLs had been built by the time production ended in February 1963.

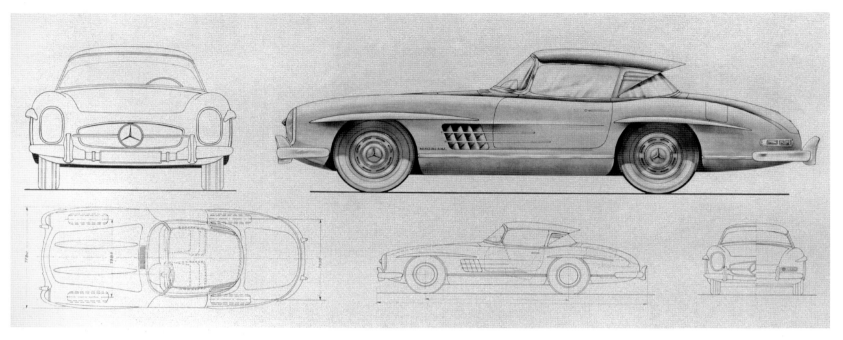

Design drawings for the Type W198 II by Friedrich Geiger.

THE SECOND GENERATION 300SL MODELS

The 300SL had been a magnificent ambassador for the Mercedes-Benz marque, especially in America. Granted, the 190SL brought greater success in the showrooms, but the glamour associated with the 'Gullwing' model was an advertising agent's dream. It was expensive to build, however, and the two SL lines were hardly close in concept. The new 300SL (Type W198 II), first shown at the 1957 Geneva Salon, would take most of the 3-litre car's attributes and package them in a roadster body, thus bridging the gap for the marketing men to go to work on a campaign that gave meaning to the SL badge – at the request of Max Hoffman in the United States, the 'Sport Licht' moniker would forever be associated with open sports cars.

Full-scale production began in May 1957. The biggest difference was found in the bodywork, with the 'Gullwing' arrangement giving way to an open structure with regular doors and frameless wind-up windows. This, of course, led to significant changes in the centre section of the spaceframe, which was further modified to allow a slightly longer tail (combined with a smaller fuel tank, this freed up more trunk space) and a fractionally wider track.

Although very similar to its predecessor in most other respects, careful observation revealed some beautiful detailing on the new car, with fabulous 'Lichteinheit' front lights (bringing headlights, foglights and indicators into a single unit, although US-spec lights were different by necessity), longer chrome flashes in the side vents, and sharper swage lines in the rear wings.

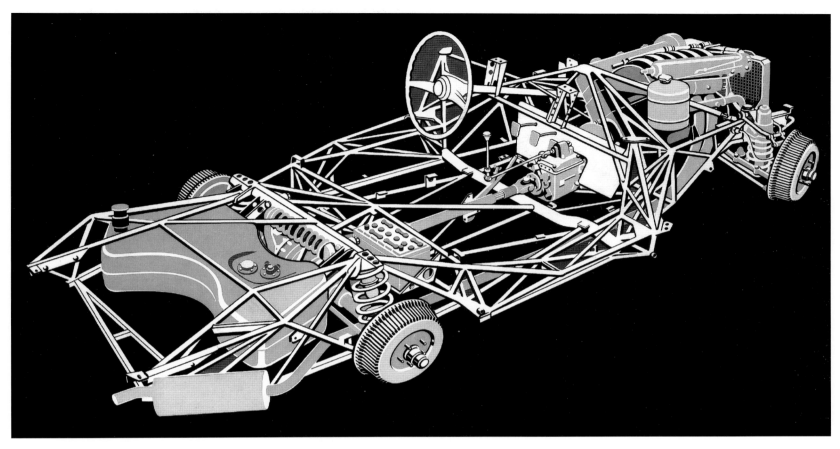

Technical drawing showing the layout and modified spaceframe of the 300SL in roadster guise.

In addition, while the 190SL soft-top required a regular tonneau cover, the 300SL hood dropped into an area behind the seats, being covered by a hinged metal panel when not in use – a very clever piece of design, and something carried over to future SL generations. Introduced at DM 32,500, the roadster was given the option of a removable hardtop in the summer of 1958.

Mechanically, the biggest change was applied to the rear axle, with a new low-pivot swing axle design that incorporated a novel, central compensating spring. The steering was slower than that of the 'Gullwing' model, though still faster than that on the 190SL, and while drums were still fitted, the latest 3-litre car gained servo-assisted discs from March 1961; the 220SE was the first Mercedes-Benz with disc brakes, although they were sourced from Girling and fitted on the front axle only in this case – the SL used a Dunlop set-up on all four wheels.

A 300SL roadster racing in Caracas in March 1957.

Atmospheric shot of one of the earliest 300SL roadsters.

Production shot from February 1958, with a 300SL body being lowered onto a built-up chassis. Note the American-spec headlights, minus their chrome trim in this picture.

English language advert stressing the value of extensive testing.

Dunlop advertising from the spring of 1961 heralding the arrival of disc brakes for the 300SL.

Also, due to the extra chassis bracing required with an open car, plus the luxurious appointments of the interior, the new 300SL was significantly heavier than the closed coupé, so a high-lift sports camshaft was fitted as standard to enhance power output (the sohc six developed 215bhp at 6100rpm). In March 1962, the SL was given an alloy block to save weight, although cast cylinder liners were employed to prolong engine life.

In the meantime, two lightweight roadsters were produced by the Works for use in the American SCCA (Sports Car Club of America) series. These so-called 300SLS models were completed in the spring of 1957, handing Mercedes stalwart Paul O'Shea that year's SCCA Class D championship by a country mile.

And once again, the SL proved to be the darling of the motoring press. *Road & Track* stated in a 1958 article: "While

the price asked seems almost astronomical, there is no doubt that the 300SL roadster is a truly great dual-purpose sports car, equally at home in traffic and the open road, or on the track."

In the spring of 1959, *Autosport* noted: "On the whole, driving this superb machine was an exhilarating experience. Only a race-bred machine could behave like the 300SL, and although

Rows of cars assembled ready for collection from the factory by their new American owners, with 300SLs in the foreground, and the same vehicles on the autobahn, en route to Hamburg, from where they were shipped.

A 1958 300SL with the hood erected, and the interior of the same car. The vehicle was also photographed with the hood down and with optional hardtop fitted.

The elegant rear quarters of the 300SL with hardtop in place. Note the tiny '300SL' badge on the base of the hardtop.

Tailpiece. A US dealership pictured in the 1960s, with a 300SL taking pride of place in the showroom.

there may be a few faster cars, it would be difficult to imagine anything else which could compete as regards sheer perfection of engineering and a remarkably high standard of finish."

Like the 'Gullwing' model, though, this second 300SL was also destined to be a rarity, with only 1858 units built by the time production ended on 8 February 1963. Historically significant in so many ways, these were to be the last Daimler-Benz passenger cars to feature a separate chassis.

4

Birth of the W113 'Pagoda' series

"A new model by the world-famed German concern of Mercedes-Benz is always an event, and the debut at tomorrow's Geneva Show of the new 230SL will be an occasion of particular interest to sporting motorists." (*Motor*, 13 March 1963 issue.)

The last of the 300SL and 190SL models were built in February 1963. However, the 300SLs were little more than exotic, small volume masterpieces. It was the 190SL that had sold in worthwhile numbers, and the next generation Sport Licht model was basically a replacement for the four-cylinder car.

Looking back, it's hard to think of a series from any maker that shared the same moniker, but was so different in appearance and performance levels. Yes, the current crop of AMG models can provide a gap in speed off the line, but they still look similar to their lesser brethren, and the difference in maximum speed is nowhere near as significant (at least in percentage terms) as that between a 190SL and a 300SL – normally the smaller-engined car would top out at around 108mph (173kph), whereas a 3-litre roadster was capable of 155mph (248kph).

In reality, of course, this meant that the two cars were able to co-exist, but volume was restricted at the top-end due to pricing and performance that, frankly, few could handle with any degree of safety, and at the lower end because the 190SL was a heavy car with too few horses – and even those that were under the bonnet were pretty lethargic compared to those of contemporary Italian stallions. The 190SL wasn't cheap either, as the way it was built and the numbers involved dictated a high premium.

What was needed was a good compromise that would meld the best qualities of the homely 190SL and the exotic 300SL in a single package – a car that was quick enough without being

The Untertürkheim works, seen here in 1960.

a handful, whilst practical and comfortable enough to use as a daily driver. At the same time, the single body would need to encompass the styling cues of the Mercedes 'family' look of the 1960s, along with the latest thoughts on safety – an area in which Daimler-Benz was leading the world.

The 220SEb Coupé was an elegant variant of the W111 'Fintail' sedan line, with softer rear quarters and less ornamentation. The styling links between this model, introduced in September 1960, and the W113 SL, are clearly evident. A Cabriolet version was added to the range in September 1961.

Key players in the Mercedes-Benz camp, pictured at the 1954 Italian Grand Prix. From left to right: chief development engineer Rudolf Uhlenhaut, Professor Fritz Nallinger (the firm's Technical Director), and Professor Hans Scherenberg, who would take Nallinger's place at the end of 1965.

Naturally, some purists were disappointed that when the W113 arrived, the SL lost its ability to be competitive on the track. However, as Reinhard Seiffert pointed out in 1963, times had changed. The days of road cars challenging for overall honours in top class racing were well and truly over – sports-racers had become specialist machines, built for the job, enabling manufacturers to make production cars that were altogether more practical, as well as safer, easier to handle, quieter, significantly more comfortable, and cheaper to buy, as volumes could be increased and more off-the-shelf parts employed. Of course, the men at Daimler-Benz would not turn their backs on traditional sporting attributes per se, just remove the rougher edges that made the difference between a good all-rounder for stress-free daily use and a weekend warrior, and replace some of the more exotic components and materials with parts offering better cost-performance.

The concept of a practical sports car that could successfully sell in volume was supported by two things: The Americans were buying more and more imported vehicles, and most of them were sporting variants, this being the heyday of the British LWS models. This bode well for the future, with US sales of Mercedes-Benz cars increasing steadily year on year during the 1950s, but for German makers, events at home were always just as important at this stage in the proceedings.

While the first SL was in its gestation and evolution period, an interesting shift in the German economy was taking place. Germany's industries were once again able to flex their muscles, with wages increasing from an average of DM 1.41 an hour in 1950 to DM 2.89 at the end of the decade.

At the same time, the number of vehicles registered in Germany rose from 787,000 to 4,800,000. Car ownership was no longer a luxury – it had become the norm for all working families. As a result, manufacturers were able to offer more exclusive and sporting variants in the knowledge there was a market for them. Planners could also work around the potential of increased volumes, which, by reducing costs and therefore end-pricing, brought with it a great deal of benefit for maker and customer alike.

The growth in motoring and the various publications that sprang up alongside it naturally gave rise to a more knowledgeable buyer, and this was especially true at the top-end of the market. The Daimler-Benz promotional paperwork of the time was quick to point out technological advances, as well as innovations that enhanced safety – the engineers in Stuttgart giving this design element far more attention than most, allowing the marketing men to use this point as an excellent new angle in advertising. Add in the traditional Mercedes strengths of longevity and build quality, and it's easy to see why people would be swayed toward the three-pointed star as they moved up the social ladder.

With the coming of a new era full of hope and potential for car manufacturers, in every respect, the SL was about to undergo a metamorphosis …

A NEW BODY

Although the older SLs will always have a special place in the hearts of enthusiasts everywhere, from a contemporary viewpoint, one has to remember the huge changes in sports

Karl Wilfert (right), shaking hands with his successor as head of passenger car body development, Guntram Huber.

Friedrich Geiger, who was head of the styling department.

car styling that were taking place as the fifties gave way to the swinging sixties. In Britain, the vintage Jaguar XKs moved over for the stunning E-type. In the States, the transformation can best be summed up by the evolution of the Chevrolet Corvette. Even in Japan, which was only just starting to make an impact in this sector of the market, the Datsun SPL213 was pushed aside by the ultra-modern SP310 Fairlady Roadster. For Daimler-Benz, the stylistic jump from 190SL to the W113 series was no less bold – the project that would bring the two-seater Mercedes up-to-date beginning in earnest at the end of October 1958, when Fritz Nallinger approved the general concept for what was then called a 220SL.

As far as the body was concerned, the main players in the team were Karl Wilfert, the new chief stylist, Friedrich Geiger, and Bela Barenyi – Daimler-Benz safety supremo. Born in Vienna in 1907, Wilfert left Steyr in 1929 to move through the ranks at Daimler-Benz to finally head the Sindelfingen-based body engineering department, although his responsibilities were far greater than simply looking after body development. Geiger, meanwhile, was born in a small town to the east of Stuttgart in the same year, and having joined Daimler-Benz after university, duly left his imprint via a series of inspirational designs in the 1930s to become the head of styling. Barenyi was born on the outskirts of Vienna in 1907, and joined Daimler-Benz just before the war, ultimately giving the German company the lead in many areas of safety innovation.

Whereas the 190SL had borrowed the 180 sedan's platform and technology, the W113-series SL was to be based on a shortened floorpan from the 'Fintail' 220SEb, a car that was introduced in the summer of 1959. The two-seater, short-wheelbase configuration ensured a unique market position for the SL within the Benz line-up, allowing buyers to choose between a pure sporting vehicle or the larger, more luxurious coupés and convertibles in the W111/W112 range. But at least the basic dimensions were in place to work around, with the donor car dictating track width and component sizes, while the wheelbase was a familiar 2400mm (94.5in), carried over from the earlier SLs.

Between 3 April 1959, when the leading dimensions that had a bearing on the car's shape were settled on, and 23 June 1961, when a full-sized clay was first presented to selected Board members for initial approval, the body had gone through countless minor changes, not just to become more contemporary (early sketches leaned heavily toward 190SL and 300SL styling cues), lithe, and aesthetically pleasing, but also to incorporate the necessary engineering hard points prescribed by the 'dream team' of Uhlenhaut and Wilfert, as well as Barenyi's various ideas on safety, which included the integration of crumple zones and the provision of seatbelts.

Bela Barenyi making a point after a 1967 crash test.

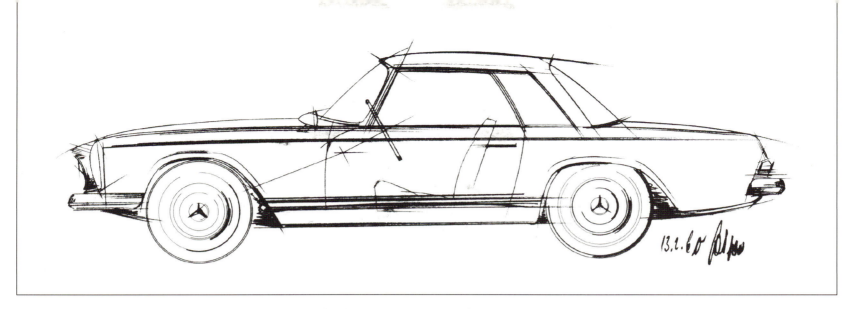

An early Geiger sketch for the W113 SL, dated February 1960. Many of the design elements were already starting to take shape.

Ultimately, by 14 November 1961, when the final rubber stamp was given by the full Board, the decidedly Teutonic body was very much in keeping with the Mercedes-Benz 'family' styling of the time. Indeed, followers of Stuttgart lore would be able to spot the likeness between the W113 and the larger W111/3 220SEb Coupé of 1960 vintage quite easily. One thing that was obvious to all, however, was how strikingly modern this new SL was compared to its predecessors.

While Friedrich Geiger had the final say, the W113's basic lines can be credited to the talented Frenchman, Paul Bracq.

Born in Bordeaux in 1933, Bracq started his career at Citroën, but transferred to the Daimler-Benz camp in 1957, where he stayed for ten years before moving on to a varied but sparkling career, highlighted by a lengthy tenure at BMW.

The frontal styling was perhaps the strongest sign of SL DNA, clearly paying homage to the last of the 300SLs, with its upright Bosch Lichteinheit headlights and a simple grille dominated by a large three-pointed star faired into the nose panel. For ease of production, though, the latest grille sat proud of the body on the latest car, instead of inside the panel. In addition, the top

Paul Bracq – the man credited with the final lines for the W113 model – seen here in his BMW days. Bracq also designed the TGV high-speed train. (Courtesy BMW)

One of the early styling bucks. The W111 model's floorpan gave the 230SL a wider track, and although it looked low and wide, the body was still narrower than that of the old 300SL. Note the Mercedes-Benz badge on the trailing edge of the front wing, and the mock-up of the soft-top in the background.

A styling prototype at a very advanced stage. The lights on the Sport Licht model always seemed to reflect the Mercedes 'family' styling from the time, so the upright headlamps were no big surprise (US light units were different, by the way). With its famous 'Pagoda' roof in place, only small items like the wheel trims, mirror, and door handles remained to be sorted.

of the grille was given a convex shape to accept the engine's height without looking too bulky, while the concave roof and taller headlight pods balanced this. It was also noticeable that the bumpers were far more integrated into the design, as earlier versions had tended to look fussy and cumbersome.

From certain angles, the bulge in the forward-hinged aluminium bonnet (a single elongated vee-shape in profile) was quite subtle compared with that of the 190SL, although body colour also made a difference on its appearance. Moving back, there was a large upright vent housing on the bulkhead, which was more practical than stylish, as it was part of a new heating and ventilation system that was far superior to earlier versions. Beyond this was a pair of 'clap hands' wipers, which were something of a departure for the SL, previous models having conventional windscreen wipers.

The front wings were an exceptionally clean piece of design, displaying a straight-line approach, with the W113 series character lines being as sharp as those of the earlier SLs were rounded. With a short overhang at the front, the various vents seen in early design proposals deleted (although, incredibly, it appears there was a last-ditch attempt to bring them back in 1962!) and modern wheelarch flares that suggested forward motion, these elegant panels were well able to stand the test of time, while the slight curve dropping down into the top of the headlight was part DNA, part aerodynamics.

The windscreen was taller and more upright, but enabled those of bigger build to drive in comfort without the need to hunker down below the top rail, or peep over the top with air blasting their head. It also gave better clearance when the hood was up or the hardtop in place, while minimal curving at the edges reduced distortion when looking through the screen. The A-post looks heavy from behind, but was broken visually at the front via the use of separate chrome trim sections for the screen and post.

After several more ornate door shapes were looked at, the aluminium doors (complete with a lightweight diecast frame) eventually featured a simple shut-line, their depth disguised by chrome strips – one filled with rubber that ran from the trailing edge of the front wheelarch to the front tip of the rear bumper, and another laying atop the rocker panel (or sill); the sill itself was painted black in another trick to visually reduce the car's bulk.

Interestingly, early design proposals had a quarter window, but this idea was dropped in favour of a single piece of glass for the side windows. Other details included a continuation of the waistline crease that ran from the headlight to the tail to break up the slab sides, fizzling out just before reaching the back, and new door handles that were not quite as elegant as those of the 300SL, but certainly more modern than those of the 190.

The slab-sided design theme continued into the rear wing, although a small kick above the waistline (close to the door handle) paid homage to the W113's predecessor, albeit in a far more subtle way than the 190SL, with its heavy bulge above the wheelwell. A carefully sculptured wheelarch flare for each wing matched those found up front (the 'eyebrows' of the earlier cars were considered but quickly dropped), while overhang was kept to a minimum.

Actually, the profile was vaguely similar to that of the 220SEb Coupé, and even the C-post on the SL's production removable hardtop was narrower at the bottom than the top, aping that of its bigger brother. The tail also followed 220SEb Coupé design practice, with a familiar bumper and bootlid style, the same small fins formed by the tops of the rear wings, and the resemblance in the rear lights and chromework surrounding them.

The rear bumper sections were quite plain to match the front blade, split to leave space for a chrome trim strip that sat below the number plate on European-spec cars, or a deeper number plate for US-bound vehicles. Another chrome piece ran below the aluminium bootlid (flat along the bottom to fit in with the SE Coupé's styling) and contained the rear light units, while a smaller piece acted as a bootlid plinth below the three-pointed star.

Badging was to the left, mounted on the convex-shaped boot panel, balancing the exposed fuel cap to the right of the registration plate and the twin exhausts below it, tucked away under the bumper of the offside (as it happens, this was one of the last details to be finalised in the design).

From behind, the general appearance aped that of the front, with the curves in the bootlid matching those in the bonnet, while the truncated fins resembled the headlight pods. Also, as at the front, the wheelarch flares could be seen peeping out, giving the car a sportier stance – an image further enhanced by the use of wider 185-section rubber and the wider track.

The main men behind the W113 – Wilfert (left), Geiger (centre, standing), Nallinger (sitting), and Bracq. They can be seen reviewing 'Fintail' saloon styling in this historic shot.

The soft-top was a beautifully-crafted hood, lined, and hidden beneath a hinged aluminium tonneau cover when not in use, as per earlier 300SL Roadster practice. When the hood was needed, the cover was tilted back to allow the front section of the soft-top to be fitted to the screen rail, then it was closed again to allow the rear of the hood to be fastened and locked down. Although a plastic rear screen was a necessity as a result of all the folding involved, the hood was an exceptional piece of design that was aesthetically pleasing, fairly quick to lower or raise, and came with locking devices that kept the Sonnenland cloth taut at all speeds.

It's worth noting at this point that some cars from the 1967 model year onwards didn't have a soft-top in order to enable a rear bench seat to be fitted. For these vehicles, the metalwork around the rear bulkhead was completely different, although a hardtop could be fitted for winter months.

As it happens, the hardtop was probably the most troublesome area of the whole design. While the body seems

A pre-production model, seen here fitted with crossply tyres (radials were adopted by the time the car made its debut). The front valance was not seen on production vehicles, leaving the tow-hook more exposed.

DIMENSION COMPARISONS

This table shows the chief differences between the W113 series and its immediate predecessors (with hood erect), as well as those dimensions that remained the same:

	300SL (W198 II)	190SL (W121)	230SL (W113)
Wheelbase	2400mm/94.5in	2400mm/94.5in	2400mm/94.5in
Front track	1398mm/55.0in	1430mm/56.3in	1486mm/58.5in
Rear track	1448mm/57.0in	1475mm/58.1in	1487mm/58.5in
Overall length	4570mm/179.9in	4290mm/168.9in	4285mm/168.7in
Overall width	1790mm/70.5in	1740mm/68.5in	1760mm/69.3in
Overall height	1300mm/51.2in	1320mm/52.0in	1320mm/52.0in
Kerb weight	1370kg/3014lb	1160kg/2552lb	1295kg/2849lb
Power-to-weight	6.4kg/hp DIN	11.0kg/hp DIN	8.6kg/hp DIN

For reference, the contemporary 2.2-litre W111 'Fintail' saloons had a 2750mm (108.3in) wheelbase, with 1470mm (57.9in) and 1485mm (58.5in) front and rear track dimensions, and an overall length of 4875mm (191.9in). The width was listed at 1795mm (70.7in), the height at 1510mm (59.4in), while the weight was 1320kg (2904lb) according to the same DIN measurement style used for the figures above.

to have come together fairly painlessly, evolving quickly into the welded pressed-steel unit construction shell that we know and love today, going through early sketches reveals countless variations on the hardtop.

The earliest proposals had very thin rear pillars, angled forward to give a dramatic overhang of the roof panel at its trailing edge. The pillar was later filled in to add strength, and later still, the overhang reduced to give a profile that closely resembled the hardtop fitted to the 300SL Roadster and late 190SLs. This was obviously not a good scenario for an all-new car!

Everybody involved in the styling side of the business duly put their thinking caps on, and, after seeing a very basic top with a slightly rounded roof, light C-posts and a wraparound rear screen, ultimately, Karl Wilfert came up with the signature 'Pagoda' hardtop.

Secured at four points, the 46kg (101lb) Pagoda roof had high sides, allowing better ingress and egress, and a larger glass area for improved visibility, while the lowered centre section visually reduced the car's height and helped keep rain off the side windows to a certain extent. The shape of the rear pillars were duly refined to give an exceptionally strong structure that was readily adapted for dedicated luggage racks that could be bought as an option. There were even vents in the back to extract stale air from the cabin via perforations in the headlining – it was a very thorough piece of design all-round.

It's fair to say the W113 was fairly conservative from a styling point of view, but the lack of ornamentation gave the new car a very clean and functional look. In combination with reduced overhangs and bigger 14-inch wheels and tyres filling out the arches (13-inch rims were used on the 190SL), the new car also managed to look lighter and more nimble than its predecessor at the same time.

Oddly, though, the aerodynamics were not as good. The Cd was far from amazing at 0.51, or 0.48 with the hood up. The 190SL displayed a figure of 0.46, and even the boxy 220SE was positively slippery by comparison. The short body length and upright window carried a lot of the blame, augmenting the normal fluttering of airflow one sees whenever a convertible runs with the hood down.

The showroom model. The hardtop was designed in such a way as to give maximum strength and increased glass area, while the signature concave dip in the centre section gave the car a lighter, more compact appearance, without detracting from the original intention of enhancing visibility through larger glass sizes.

Lengthy sessions on a four-poster 'shaker' and testing in France in July 1962 revealed the body to be strong and free from any obvious design defects, so the green light was given for production. Ultimately, the SL's styling bridged the existing range and the 250/300-series saloons that heralded a new era. Many of the sports car's styling cues, including wheelarch profiles, tail detailing (including rear lights and bumpers) and blacked-out sills were duly carried over into the new breed.

Another aspect in which the W113 lead the way was in safety. As one of the brochures noted: "Some aspects of the car were developed with aesthetics in mind, many features help to enhance comfort, but everything – every single detail – was designed to promote active safety."

The 230SL was the first sports car to feature Barenyi's stiff passenger cell and deformation 'crumple zones' built into the structure at the front and rear, which had been used for the first time in the Fintail sedans. Other safety innovations were duly built into the interior.

A FRESH INTERIOR

The dashboard was a mixture of contemporary saloon practice and the traditional 300SL Roadster instrument pack, with its minor gauges (fuel level, water temperature, oil pressure and warning lights) grouped in a single vertical section with a small rheostat knob at the bottom, surrounded by a round VDO tachometer on the left and a matching speedometer on the right for lhd cars, or the opposite for rhd vehicles.

Compared to the 300SL, though, the layout was less fussy, and a good deal more functional. The controls for the two-speed windscreen wipers and electric screen washer were integrated into a new multi-purpose stalk that was also used for indicators and flashing headlights (a small switch was fitted to the left of the clutch pedal, or under the dash on the first 650 or so cars, for dipped beam activation). The W113 was the first model to employ this modern wand, but its use later spread through the entire Daimler-Benz range.

The steering wheel sat lower than it had in the 190SL, and was a two-spoke affair, as before, but the spokes were straight and the centre boss padded to reduce head injuries in the case of a heavy accident. In extreme circumstances, the steering column collapsed – another safety feature, this time to reduce chest injuries. The horn ring was a full circle originally, but later kept to the lower section only, giving a better view of the instruments. Officially, production steering wheel rims and centre bosses were black, with ivory becoming a no-cost option (NCO) in time for the 1964 season (it should be noted that a handful of earlier cars have this feature, though), along with a matching gearknob.

Although the top roll and instrument binnacle was padded, along with the lower section to protect the knees, as per tradition, the dash panel was painted in body colour. The centre section housed the illuminated heating and ventilation controls, with round directional vents on the outer edges (complete with their own sliders for air volume control), augmented by smaller fixed side window demister vents placed to the side of them.

Below the heater sliders and fan blower switch was the radio slot (a blanking plate with the model designation was supplied if a radio wasn't fitted), while the speaker and grille were placed above it in the top roll. A clock was placed next to the radio slot (always furthest from the driver compared to the radio, as lhd and rhd cars had different layouts), with a cigarette lighter on the opposite side.

The glovebox was lockable, and played host to a small map reading light that sat flush on the glovebox lid. The only other items of note were the ignition barrel and main lighting switch, which sat underneath the speedometer and tachometer respectively. The speedo, incidentally, was calibrated to 220kph (upped from 210kph on prototypes) or 140mph, while the 7000rpm 'rev-counter' was red-lined at 6500rpm. There was no choke control, as the AED in the fuel-injection system looked after the mixture automatically.

Meanwhile, in addition to the oddment storage provided by the glovebox, door pockets were fitted to the lower section of the inner door trim. This was one of the few areas where the design was reviewed time and time again, with longer, narrower armrests, integrated door pulls, and pocket shapes under constant review. Eventually, in the summer of 1962, a very short armrest was chosen, thus giving better access to the bin below. Most of the other door furniture was familiar to W111 drivers.

The gear selector was fixed to the top of the centre tunnel, which also featured a shallow wooden tray between the seats. It was ideal for loose change and so on, and had a covered ashtray fitted at the front end. The handbrake sat to the left of the tunnel, and stayed in this position regardless of whether the car was left- or right-hand drive.

The seats – fitted slightly lower than they were in a 190SL, thanks to the reduced scuttle height – were touted as 'buckets' in promotional paperwork, but there's probably just a touch of artistic licence in that description. There was definitely a certain amount of curvature on the outer edges to hold and support occupants, but comfort was given priority over sporting character.

Indeed, contemporary advertising for the car noted that the SL came "... with the chassis and engine of a sports car, but the comfort of a touring saloon." As it happens, comfort was considered another safety feature, as a driver could "... stay fresh for longer" – a situation further helped by the large amount of fore and aft movement provided and almost infinite range of adjustment in the seatback.

Behind the seats was a carpeted shelf that could be used for carrying luggage, or put to work as a 'jump-seat' for occasional use.

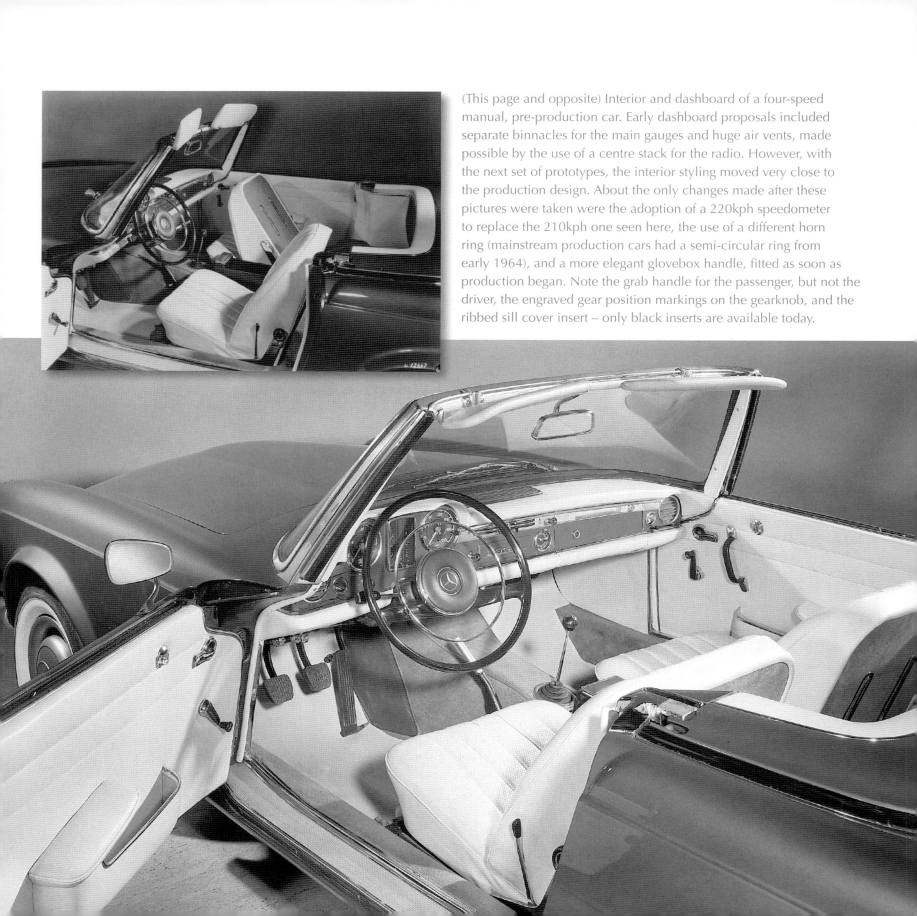

(This page and opposite) Interior and dashboard of a four-speed manual, pre-production car. Early dashboard proposals included separate binnacles for the main gauges and huge air vents, made possible by the use of a centre stack for the radio. However, with the next set of prototypes, the interior styling moved very close to the production design. About the only changes made after these pictures were taken were the adoption of a 220kph speedometer to replace the 210kph one seen here, the use of a different horn ring (mainstream production cars had a semi-circular ring from early 1964), and a more elegant glovebox handle, fitted as soon as production began. Note the grab handle for the passenger, but not the driver, the engraved gear position markings on the gearknob, and the ribbed sill cover insert – only black inserts are available today.

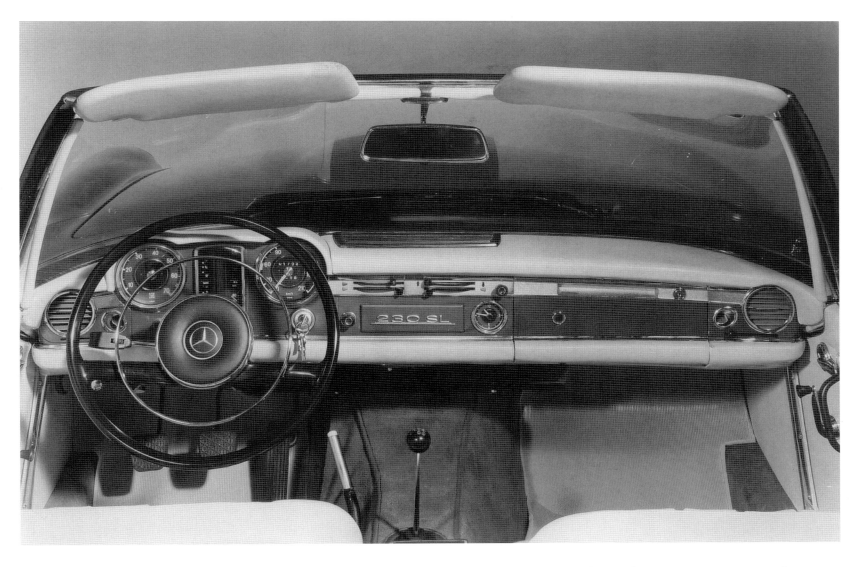

In fact, a third transverse seat was made available from the off, and a bench seat was eventually put on the market, too, although fitment of the latter meant losing the hood mechanism.

Final interior details, such as the use of carpet on seatbacks, padded sunvisors, the provision of a dipping, anti-dazzle rearview mirror, and so on, were outlined and approved in August 1962, by which time the anchors for the optional, diagonal-pattern seatbelts had been integrated into the design.

As well as providing faultless ergonomics, such was the progress in modern packaging, despite being slightly shorter than a 190SL, the 230SL offered a far greater level of safety, 14 per cent more space in the cockpit, 38 per cent more glass area, and 26 per cent more luggage space.

The last-mentioned improvement was made possible by a late design change. At one point, the battery was to have been placed in the boot, although it was eventually tucked in behind the front grille, low down on the nearside. From a handling point of view, the original idea would have been better, but at least this position offered easier maintenance and a great deal less wiring, with heavy cables that would have ran almost the entire length of the car. It also freed up a significant amount of luggage space, now put at $0.34m^3$, or $12ft^3$.

ENGINE & TRANSMISSION

The 190SL had been tested with a 2.2-litre six from one of the contemporary Mercedes saloons as early as June 1956, with Erich Waxenberger (who would later run the works rally team after making his name tuning and occasionally racing touring cars) in charge of the transplant. The difference was notable, to say the least, with a full 29 seconds knocked off the time taken to lap the Nürburgring. It was an indication of things to come, with the first signs of Waxenberger's shoehorning habits (he is the person responsible for creating the 300SE 6.3) and a promise of better performance for the base SL in the future.

In fact, there were thoughts of a 220SL entering production as a 1958 model using the 190SL body. Discussions then moved toward employing new styling for the 220SL, but costs ruled this out, and, with other more pressing concerns to think about, talks concerning the project dragged on to such an extent that it was decided to simply use the six-cylinder engine for the next generation SL instead. So, just as the 190SL had used a special version of the 180 saloon's engine, it was decided that the W113 SL would also borrow its motive power from the contemporary sedan family.

Production of the 220SL was as good as approved using an evolution of the final six-cylinder 'Ponton' unit – the M127 II (127.980) – when it was suddenly realised that competitors in the GT arena, such as Alfa Romeo and Porsche, were starting to field faster and ever-more powerful cars. The Jaguar E-type had also put in an appearance (having made its debut at the 1961 Geneva Show), bringing with it racing car levels of performance. In a bid to bring the SL in line with the new benchmarks set in Milan, Stuttgart and Coventry, the engineers at Daimler-Benz thus decided it was time to up the ante with their new two-seater.

Andreas Weber started work on the 2.2-litre engine fitted with an experimental six-plunger pump for the mechanical fuel-injection system. Using a higher 9.5:1 compression ratio, a test carried out on 8 January 1962 showed that the unit developed a healthy 142bhp at 5300rpm in this state of tune. The torque curve dropped off quicker than those plotted for the Porsche Carrera 2 and Fiat 2300S engines tested the same day, but the power delivery was remarkably linear, and peaked a fair bit higher, too.

Encouraged by this result, Weber decided to bore out the engine by 2mm, taking it from 80mm to 82mm, whilst retaining

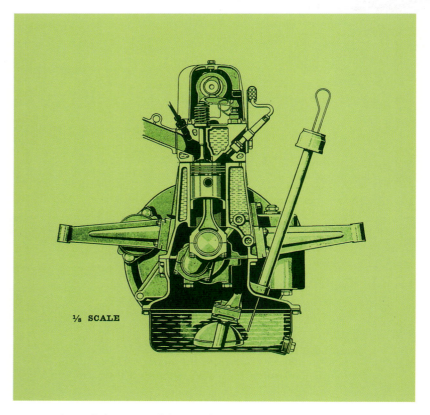

Technical drawing of the 2.3-litre, fuel-injected sohc engine.

the 72.8mm stroke. This gave a displacement of 2306cc, instead of the 2195cc listed against the M127 III (127.982) engine found in the W111 'Fintail' 220SEb models.

With this increased capacity, the oversquare 2.3-litre six would form the basis of the 230SL's M127 II (127.981) production unit. Initial experiments with the 2306cc displacement, a 9.5:1 compression ratio (the 220SEb saloons used an 8.7:1 ratio) and a new camshaft resulted in very little difference compared to the 142bhp seen on the dynamometer a week earlier, although there was no doubt progress was certainly being made, with the power delivered in a less stressful manner.

Ultimately, the 2.3-litre engine was signed off in principle (at 2306cc, it was classed as 2290cc – or under 2.3 litres – using the German tax formula), and the 230SL moniker was approved for the new car at a meeting held on the 14 January 1963. This allowed technical and sales information to be gathered, processed, printed and distributed, albeit at a late hour

The straight-six was a tight fit in the W113 engine bay, but access was excellent for all maintenance points. The throttle body was attached to a single plenum chamber with six ram tubes, giving a similar layout to the 300SL, albeit not quite as exotic-looking. Note also the brake servo and radiator header tank locations – swapped over on rhd cars. This was the first time Daimler-Benz had used an alternator instead of a dynamo for charging the electrical system, incidentally.

considering the Geneva Show had been chosen for the launch, and that was only two months away.

There was still work to do, though. Several months of refining the design resulted in the adoption of a brand new alloy head (while the main block was cast-iron, the lower section of the crankcase was also made of aluminium alloy to reduce weight) that played host to bigger valves and a hotter chain-driven sohc to give revised timing and greater overlap. Intake valves were 39mm (1.54in) in diameter, while the sodium-cooled exhaust valves were 35mm (1.38in) across and given a so-called 'rotocap' device to turn them each time they were opened to spread the build-up of heat more uniformly.

The intake system was fine-tuned, with new aluminium alloy manifolds to allow the Bosch port injection to work at its best, the ram tube lengths giving a good compromise on low-end torque and top-end power. The six-plunger pump proved reliable enough for production (saloons continued with a two-plunger type), while the injection nozzles were ultimately placed close to the inlet valves so that half the total spray volume went straight past the valve and into the cylinder. This then evaporated to contribute to the internal cooling of the head. As *Autocar* noted: "The system would appear to be a compromise solution between that giving maximum power, as in the 300SL, and the desirability to provide the flexibility of the 220SE."

There was also a modified exhaust system to give freer engine breathing, the pair of lightweight, three-into-one fabricated tubular steel manifolds giving a perfect starting point for the twin-pipe exhaust system, which incorporated a central silencer and a back box; the pair of exhaust tips were duly lengthened in September 1963, finished by stainless sleeves that protruded well beyond the bumper but slid forward if they were hit to avoid damage.

Despite the many changes at the top of the engine, the components in the lower section were kept pretty much the same. The forged crankshaft ran in four plain main bearings with a vibration damper on the end (duly modified to become a unique SL item in September 1963), while the Mahle alloy pistons were attached to the crank by forged steel connecting rods.

Some of the engineering team requested an oil cooler, but Professor Nallinger declared that the additional weight and cost couldn't be justified on production cars, although certain vehicles entered in competition would ultimately be fitted with the device.

As for the 12-volt electrical system, naturally supplied by Bosch of Stuttgart, the most notable thing was the use of an alternator used for charging the 55Ah battery. In fact, the 230SL had the honour of being the first German car to be fitted with one.

With the compression ratio finally set at 9.3:1 (still quite high, but *Motor* noted it could detect no pinking on Four Star, 97-octane fuel), the 2.3-litre unit developed a healthy 150bhp DIN – an increase of 35bhp on the 127.980, or 30bhp on the 127.982. On saying that, one wonders if the catalogue rating was perhaps a touch optimistic, as most of the test engines were listed as having between 140 and 143bhp DIN on tap.

The standard G72 transmission was a Daimler-Benz (albeit built by Getrag!) four-speed unit tacked onto the back of the engine and joined by a 228mm (9in) diameter Fichtel & Sachs single dry plate clutch. This came with baulk-ring synchromesh on all forward gears, which were shifted in a regular 'H' pattern, with reverse outside it, up and to the left of these. Internal ratios were 4.42 on first, 2.28 on second, 1.53 on third, and a direct 1.00 for top, while a 3.75:1 final-drive was specified for the rubber-mounted hypoid-bevel rear axle.

For the first time on an SL, a Daimler-Benz automatic gearbox was available as an option, sporting the now-famous staggered selector gate to reduce the chances of unwanted changes. Interestingly, throughout the W113 era, its layout was the opposite of today's quadrant, with 'Park' at the bottom of the gate. Available fairly soon after full-scale production started, this four-speed epicyclic unit lacked a torque converter but came with a hydraulic coupling and ratios of 3.98, 2.52, 1.58 and 1.00, along with the same 3.75:1 final-drive.

A five-speed ZF gearbox was still being tested as late as the summer of 1963, with a dog-leg first under the reverse position, and second through fifth in a conventional 'H' pattern to the right. It would be quite some time before the 5MT unit made it into the showrooms, though.

The engine and transmission were mounted to the body at three attachment points – via arms on either side of the power-unit that bolted onto the front subframe with HVH insulated by special rubber bushes, and a rear support bracket to balance the weight.

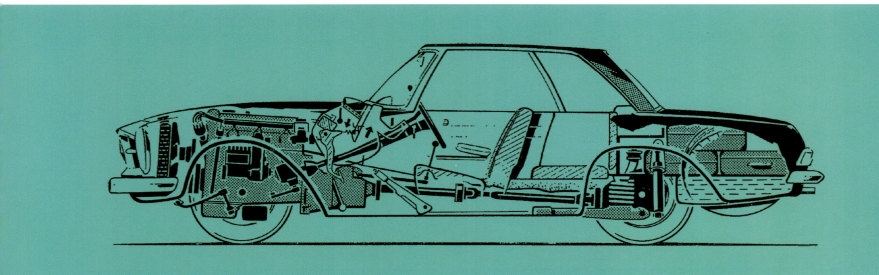

General layout of the 230SL.

CHASSIS DETAILS

Most of the suspension components were taken directly from the 220SEb, although the SL had a different front subframe that featured heavier tubular-section mountings for the anti-roll bar brackets. In its basic layout, it was actually quite similar to that of the 190SL up front, albeit with detail improvements. The rear, too, was also fairly familiar, although a transverse compensator spring (as used on the later 300SLs) was added aft of the differential, allowing engineers to adopt softer road springs combined with firmer damping for enhanced comfort and anti-roll characteristics.

For the record, the independent front suspension system comprised of unequal length upper and lower wishbones, separate coil springs and gas-filled Bilstein telescopic dampers, and a 22mm (0.87in) diameter anti-roll bar. As it happens, the W113 body was 40 per cent stiffer than the 190SL shell, providing a good base structure for the suspension to work properly.

The independent rear suspension was made up of a single-joint, low-pivot swing axle with a transverse compensator spring, coil springs mounted on trailing arms (just before the axle line), and telescopic shock absorbers, mounted in a similar position but on the opposite side of the driveshaft casings. There was no anti-roll bar at the back.

Front suspension layout of the W111 saloon. The W113 SL was basically the same, except for a mounting for the anti-roll bar hangers on the subframe.

Rear suspension of the W111. Again, the W113 was much the same, although the wheels, tyres, and hubcaps were different on the SL. The round bases on top of the trailing arms (close to the driveshaft casings) were spring seats, while the dampers were attached aft of the axle line.

The W113 series was originally scheduled to have been equipped with 7.25 crossplies on 13-inch rims, as per the 'Fintail' models from 1960 onwards (the earliest cars were fitted with 6.70-width tyres). The decision to plump for radial tyres was not officially taken until October 1962.

The latest low-pivot swing axle and extra width of the 220SEb platform (thus allowing a wider track) enabled Daimler-Benz to take full advantage of radial tyre technology, which was still pretty much in its infancy compared to the development time that had gone into crossplies.

This move naturally meant more last-minute testing was necessary to fine-tune the chassis to suit the new rubber. By the end of November, though, the testing staff – led by Rudy Uhlenhaut, of course – had already declared the change a great success, achieving higher cornering power and improved driver feedback whilst perfecting the ride/handling compromise, and all the chassis settings were ready for production specification. This was done with remarkable speed, considering the 230SL was the first series-production Mercedes-Benz to be fitted with belted radials.

The 185 HR14 tyres were initially supplied by either Continental AG (which made a new tyre called the Halbgurtel)

Mercedes' reputation for toughness was hard-earned, and used to great effect in advertising, as seen in this UK piece dating from March 1962. The same 'unbreakable' quality had to be built into the new SL.

Safety was another watchword that had helped Daimler-Benz rise to the top of the pack. The company built its one-millionth post-war Mercedes-Benz passenger car in September 1962.

or Phoenix AG, the latter (ironically, taken over by Continental in 2004) using Firestone tread patterns at the time. One will also see German-made Dunlop SPs fitted on test cars occasionally.

Ultimately, the tyres, which were quite fat for the day, rode on 5.5J x 14 steel rims, at least until July 1964, when a 6J rim width was adopted. Hubcaps started off quite ornate, although the centres were eventually painted to take away at least some of the flashy chrome, while the outer trim rings were further simplified. Ironically, one of the proposals used on the W111 saloons was later reappraised and adopted on the 280SL, but for early cars, it was decided during a meeting of department heads in the spring of 1962 to go with a simple outer chrome ring matched with a simple nave plate mounted on a painted wheel; the hubcap was usually colour-keyed to the body, although it often matched the hardtop colour on later cars supplied with 'two-tone' paint.

Behind the wheels, the majority of the braking system would have been familiar to Benz buffs, with solid 253mm (10.0in) diameter discs up front, straight off the 300SE and adopted on the 220SEb from April 1962. These brake discs were mated with three-pot calipers made under licence by ATE in the Alfred Teves factory in Frankfurt, using a Girling design. At the back, the SL was considered light enough for the drums of the lower-powered W111 machines, despite the 300SE having 255mm (10.0in) discs from the off. These Al-Fin drums were 230mm (9.1in) in diameter and 65mm (2.6in) wide, and whilst not quite as good at pulling a car down from high speed, at least they gave a strong handbrake.

In addition, a major advantage for the 230SL was the adoption of split front/rear circuits for the brakes for added safety, and the use of an ATE vacuum servo (soon adopted on the 1964 model year 'Fintail' cars).

Finally, completing the chassis specification, the recirculating ball steering was a carry-over from the saloons, with a damper to reduce road shock transmission, while a well-weighted PAS system was offered as an option. As it happens, the power assisted steering had a faster ratio, with three turns lock-to-lock instead of the regular three-and-a-half.

A GENEVA DEBUT

Prototype vehicles were spotted throughout Germany and the South of France during the autumn and winter of 1962, and testing continued at the works facilities, even during the heavy snow that fell in the opening months of 1963. Most of the time, these cars had disguise panels fitted, such as fake tail-fins, dummy grille emblems, odd chrome pieces to break up the lines, and smaller headlamps that looked like they'd come off a 190 saloon. Come March, however, the need to run in camouflage soon came to an end …

With the Cuban Missile Crisis thankfully fizzling out in the background, motoring enthusiasts could once again look forward to an exciting future. As the infamous winter of 1962 – which saw the world wondering if another major war was inevitable – gave way to spring, the 1963 Geneva Show witnessed some interesting debuts, such as the Michelotti Jaguar, Pininfarina's convertible body on the Fiat 2300 chassis, and a special Bertone-bodied Alfa Romeo. But the star of the show was undoubtedly the Mercedes-Benz 230SL.

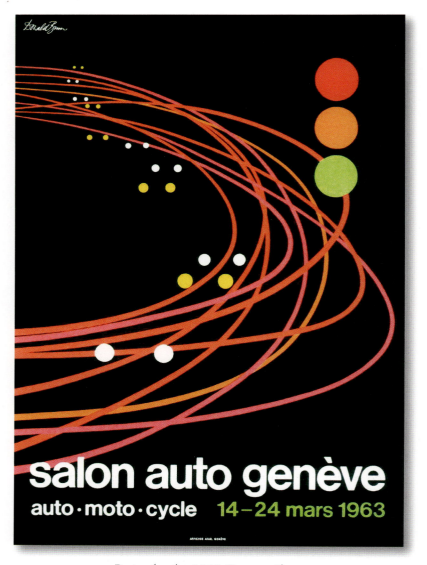

Poster for the 1963 Geneva Show.

Indeed, Daimler-Benz put two 230SLs on display at the Swiss event. By the end of the show, held during the second half of March, almost 380,000 visitors had been able to see the new Mercedes in open and hardtop guise.

The first price list was issued on 15 March 1963 to coincide with the Geneva Show, with the 230SL Roadster quoted at DM 20,600 including a soft-top, although deletion of the cloth hood reduced the invoice by DM 750. This normally implied a hardtop was ordered, and this was a DM 1100 extra.

Debut time in Switzerland. With the wheelbase shortened to the same length as that of the earlier SLs, the bigger wheel and tyre combination, and reduced overhangs at both ends, gave the W113 an altogether more modern appearance compared to its predecessors.

Standard equipment included manual transmission, radial tyres, foglights (built-in units within the lower section of the headlight enclosures), MB-Tex vinyl trim, a locking fuel cap, manual radio aerial, glovebox with map reading light, and a driver's-side mirror, even though some of the earliest pictures released show cars without one.

Other options not already mentioned included spotlights (DM 50), ornamental parallel chrome strips on the upper surface of the hardtop to allow roof-racks to be fitted (DM 40, with luggage or ever-popular ski-racks available as accessories), power-assisted steering (DM 550), leather trim (DM 800), Unica seatbelts (DM 55 per side), a transverse rear seat (DM 200, or DM 250 in leather), fire extinguisher (DM 60), fitted suitcases (DM 365), a first aid box (DM 30), and a 'D' country recognition emblem for DM 8.

Audio equipment included the contemporary Becker Grand Prix radio at DM 650, the Becker Mexico at DM 630, or the Becker Europa at DM 490. One could also order an automatic aerial to replace the standard item for an additional DM 180.

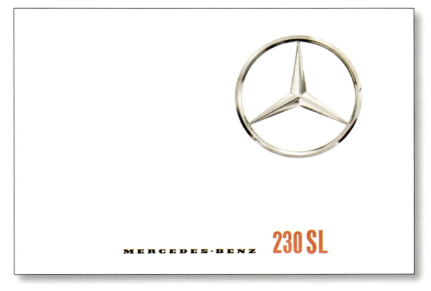

Cover and one of the more interesting pictures from the preliminary 230SL catalogue produced in time for the Geneva Show. The proper brochure, issued for the Frankfurt Show, had twice as many pages and more accurate photography.

Standard coachwork colours (to September 1963)
Black (040), White (050), White-Grey (158), Light Beige (181), Graphite Grey (190), Dark Green (268), Dark Blue (332), Signal Red (568), Dark Bordeaux Red (573), Ivory (658), and Papyrus White (717).

Hood colours (to September 1963)
Black, Marine Blue, Grey or Brown.

Trim colours & materials (to September 1963)
Turquoise (112), Bronze (113), Light Natural (114), Dark Blue (115), Caviar (116), Red (117), Light Grey (118), White-Grey (119), Cognac (120) or Cream (121) MB-Tex vinyl, or Black (201), Red (203), Light Grey (207), Cream (209), Cognac (216), Turquoise (217), Bronze (218), Light Natural (219), Dark Blue (220) or White-Grey (221) perforated leather.

Carpet (to September 1963)
Black, Cream, Graphite Grey, Dark Grey, Turquoise, Medium Red or Brown.

The colour range and trim options were fairly limited initially, although only around 450 cars had been built by the time the Frankfurt Show was held in September. As it happens, the Geneva Show was something of a preview, as there was still a great deal of development work going on behind the scenes. Granted, only minor details were changed, such as camshaft construction rather than lobe profiles, some changes to the hydraulics on the power-assisted steering, and subtle tweaks to the cooling and lubrication system, but it's interesting to note

One of the pre-production cars, used extensively by the press, being hurled around by Erich Waxenberger. Pilot production began in March 1963, with full-scale production starting four months later, in July. As many as 30 'zero series' cars (all with unique chassis numbers distinct from the regular codes) were built in the pilot run to use for show, demonstration, testing, and publicity purposes.

(Above and opposite) Two pieces of German advertising from the time of the 230SL's debut. The 'Händlerschrift' text on the one above is where the dealer name would go.

that even as late as 17 April 1963, Professor Nallinger declared the 230SL was "... almost ready for series production."

Between the Geneva Show and the Frankfurt Show, work continued on refining the PAS system, eliminating sources of NVH (leading to the replacement of the rear springs in August 1963), and the door locks.

There was also a great deal of R&D time allocated to curbing piston failures. While most manufacturers would have been more than happy with the level of reliability shown by the SL, a 1.73 per cent failure rate was not good enough for Uhlenhaut and his men, especially when the 220Sb figure was 0.04 per cent, and even the higher-stressed injected version had an average failure rate of 0.13 per cent.

Countless experiments were carried out using different piston clearances, new rings, and oil routing and pressure variations. In fact, it appears the problem was never really cured to the exacting standards prescribed by Daimler-Benz. A new crankcase and con-rods were used from December 1963, and several modified pistons followed over the next couple of months. Ultimately, two full years into the 230SL run, new Mahle pistons with molybdenum-filled piston rings were specified in April 1965, along with shorter connecting rods to suit.

INITIAL PRESS REACTION

May was supposed to have been the full production start date, but suppliers were not up to speed. Not until July did the lines work at full steam. Meanwhile, thanks to a preliminary ride-and-drive session held at the small Monthoux circuit close to Geneva, quite a few important road tests had appeared across the globe.

In its introduction of the 230SL, *Autocar* observed in March 1963: "Sports cars have progressed from the days when they were invariably uncomfortable to ride in, had cramped accommodation and poor weather protection. In other words, the modern idea is a fully equipped and sophisticated car, designed for long distance touring in all climates and having excellent luggage accommodation for two people. The 230SL is fully in keeping with this concept."

Motor Revue, in its first quarterly issue of 1963, echoed this point: "Though the 230SL deserves the eye of the really 'fast' crowd far more than its [190SL] forerunner, it has all the qualities of a boulevard ride, with excellent fusion of the two poles."

Most people seemed happy with the styling, which *Sports Car Graphic* described as "... well-balanced, with very personal lines, which are much emphasised by the unusual concave hardtop."

Car & Driver added: "The angular body lines arouse very little wind noise (except when a window is open) and directional stability is never a problem; the 230SL seems even less sensitive to crosswinds than the Gibraltar-steady 220SE coupé."

That doyen of motoring scribes, Bernard Cahier, wrote: "The body itself is beautifully finished all-round, and the luxurious, tasteful interior is of the highest quality. The well-conceived dashboard is very elegant and all instruments are concentrated in a clear, compact unit. Lovely glove quality leather is used to cover the dashboard and trimmings, while, if wanted, the large comfortable bucket-type seats can also be had in leather. These seats are fully adjustable (reclining type) and the driver finds an excellent driving position right away. The floor-type stick shift (which is of a similar type in the automatic version) is well-placed, quick and pleasant to use. The handbrake, however, which is located against the gearbox tunnel, has a rather crude appearance, which contrasts with the general plush appearance of the rest of the car. Another feature which I noticed (although many did not seem to mind at all) was the rather large steering wheel, which in my opinion, took too much room and could even be an inconvenience for a tall person driving close to it."

But once on the move, Cahier was impressed: "When at the wheel of the 230SL for the first time, one is immediately impressed by the sensation of comfort, luxury, and outstanding visibility about you. The convenient instruments are easy to read, the turning signal, wipers, washers and light are all concentrated into one practical stick gadget on the steering column, easy to use once accustomed to it. The gearbox is quick to respond and the engine, although not entirely dead quiet at maximum revs, is very smooth. It is so smooth and flexible, in fact, that you can actually drive to under 10mph in top gear without making the engine suffer, and then accelerate away briskly."

However, some journalists were unhappy with the 4MT's gear ratio spacing (first was very low, while there was a very big gap between third and fourth), and at least one stated that the "... shift itself is a little vague in its gate."

Cahier continued: "I found the optional, stiffer type of suspension to be the best of the two, as it still gives a comfortable ride while it provides the car with more precise, better handling, and a minimum of body roll ... The brakes proved to be up to the performance of the car, and no trace of unpleasant fading was noticed during all my driving."

Posing the question over whether the W113 provided better performance, *Road & Track* said: "The 230SL is not meant to show a clean pair of heels to GTOs and Cobras. However, if better performance means a well-balanced combination of solid acceleration, faultless engine flexibility, cruising speeds adequate for any highway, and road manners capable of coping with surfaces and bends of every description, then the Mercedes definitely qualifies."

As far as the fuel-injection was concerned: "The new arrangement seems to be worth what it costs. Getaway can be as smooth as that of any luxurious town carriage; pedal response is always the same, and perfectly predictable; and when the foot goes to the floorboards, the power comes in with convincing eagerness. The engine note is crisp, but probably will not offend the ears of sensitive policemen. Even at high speeds (6500 is quite something for a 2.3-litre, after all) the engine operates freely and without any suggestion of strain. The hard, metallic note so typical of the 300SL and SE has disappeared, and the general impression is that of a powerful, very well tamed animal. Slow speed behaviour is equally convincing: With the car slowed down to only 1200rpm in fourth gear and the throttle then floored, there is smooth acceleration, no jerks, no coughing. It really seems impossible to catch this unit on the wrong foot.

"The performance figures prove that the 230SL really belongs to the fast car group. A standing-quarter mile in 17.3 seconds is not bad, and on most highways, traffic or speed limits will decide the average speed – not the car. Because the 230SL takes the place of the 190SL, this is real progress. Actually, the smaller newcomer will not be appreciably slower from A to B than even its glamorous aunt, the 300SL."

Of the handling, *Car & Driver* observed: "The car's cornering power is unusually high, but, with a nose-heavy weight distribution (52.5 per cent on the front wheels) and a 'sticky' rear suspension, there is quite a bit of built-in understeer which Mercedes-Benz likes to think of as a safety factor – if you close the throttle in the middle of a turn, there is a smooth transition to what feels like a neutral steering condition. It's all very stable – you simply steer your way around the turn until you feel like applying power again.

"Somewhat surprisingly, opening the throttle wide in a turn will increase the understeer, though not to the extent that the front end ploughs. Steering with the throttle, ie, utilising the variable slip angles of the Continental radial tyres, thus becomes a highly practicable cornering method, obviating the necessity for anything as Wagnerian as a four-wheel drift.

"As the centre of gravity of the 230SL is located about 16.5in [420mm] above the ground, the front anti-sway bar does not have to work terribly hard at keeping the car level in corners. The driver, in fact, feels no roll at all, but spectators do note a definite lean.

"The front roll centre is only 4.8in [122mm] above ground level, while the low-pivot, single-joint swing-axle rear end (pioneered by Mercedes-Benz in 1951) has its roll centre at 8.4in [215mm]. There is no anti-sway bar at the rear, as the Mercedes-Benz system has much the same roll stiffness as a normal rigid-axle layout. In addition to the coil springs taking vertical loads from the rear axles, there is an auxiliary horizontal coil spring behind the differential carrier coupled to both axle halves which resists large vertical axle movements while allowing a lower roll couple – the same effect Porsche achieves with a transverse 'camber compensator' leaf spring.

"Wheel travel is normal for a sports-touring car; in compression, the front springs allow 4.5in [115mm] and the rear springs 4.1in [105mm]. On rebound, front wheel travel is 3.7in [95mm] and the rear wheels 5.2in [132mm]. The normal rear wheel camber setting is slightly negative; it is only on severe rebound that the camber becomes positive enough to materially affect the 230SL's handling characteristics.

"The steering box is the recirculating-ball type; the linkage has the well-known Mercedes-Benz shock absorber which reduces or eliminates road shock transmitted to the steering wheel. As on the 220SE, some muscular effort is required for hairpin turns and parking manoeuvres. For the not-so-sporty, there is a power steering option. Don't sneer – this is the same praiseworthy item we noted in our road test of the 300SE which always retains feel of the road and requires purposeful effort. True, there is less feedback than with manual steering, but there's enough to give the driver a pretty fair idea of how much 'tiger' he is unleashing on the corner.

"The power steering has a slightly quicker ratio, so you have to alter your methods when going from one system to another. With manual steering, you normally set the car up for the corner with a fast flick of the wheel, to overcome the initial oversteer. With the power assist, you begin as early, but put less lock on the wheels at first, then more and more as you go deeper into the turn and ease off lock just as leisurely on the apex."

Legendary British writer and occasional race and rally driver, Gordon Wilkins, also gave his angle: "With every new Mercedes-Benz introduced since the war, it has been my privilege to have my first ride in it with Rudolf Uhlenhaut, the brilliant engineer in charge of passenger car development. It is the quick, electrifying but painless way of exploring the uttermost limits of the car's capabilities.

"Our test track was part of a new forest circuit being built by a French club near Annemasse. It was a tight and difficult little loop with seven severe corners in just under three-quarters of a mile. Uhlenhaut hurled the 230SL round it in continuous controlled drifts. It felt as if the tyres must come off the rims, but the car stayed on course at seemingly impossible speeds. Shortly before, in a friendly beat-up with Mike Parkes in a 250GT

Ferrari Berlinetta, Uhlenhaut had lapped in 47.5 seconds in this comfortable, lavishly equipped road car of 2.3 litres against 47.3 by the young racing engineer in the lightweight 3-litre Ferrari.

"Having seen what astonishing things the 230SL could do, I took over and was soon getting it round in about 49 seconds. It seemed to be time to find out where the snags might be. I tried changing course in a corner. No problem. I shut the throttle abruptly in the middle of a full power four-wheel drift. The car slowed down but continued on course.

"So next I tried tramping on the brakes right in the middle of a corner while going as fast as I knew how. The car should have spun off. It held right on course. These were no 100mph bends, but on the available evidence I am tempted to rate this as just about the most forgiving fast car I have ever driven. Yet it is quiet and docile with all home comforts, perfectly suitable for a dinner date on a wet winter's night."

The final words in this section go to Bernard Cahier, who summed up the W113 model with the following prose: "The miracle of the 230SL is that the car is free of handling vices, it is almost neutral with a very slight understeer, and you can place it where you want in a curve while staying in full control, plus feeling safe and comfortable. Take a wrong line, brake in the middle of a curve, and before you know it you find yourself in perfect shape again. Remarkable! Why? The answer is that the 230SL is an outstanding road car (and even track car, although not built for racing) because Technical Director Nallinger, Chief Engineer Uhlenhaut and their team of first class men have the unique and precious background of having produced some of the world's most successful racing cars. They have constantly applied their immense racing experience, plus practical knowledge, to the benefit of a fast, safe, superbly handling series of touring cars, the most recent example being the 230SL. What a lesson learned, and what an example for manufacturers who do not yet believe that racing plus exceptional high-speed testing, as always carried out by Uhlenhaut, is not really necessary to producing a modern, fast touring car."

"With the new 230SL Mercedes, Daimler-Benz has produced, in my opinion, one of their very finest cars of the post-war period – a car capable of pleasing both the sportsman and those looking for a prestige 'quality' automobile. Technically superbly designed, its styling is good, its performance high, and its handling among the finest in the world. The 230SL should have a tremendous commercial success and I will be curious to see what it will do in rallies and production car racing, although Daimler-Benz, of course, claims that this car was never made for such purposes."

A BELGIAN EXCURSION

Just prior to the Frankfurt Show, the new SL was entered in one of the most famous European marathons – the highly competitive Spa-Sofia-Liege Rally. Ex-racer Karl Kling was in charge of the single-car entry (the big SE saloons were still the weapon of choice in the Benz camp), and it was he who chose the hugely experienced team of Eugen Böhringer and Klaus Kaiser to drive the vehicle.

The 230SL was tuned to deliver 165bhp, a jump in power that justified the installation of an oil cooler, while different gearing made the most of the spread of horses. Spotlights were fitted inboard of the headlights and in front of the grille emblem,

Mercedes-Benz had a strong history in long-distance rallying. This picture shows Karl Kling and Rainer Gunzler after winning the 1959 Algiers-Cape Rally. Kling (seen here standing by the driver's door) was duly placed in charge of the 230SL's first competitive event three years later.

Eugen Böhringer in action during the 1962 Liège-Sofia-Liège Rally. His superb performance on the event helped him become 1962 European Rally Champion, and made him the obvious choice to drive the 230SL in the 1963 edition of the Liège.

Böhringer about to take a break in the passenger seat in the early stages of the Spa-Sofia-Liège Rally.

(Above and opposite) The 230SL making progress on some very varied roads, which is the reason why Kling wanted several wheel and tyre options.

Waving to a friend in the crowd, Eugen Böhringer drove a superb rally to win the 1963 Liège (also known as the Marathon de la Route), ably assisted by Klaus Kaiser (seen here in the padded jacket). The battered car graced the cover of *Autosport* magazine, giving the new model some excellent publicity.

and various wheel and tyre combinations (centred on 13- and 15-inch rims) were tried to best match conditions.

Running from the 27-31 August, Eric Carlsson described the 1963 3430-mile (5488km) event as "... the toughest yet" Marathon de la Route, which explains why only 20 of the 120 starters made it to the end. However, not only did the Böhringer/Kaiser pairing finish in their red 230SL, they made it to Liège in first place – a remarkable achievement for a new car.

For the record, Böhringer won with only eight minutes of penalties, while Carlsson's second-placed Saab chalked up 23. Three Citroëns were in the next five places, joined by a Ford and an Austin-Healey; a Mercedes 220SEb came 11th.

5
The 230SL evolves

Konrad Adenauer retired as the long-running Chancellor of Germany in October 1963, having weathered a number of political storms, not least the division of Berlin and subsequent building of the Berlin Wall; he was duly succeeded by Ludwig Erhard. However, for motoring enthusiasts, it was the Frankfurt Show, held the month before, that provided the most interest in an autumn of change …

The 41st Frankfurt Show, or 1963 IAA, opened its doors on 12 September. Daimler-Benz had its main stand in Hall 3 (occupying Stand 256), although Hall 9, Stand 767 was also used, while Peter Lindner Automobile (the local Mercedes dealership owned by the famous German racing driver), had a smaller display in Hall 1A.

The price list issued in September 1963 to coincide with the German event still had the 230SL Roadster listed at DM 20,600. While the standard equipment remained unchanged (manual transmission, foglights, MB-Tex vinyl trim, a locking fuel cap, driver's-side mirror, manual radio aerial, and a lockable glovebox with built-in maplight); more paint, trim, and hood colour choices were made available.

As before, a hardtop was DM 1100 extra (or DM 1140 with the chrome trim strips needed for fitting roof-racks), whilst dispensing with the soft-top reduced the initial cost price by DM 750.

The other main options outlined earlier (including spotlights, PAS, leather trim, seatbelts, a transverse rear seat, fire extinguisher, first aid box, and a 'D' emblem for the tail) continued at the same price, although the fitted luggage set went up to DM 380 – an increase of DM 15. While the Becker Mexico radio was deleted, the Grand Prix and Europa units remained unchanged, along with the electric aerial upgrade.

New additions to the option list at this time included automatic transmission (DM 1400), metallic paint (DM 380 for the main body, or DM 130 for the hardtop only), and whitewall tyres, priced at DM 150.

Catalogue for the 1963 Frankfurt Show.

(Above and opposite) A couple of scenes from the Frankfurt Show. Daimler-Benz officials must have been overjoyed at the public's reaction to the SL.

Also, an ivory steering wheel was officially listed as a no-cost option (or NCO) to replace the standard black item if the owner preferred, although some prototypes were seen with the lighter rim, and records show that a handful of cars were shipped from the factory with ivory steering wheels from as early as June 1963.

It was probably more a case of making the option's availability that much clearer, rather than the start date with regard to this particular item.

Initially, there was a long waiting list for the new SL, which only seemed to add weight to its exclusive image. Some

Two pieces of German advertising from around the time of the Frankfurt Show. Despite weight-saving techniques, such as the use of aluminium doors and lids, the 230SL still tipped the scales at a hefty 1295kg (2850lb).

customers were quoted up to 18 months for delivery, but even this potential dampener was somehow turned into a marketing triumph – "A Mercedes-Benz is worth the wait," said the copy in one notable advert.

New engines mounts were fitted from the end of October 1963, along with revised fasteners for the soft-top, and a foot-operated switch was employed for dipping the headlights. Shortly after, the heater was upgraded, the Al-Fin drums were strengthened at the back, the driver's-side armrest was modified to make it more suitable as a door pull, the side window winding mechanism was changed, and hardtop sealing was improved.

Most things were carried over in the February 1964 price list, although the manual aerial was now an option (DM 40) instead of a standard fitment, and there were also more specific hardtop purchase plans – mounted or provided separately (still DM 1100 either way), or supplied minus the soft-top for DM 350.

A new catalogue was issued in September 1963, and while the cover artwork was the same as that for the Geneva Show edition, internal photography was far superior. This delightful shot is one of the best pictures ...

In other words, the soft-top, which had been given subtle frame modifications at the same time, was no longer a straightforward 'delete option,' to coin a trade term.

In addition, the cost of the two-tone metallic paint option, although implied in the September list, was made crystal clear, priced at DM 510 – the combination of DM 380 for the lower body and DM 130 for the hardtop. The fitted suitcase format was changed, bringing down the price to DM 370, and seatbelts were now sold only as a pair (DM 110). All-weather tyres were made available at DM 444, and preparation for audio equipment without buying a radio added DM 35 to the invoice.

A 1963 230SL in idyllic surroundings. Whitewall tyres were listed as an official option from September that year.

Although promised from the off, the automatic transmission option didn't appear on price lists until September 1963. Note the staggered selector gate, which allowed manual-style changes without fear of jumping gears too high or too low, or, worse still, selecting neutral (marked by an 'O' on early cars, but later changed to a more traditional 'N' used by other makers, first on US-spec vehicles, then all SLs). Park was closest to the driver on W113 cars, although the positions were reversed when the 107-series was introduced.

Cars built from this date onward (from February 1964) had the familiar semi-circle horn ring in place of the full circle version used on the earlier vehicles (just over 2000 in all) and a modified steering wheel, designed to reduce unwanted vibrations. With so few readily available identifying features, this at least helps narrow down the first of the breed from the machines that followed.

By the middle of March, manual cars had gained a new synchromesh mechanism, and all vehicles received improvements in the seat springing and backrest adjuster.

Standard coachwork colours (September 1963 to April 1964)
Black (040), White (050), White-Grey (158), Light Beige (181), Graphite Grey (190), Dark Green (268), Dark Blue (332), Dark Red-Brown (460), Signal Red (568), Dark Bordeaux Red (573), Ivory (658), Light Ivory (670), and Papyrus White (717).

Metallic coachwork colours (September 1963 to April 1964)
Anthracite Grey (172), Silver-Grey (180), Blue (387), Beige (462), Varnish Red (567), Red (571), and Moss Green (834).

Hood colours (September 1963 to April 1964)
Black, Marine Blue, Cream, Beige, Grey, Light Grey or Brown.

Two-tone combinations (September 1963 to April 1964)
Solid shades: White, Graphite Grey, Dark Green, Dark Blue, Signal Red, Dark Bordeaux Red, Light Ivory or Papyrus White with a Black hardtop; Graphite Grey or Signal Red with a White-Grey hardtop; Papyrus White with a Blue-Grey hardtop; Black with a Light Beige hardtop; White, White-Grey or Papyrus White with a Graphite Grey hardtop; Papyrus White with a Dark Green hardtop; White or Papyrus White with a Dark Blue hardtop; White-Grey, Light Beige, Ivory or Light Ivory with a Havanna Brown hardtop; White, Light Beige or Light Ivory with a Dark Red-Brown hardtop; Papyrus White with a Dark Bordeaux Red hardtop, or Dark Blue with a Papyrus White hardtop. Metallic shades: Anthracite Grey, Varnish Red, Red or Moss Green with a Black hardtop, or Silver-Grey with a Graphite Grey hardtop.

Trim colours & materials (September 1963 to April 1964)
Turquoise (112), Bronze (113), Light Natural (114), Dark Blue (115), Caviar (116), Red (117), Light Grey (118), White-Grey (119), Cognac (120) or Cream (121) MB-Tex vinyl, or Black (201), Red (202), Red (203), Light Red (204), Blue (205), Medium Blue (206), Light Grey (207), Cream (209), Natural (210), Dark Green (211), Reseda Green (212), Antique Yellow (213), Rust Red (214), Cognac (216), Turquoise (217), Bronze (218), Light Natural (219), Dark Blue (220), White-Grey (221), Wine Red (222), Medium Grey (223), Light Olive (224), Eggshell (230), Anthracite Grey (231) or Brown (232) perforated leather.

Carpet (September 1963 to April 1964)
Black, Cream, Anthracite Grey, Graphite Grey, Dark Grey, Blue, Turquoise, Green, Wine Red, Rust Red, Medium Red or Brown.

Note: Three metallic shades (172, 571 and 567) were only available when selected with a 040 Black hardtop until April 1964, while two other shades (162 Blue-Grey and 408 Havanna Brown) were reserved for the hardtop only. Metallic paintwork was always matched with leather trim as standard until April 1964.

Work also began on solving the problem of the side windows lifting off their seals at high speeds – a fairly common failing on cars without the additional strength offered by an upper and quarter-glass frame. Rounding off the changes from this period, the flywheel was modified in April, followed by the crankshaft and distributor internals in the following month, while oil bath air filter assemblies were made available for countries with dusty road conditions.

The earliest style fitted luggage for the 230SL.

Cover of the driver's handbook, this edition being in German and English, written side by side.

Instructions for the soft-top and hardtop. Although it looks complicated compared to an Alfa Romeo top, for instance, after a couple of times opening and closing the hood, the operation becomes second nature.

101

THE NEW SL IN THE STATES

The Americans had first become involved with the W113 project in July 1961, when a couple of executives crossed the Atlantic to see the full-sized styling prototype, which was still badged as a 220SL at the time. That they were consulted at all showed the growing importance of the US market for the German car maker, as normally the first view of a new car Stateside was via photographs, or as it rolled off a ship as part of an initial consignment.

A couple of years later, Lon Fleener, the President of Mercedes-Benz Sales Inc, stated at the time of the car's launch: "Being safe, fast, comfortable and luxurious, the new 230SL continues the Mercedes-Benz tradition of applying the latest automotive engineering developments to its passenger cars. Its roadholding, power, and braking systems guarantee outstanding performance …"

At this time, in the carefree days of the early-1960s, most leading features were as per the domestic vehicles, with only speedometer calibrations and minor differences in the lighting, underlined by the novel front light enclosures to cope with the sealed beams required by Federal law.

One of the biggest differences was in bulb location – European cars having bulbs placed within the headlight bowl attached to the body, with the trademark single piece of glass covering them, before a chrome frame was applied to hide all the fixing and adjusting screws. With the US-spec cars, the sealed beam was a separate unit, and the clearance light, parking light, indicator light, and foglight were housed in a casing attached to the bottom of the outer chrome

Early US advertising introducing the 230SL. Note the distributor's details at the foot of the advert.

trim piece. It was actually quite a good compromise that met all the regulations of light fittings and height requirements, although things would become more and more complicated as the sixties progressed.

(Pages 103-105) The first North American catalogue, with four pages and a grey fold-over section on the right-hand side to keep the brochure closed. It's interesting to note that only the inner pages were in colour to save on printing costs!

Command Performance

MERCEDES-BENZ
230 SL

In the select international set of truly great motor cars, debut of a new member is an auspicious event. This is particularly true when this new member comes from the historic Mercedes-Benz family, for more than 3-quarters of a century one of motordom's most honored names.

The Mercedes-Benz 230SL brings a dramatic new look to the world of fine sports cars. Low-slung, fast and powerful, it comes as a soft-top roadster which is available with an optional hard top. The sports car contour is accentuated by elegantly slim roof and window posts and a flat sheath roof over extensive window areas. Visibility is excellent.

Mercedes-Benz has given this car an improved fuel injection system... a fully synchronized four-speed transmission, actuated by a short stick, designed for fast gear changing. (A four-speed automatic transmission is available as an option—see specifications on back page).

Mercedes-Benz "built-in traffic safety features" are further enhanced in the 230SL through use of Girling front disc brakes and aluminum Alfin drum brakes in the rear.

The standard version of the 230SL is equipped with all those extra touches that combine to give the deserved impression of luxury. These include a non-glare rear view mirror inside the car, along with a door-mounted exterior mirror; a handsome hand-finished console with ash tray; two-speed electric windshield wipers and washers; padded adjustable sun visors; illuminated heat-fresh air control knob; illuminated glove compartment with map light and back-up lights.

Safe... fast... comfortable... luxurious... once you have taken the wheel of the new Mercedes 230SL and experienced its incomparable performance... you'll be satisfied with nothing less.

Another minor difference in the lighting was the lack of a headlight 'flash' facility on US cars at this time, as it was illegal in certain states.

The 230SL was announced at around $6700 in the US – about $2000 less than a 300SE sedan – but with options, most cars left the showroom at well over $7000 by the time JFK was assassinated in November 1963; an historic moment that put Lyndon Johnson into the White House.

A total of 11,234 Mercedes vehicles were sold in the US in 1963, all moved through Mercedes-Benz Sales Inc, which had 343 dealers controlled by the Studebaker-Packard Corporation of South Bend, Indiana. As it happens, only 140 230SLs were exported to the States in 1963 (CY), meaning most SL sales were made up of the $5215 190SL and $11,099 300SL during this particular year.

Sleek, continental styling... motordom's thoroughbred look

An interior that is luxurious in appointment and finish

High visibility control panel in precious wood and matt leather

Engineering Excellence — A Mercedes-Benz Tradition

SPECIFICATIONS 230SL

ENGINE
- Type...............6-Cyl. Overhead Cam and Valves
- Bore and Stroke......................3.23/2.87
- Piston Displacement..................140.71 cu. in.
- Horsepower....................170 @ 5600 r.p.m.
- Compression ratio............................9.3:1
- Oil cooling...............Oil-Water Heat Exchanger
- Capacity of crankcase........11.6-7.4 pts. (V.S. PTS.)
- (max - min.)...................9.7-6.2 (IMP.PTS.)

PERFORMANCE DATA
- Maximum speed.................1st gear 27.9 mph
- 2nd gear 55.9 mph
- 3rd gear 83.8 mph
- 4th gear Top speed

FUEL
- Fuel System............Intermittent Fuel Injection
- Capacity of fuel tank....U.S. gal. 17.2, imp. gal. 14.3
- Including spare supply.....U.S. gal. 1.8, imp. gal. 1.5
- Type of fuel.................Commercial premium

CHASSIS
- Suspension, front—Independent suspension with coil springs, telescopic shock absorbers and torsion bar stabilizer.
- Suspension, rear—Independent suspension with coil springs and shock absorbers.
- Rear Axle—Single joint, low pivot point swing axle with horizontal compensating spring.
- Transmission—4-speed fully synchronized.
- Steering—Recirculating ball-type with self adjustment and shock absorber.
- Brakes (Power)—Hydraulic, disc brakes front, turbo-cooled rear drums.
- Battery—12 volt—55 amp. hrs.

DIMENSIONS AND WEIGHTS
- Overall length............................168.7 in.
- Overall width..............................69.2 in.
- Overall height, unloaded....................51.5 in.
- Wheelbase..................................94.5 in.
- Size of tires (Tubeless)....................185 x 14
- Tread, front................................58.5
- Tread, rear.................................58.5
- Turning circle..............................33.4 ft.
- Curb weight...............................2855 lbs.

SUBFRAME and single-joint swing axle. The high output engine of your 230SL is mounted together with the transmission, the front wheel suspension and the steering in the "subframe". This practical system makes possible economical removal and re-assembly of the entire unit for maintenance, and absorbs possible additional vibrations of the front wheel suspension. The rear single-joint swing axle with only one low pivot point is guided by two longitudinal pull rods. Large internally friction–free coil springs absorb every road jolt before it can take effect.

STEERING. Recirculating Ball-Type Steering with automatic adjustment and steering shock absorber is so easy to handle and obedient that even very delicate hands can effortlessly master the 230SL. With this advanced Mercedes-Benz steering design, you thread through traffic with finger-tip ease, and on the open road you can forget about "wind wander"— you simply point the car where you want it to go.

AUTOMATIC TRANSMISSION. Lighter, smaller and much more versatile than most transmissions, the new Mercedes-Benz assembly operates as fully automatic when in fourth position, providing a shift sequence from 2nd through 4th gear, with a full sequence from 1st possible by depressing the accelerator to full throttle. However, the car can be manually shifted through any gear sequence desired for maximum control and acceleration.

POWER TRAIN. Here the 230SL shows you its strong "heart", its spirited 170 HP fuel injection engine. The modern design innovations are clearly recognizable. Due to the short stroke, the larger bore and the overhead cam shaft and overhead valves, the engine will maintain safely a maximum of 6,500 r.p.m.

PRINTED IN U.S.A.

Mercedes-Benz

Mercedes-Benz Division
STUDEBAKER OF CANADA, LTD.
HAMILTON, ONTARIO, CANADA

THE RHD MARKETS

The announcement in *MotorSport* had been very low-key, with one small photo and the following prose: "Announced at the Geneva Show, the new Mercedes-Benz 230SL, which replaces the 190SL, is fitted with a six-cylinder engine derived from that of the 220SE. The size has been increased to 2.3 litres and the injection system now feeds into the intake duct on the cylinder head. With a compression ratio of 9.3:1 the engine develops 170bhp at 5600rpm. The chassis closely follows the design principles of the other six-cylinder Mercedes but the front and rear track is wider. The swing-axle rear suspension is retained and Girling disc brakes are fitted at the front in conjunction with Al-Fin drums at the rear. Speeds in the three upper gears of 56, 84, and 124mph are claimed. The price in Britain is £3414 2s 1d."

The lack of words can be put down to two things – a restriction on column inches in that particular issue, and the knowledge that only left-hand drive cars were being made in the first few months. Although orders could be placed, buyers were informed they'd have to wait a while before they could take delivery. In fact, imports didn't really start flowing into the UK in any worthwhile numbers until November, eight months after the Swiss premiere.

Notwithstanding, the 230SL was listed immediately after the Geneva Show in the UK, priced at £3414 including taxes, while the 300SL continued at £4760, or £4885 with a hardtop. This was probably a bid to prompt those still considering the 3-litre car to make the jump and secure one of the final few in stock, as the 190SL had already disappeared.

As it happens, the 300SL had gone by the middle of 1963, leaving the 230SL in Roadster guise at £3414, as a Coupé at £3462, or a Convertible (supplied with both tops) at £3595. To put that into perspective, the Aston Martin DB4 was priced at £3504, while the Jaguar E-type could be picked up for under £2000! Even the top Porsche 356 (the 1600 S90 Cabriolet) was only £2527, allowing one to put a Morgan Plus 4 in the garage with the change left over if an enthusiast had budgeted for the cost of the new Benz. In other words, the 230SL was an expensive tool, with the only consolation being that the British prices held steady until the end of 1964.

Opening on 16 October, the 1963 Earls Court Show was largely overshadowed in the news by the Profumo Affair, with Harold Macmillan resigning as PM on 18 October, and handing the reins to Alec Douglas-Home. What a scandal!

But at least the London event gave people a chance to see the new SL, displayed alongside a 600 limousine on the Mercedes-Benz GB stand. In the words of *MotorSport*: "Vast crowds stood around, sat in, and stared at the 600 model, while the sporting enthusiasts drooled over the 230SL."

The 230SL was slow to find its way to Australia, but the growing importance of the Japanese market was clearly illustrated by the appearance of the new Benz at the 5th Import Car Show in Tokyo, timed to display the 1964 models on offer from foreign manufacturers. The white left-hand drive SL displayed there (priced at 4,300,000 yen, and featuring American-style lighting, an ivory steering wheel and matching gearknob, and a transverse rear seat) was given three pages in the January 1964 edition of *Car Graphic*, so it certainly made an impression on Shotaro Kobayashi and his editorial team.

THE W113 ESTABLISHED

A passenger-side mirror was added to the options list in April 1964 (priced at DM 15), making kerbside parking easier on lhd machines and meaning right-hand drive cars could at last have exterior mirrors of the 'correct' type fitted – buyers of the earliest rhd vehicles had to make do with the rearview mirror only.

Other new items included uprated road springs (DM 12), tinted glass (DM 90, plus DM 25 extra for the hardtop), a luggage compartment light (DM 35 at this time, but made standard in August 1965), coconut floormats (DM 35), and an uprated heater (DM 12). The fitted suitcases were shuffled around again, too, along with the paint and trim colour palette.

Revisions took place to the clutch plate on manual cars, along with the front brake calipers and road springs for all SLs in June 1964. Changes to the heater meant modifying the front bulkhead, and the engine mountings received attention at the same time. At the start of July, there were changes to the gearlever and synchromesh, while the lower wishbones were revised, and the road wheel rim width was increased from 5.5J to 6J at the end of the month.

The cost of servicing plans went up during August, and the check valve on the rear brakes was modified, along with the

A Frankfurt-registered 230SL pulling a Dethleffs caravan. As camping and boating became increasingly popular, manufacturers had to think seriously about providing a towbar.

engine's big-end bolts and water pump, but otherwise, there were no other major changes applied to the SL during the summer, and the two-seater's basic price remained at DM 20,600.

In October, the automatic gearbox code changed on the option list, although it continued at the same price, and the only way customers could identify a difference was on the tail, where an 'AUTOMATIC' badge was added beneath the '230SL' one. Internally, there had been new brake bands adopted, hence the new number.

The Becker Mexico radio made a comeback at this time, commanding a hefty DM 630. However, the price of tinted glass was reduced to DM 20, as the laminated front screen was no longer included; an extra DM 25 was needed to put tinted glass in the hardtop.

The fitted luggage and bags were revised again, thus rounding off the major changes. This was a necessary move rather than pure cosmetics, as the spare wheel had been relocated, from an upright position in the nearside corner of the boot, to one laying

Standard coachwork colours (April 1964 to August 1965)
Black (040), White (050), White-Grey (158), Light Beige (181), Graphite Grey (190), Dark Green (268), Dark Blue (332), Dark Red-Brown (460), Signal Red (568), Dark Bordeaux Red (573), Light Ivory (670), and Papyrus White (717).

Metallic coachwork colours (April 1964 to August 1965)
Anthracite Grey (172), Medium Grey (178), Silver-Grey (180), Blue (387), Medium Blue (396), Bronze-Brown (461), Beige (462), Copper (463), Varnish Red (567), Red (571), and Moss Green (834).

Hood colours (April 1964 to August 1965)
Black, Marine Blue, Cream, White-Grey, Brown-Beige, Beige, Grey, Light Grey or Brown.

Two-tone combinations (April 1964 to August 1965)
Solid shades: White, Graphite Grey, Dark Green, Dark Blue, Signal Red, Dark Bordeaux Red, Light Ivory or Papyrus White with a Black hardtop; Graphite Grey, Dark Blue or Signal Red with a White-Grey hardtop; Papyrus White with a Blue-Grey hardtop; Black with a Light Beige hardtop; White, White-Grey or Papyrus White with a Graphite Grey hardtop; Papyrus White with a Dark Green hardtop; White or Papyrus White with a Dark Blue hardtop; White-Grey, Light Beige or Light Ivory with a Havanna Brown hardtop; White, White-Grey, Light Beige or Light Ivory with a Dark Red-Brown hardtop; Papyrus White with a Dark Bordeaux Red hardtop, or Dark Blue with a Papyrus White hardtop. Metallic shades: Anthracite Grey, Silver-Grey, Copper, Varnish Red, Red or Moss Green with a Black hardtop; Varnish Red or Red with a White-Grey hardtop, or Silver-Grey with a Graphite Grey hardtop.

Trim colours & materials (April 1964 to August 1965)
Turquoise (112), Bronze (113), Light Natural (114), Dark Blue (115), Caviar (116), Red (117), Light Grey (118), White-Grey (119), Cognac (120), Cream (121), Light Red (122), Medium Blue (123) or Green (124) MB-Tex vinyl, or Black (201), Red (202), Red (203), Light Red (204), Blue (205), Medium Blue (206), Light Grey (207), Cream (209), Natural (210), Dark Green (211), Reseda Green (212), Antique Yellow (213), Rust Red (214), Cognac (216), Turquoise (217), Bronze (218), Light Natural (219), Dark Blue (220), White-Grey (221), Wine Red (222), Medium Grey (223), Light Olive (224), Eggshell (230), Anthracite Grey (231) or Brown (232) perforated leather.

Carpet (April 1964 to August 1965)
Black, Cream, Anthracite Grey, Graphite Grey, Dark Grey, Blue, Turquoise, Green, Wine Red, Rust Red, Medium Red or Brown.

Note: Four shades (268, 463, 568 and 573) were only available when selected with either a 040 Black or 158 White-Grey hardtop until the end of the 230SL run (except for Dark Bordeaux Red, as this was deleted earlier), while two shades (162 Blue-Grey and 408 Havanna Brown) were reserved for the hardtop only.

An English language advert that would have appeared in the likes of *National Geographic*, and other international publications.

This German advert shows the post-February 1964 steering wheel, and a good view of the 'AUTOMATIC' badge mounted below the model designation in time for the 1965 season.

flat on the floor on the opposite side. The floorpan was changed as a result, too.

By November, all cars were leaving the line with a new soft-top, and this is actually a useful distinguishing feature. Although the bows themselves cannot be seen all that easily (they were changed from lightweight aluminium and wood to stronger steel items to keep the cloth taut at high speeds), the highly visible chrome trim on the outer trailing edge (above the rear window) was deleted at the same time.

There were also changes to the side windows to keep them tight to the hood or hardtop seals, the crankshaft, and a new vibration damper for the latter. Shortly after, the timing chain tensioner and AED were improved, and in the New Year, the clutch pressure plate was revised again (as it happens, the clutch

A 1965 230SL at the Stuttgart TV Tower, an advanced concrete structure completed in 1956.

The luggage compartment of a 1965 model year car, seen here with fitted luggage, but it also had to play host to the spare wheel, jack, and 11-piece toolkit, the latter kept in a slotted tool-roll. The underside of the bootlid was always flat black (like the luggage compartment itself), while that of the bonnet was usually finished in body colour, like the rest of the engine bay.

was uprated yet again in August 1965). There were also modifications to the front section of the body to allow more space for bigger tyres if required, even though the standard wheel and tyre combination remained the same.

In February 1965, luggage and ski-racks became listed in the options list rather than as accessories, priced at DM 275 and DM 130 respectively; a hardtop carrier was also listed, made available for DM 125. Otherwise, there was a significant reduction in the price of all-weather tyres (down from DM 444 to DM 272), and that was about it.

Minor changes abounded, however. Of the more important modifications, the shape of the fuel filler pipe was revised to make top-ups easier, fresh main bearing caps and crank counterweights were employed, the crankshaft pulley was changed on cars with PAS, and there were a number of revisions to the pistons and rings, as mentioned in the previous chapter.

RALLYING REVISITED

Joining a pair of big saloons, the 230SL was called up for duty for the Spa-Sofia-Liège Rally, the 1964 edition running from 25-30 August. S-RV 441 was rolled out for service again, joined this time by a second car, registered S-TT 473. Both cars were given US-spec headlights, allowing quicker repairs, and the bumpers were removed at both ends to reduce weight, although quite a bit of it was put back on by the adoption of no less than five driving lights up front.

The SLs were assigned to Dieter Glemser and Martin Braungart (number 19, 'S-RV'), and Eugen Böhringer and Klaus Kaiser (number 31, 'S-TT'). As usual, though, the Marathon – 1964 being the last year it was held in its classic road rally format – was hard on man and machine alike.

The rally team posing for the camera in Stuttgart. From left to right: Martin Braungart, Dieter Glemser, Alfred Kling, Ewy Rosquist, Manfred Schiek, Eugen Böhringer, Rolf Kreder, and Klaus Kaiser.

As the cars turned back towards Belgium at the Yugoslavian border, Rauno Aaltonen's 'Big Healey' had a half-hour lead over Erik Carlsson (Saab) and Eugen Böhringer in the 2.3-litre SL. This is ultimately the way things stayed, with the Austin-Healey winning the event on 57 minutes of penalties, the Saab second on 85 minutes, and the Böhringer/Kaiser 230SL in third (second in Class), two minutes down on the Swedish entry, but a full 36 minutes ahead of the fourth-placed Saab, despite ignition problems.

Meanwhile, the Glemser/Braungart SL retired through electrical maladies. Of the two works SEs, one crashed out, while the other came sixth, beaten into fifth by just one minute, by one of the eight factory-entered Citroëns. From 97 starters, only 21 cars made it back to Belgium.

There was one other rally in which the 230SL was entered – the 1965 Acropolis. Mercedes had a good record on this Greek classic, which was part of the European Rally Championship, so there was a lot of pride at stake.

The red works car, registration S-TT 473, was refurbished, and given back its bumpers and European headlights. Wearing number 12 in the tough May event, it was driven by Dieter Glemser, who was partnered by Martin Braungart again.

The Glemser/Braungart car retired from the Spa-Sofia-Liège Rally with electrical problems.

(Opposite) Looking surprisingly fresh after their ordeal, Eugen Böhringer (left) and Klaus Kaiser captured on film after managing to secure second in Class, and third place overall on the 1964 Liège.

A series of action shots following the fortunes of the Böhringer/Kaiser 230SL on the Spa-Sofia-Liège Rally (or Marathon de la Route).

As always, the Greek rally provided the scene for a great deal of drama. Böhringer's saloon blew its engine, leaving Glemser representing the Stuttgart marque. Unfortunately, a wrong turning led to a loss of 20 minutes, and the SL was effectively out of the running.

A Volvo Amazon won, followed home by a Saab, a Lancia and another Saab. The 230SL was fifth, a long way ahead of the next-placed Citroën DS, but this would be the SL's swansong in the field of rallying …

EXPORT REVIEW

The 1964 model year was the first full season of 230SL sales in the States. A total of 782 cars made it across the Atlantic in 1964, followed by 1429 the following year – a figure that represents just over ten per cent of the 12,100 units sold by around 400 US dealers during 1965. Interestingly, Daimler-Benz built around 175,000 cars in 1965, so the SL run was small compared to future R107 figures, but in line with the overall production versus SL production ratio.

While America was drawn into the Vietnam War in August 1964, which tended to overshadow most Stateside events, the 230SL continued on a steady path to popularity, despite its $6724 price tag. Options, naturally, took the price well beyond $7000.

As it happens, 1964 was to be the final year of Mercedes cars being sold through Studebaker-Packard dealers, with the Fort Lee, New Jersey-based Mercedes-Benz of North America Inc (or MBNA) concern taking over the distributor network from 1 January 1965. (This was a subsidiary of Daimler-Benz AG.)

In Britain, the other major export market, power switched from Conservative to Labour in October 1964, with Harold Wilson named as PM. At this time, the 230SL Roadster commanded £3482, while the Coupé was £3532, and Convertible £3668. Without extras like an automatic gearbox (£198), leather trim (£125), PAS (£93), and an occasional rear seat (from £31), the SL was bracketed in a range going from £1727 for the 190C saloon, all the way up to £9994 for a 600 Pullman Limousine. The latter actually cost substantially more than a coachbuilt Rolls-Royce!

Whilst commenting on the general refinement of the engine from above 2500rpm out to the red-line, *Autocar* noticed "... [an] absence of low-speed torque accentuates the

Servicemen stationed in Germany still accounted for a large chunk of the export market for Mercedes-Benz. Note this advert now has the MBNA address as the US sales and service contact in America.

A mixed bag of export models pictured in the summer of 1964, including UK, Italian, French, and US-bound cars going down the line. It was extremely difficult to date this picture, but the wheels on the vehicle to the right narrow it down to the 230SL or 250SL run, and indeed, the image was used in the 250SL catalogue. However, the giveaway was the original-style soft-top on the red right-hand drive car in the foreground – it's possible to just spot the chrome trim on the trailing edge of the hood.

unsuitable gear ratios, because although top is not high – it gives only 19.6mph per 1000rpm – acceleration in that gear is sufficiently limited to call for over-frequent use of a third gear which is decidedly low for a sports car; it allows a maximum of barely 80mph, just within the red mark on the rev counter. With 2000rpm on the clock in top, for instance, one needs 3000rpm for a smooth down-change to third. Quickly, the driver learns to take advantage of the high crankshaft speeds attainable, and finds that the harder the Mercedes is pushed along, the more the car can be enjoyed in its true element as a Grand Tourer.

Mercedes-Benz automobilia sold in Britain during the summer of 1964.

"Bottom gear ratio at 16.6:1 also seems somewhat low, but allows brisk starts from rest up to a 27mph maximum – a deliberate move for long clutch life, which certainly made the car one of the easiest to restart on the one-in-three test hill. Travel and load of the clutch pedal are not excessive for a powerful car ... For synchromesh efficiency and the easy, rapid movements of the change, the Daimler-Benz gearbox is good; and the gears are remarkably quiet."

There was no way for an SL to stay with a Jaguar E-type in terms of outright performance, but the 2.3-litre machine held its own against a Big Healey, and was able to dispose of cars like the Triumph TR4 with ease, returning better fuel consumption figures along the way – an average of 22.3mpg was quite remarkable for such a heavy car.

For the record, *Autocar* clocked a 0-60 time of 10.7 seconds, a 17.5 second standing-quarter and a top speed of 121mph (194kph) with a 4MT vehicle, and figures that were only a fraction slower for the 4AT car, despite the heavy hardtop being in place on the latter – respectively, 11.4 seconds, 18.1 seconds, and 119mph (190kph), although fuel consumption dropped to 17.7mpg, mainly due to the nature of test reporting, as the estimated DIN mileage was exactly the same for both transmissions (27.3mpg).

"Just as the character of the car brings out the best in a driver and invites him to really get a move on," continued *Autocar*, "so does the ride improve as speeds increase, and when being really hustled along, the 230SL sits down on the road beautifully, sweeping over bumps and undulations with the minimum of vertical movement, and no sensation at all of wheels pattering up and down. The

British advertising from 1965, linking past and present.

bodywork also has that feeling of rigidity and immense strength which is exceptional for a sports car – there is no scuttle shake when it is open," although it was noted that the stiffness of the damping produced some NVH on rarely-encountered cobbled sections of road.

Summing up, the long-running weekly said: "There is much to admire in the Mercedes-Benz 230SL – the high standard of finish and workmanship, comfort, tasteful styling and interior appointments; the quality of engineering skill in its construction almost goes without saying. Leech-like adhesion to the road on fast corners makes the greatest dynamic impression."

In a separate test, the same magazine tried an SL with automatic transmission and PAS. The gearbox was described as "... among the best in our experience" in the text, with its manual hold functions in the staggered, nylon-lined gate (the gear markings stayed on the left on earlier cars, but changed to the right after the quadrant was illuminated later on in the W113 run), and second-gear starts unless kickdown was activated or the '2' position selected, which would give first-gear starts and then stay in second until '3' or '4' (basically 'D') was chosen.

It was noted: "For fast cornering, overtaking or zooming up hills, the ease with which the lever can be slipped from '4' to '3' is delightful, allowing a smooth change down to third, with full engine braking."

The PAS also received high marks, the level of assistance making "... the steering delightfully light without introducing any of the weaknesses of inaccuracy or too-lively response. It is completely unobtrusive and there are no side-effects to tell a newcomer to the 230SL that the lightness of the steering is due to power assistance. Of the transmission, too, no better car could be picked to persuade the most ardent diehard to surrender his allegiance to the old concept of clutch and gearshift."

Trying a slightly newer car, *Motor* felt that the four-speed manual without PAS was the best combination "... if you drive for pleasure," adding: "There are very few production cars in the world that can match the 230SL's uncanny roadholding. The handling inspires a feeling of tremendous command and confidence, which, even under the hardest cornering, the car always justifies. There must be a limit, but on a dry road we never found it, even when accelerating faster and faster round the MIRA steering pan in second gear.

"It is the combination of virtues that makes the 230SL so notable – scarcity, speed, handling, comfort, finish, and prestige in one beautiful package. From our own experience, its dual personality does not evoke the universal appeal one might expect. It seems to inspire either detached admiration or fanatical love. It is that sort of car."

Motor's performance figures were similar to those recorded by *Autocar*, with the automatic SL giving a 0-60 time of 11.5 seconds if left to its own devices, or 10.5 seconds if the gears were held until the red-line in each gear. The top speed was a fraction down, while the standing-quarter time was 18.4 seconds, reduced to 17.7 with some trickery on the gear selector.

William Boddy of *MotorSport* borrowed the automatic vehicle tested in *Motor* for a while, and concluded: "It is the manner in which the 230SL runs, its impeccable finish and comprehensive specification, as much as the performance which is available, that makes this a supreme sporting car for the discerning."

Down Under, the November 1964 issue of *Australian Motor Sports* introduced the W113 with the following words: "Mercedes-Benz has a name for thundering race cars from the time when men were men and cars took a superman to control them at speed. The 230SL doesn't live up to this image at all, but we don't condemn it. The men of today will find it just as exciting.

"Impressive is the way that, despite comparatively large dimensions and not inconsiderable weight, it can be flicked through bends in a manner that would credit the best of small sports cars. With two people aboard, the 230SL has almost 50/50 weight distribution which is reflected in its unshakeable balance and aplomb."

In another magazine, Bill Tuckey summed up his 230SL experience thus: "Its memory will linger long with us, mainly for its astonishing roadholding, first-class design, extremely comfortable interior, and distinctive looks. And because girls blow kisses at it …"

Australia was still using the pound at this time (the Australian dollar was not introduced until February 1966), although it wasn't directly related to UK sterling – it just had the same name and symbol. The Roadster was priced at £4382, the Coupé at £4449 and Convertible at £4605; automatic transmission was a £261 extra, while PAS added £112 to the invoice.

Two views of the Pininfarina SL, which has recently been restored to its former glory.

SL ODDITIES

Pininfarina, the famous Italian styling house, presented its vision of the 230SL in the autumn of 1964, although records in Stuttgart show that the base car had been requested as early as May 1963.

Tom Tjaarda, who had a stunning career as a stylist, mainly based in Italy, came up with a compact closed coupé, which featured a tilted grille in an extended nose, wheelarches that were pulled tighter to the wheels and with less chrome running between them, a very strong waistline, a slightly rounded tail with new rear lights more in keeping with contemporary Italian tastes, new, slimmer bumpers at both ends, a sharper roofline, and a lot of glass to provide an airy feel to the cockpit, fitted with new bucket seats.

First shown at the Paris Salon in early October, it had auxiliary turn indicators on the front wings, which had disappeared by the time the car was displayed again at the Turin Show, held during the last days of October into early November. This was the last public appearance of the Pininfarina SL, for after that, it went into the collection of Axel Springer – a German media magnet.

Frua made a 230SL into a shooting brake at around the same time. Compared to Frua's usual work, it was not the prettiest thing to ever leave the workshop, with its heavy grille and awkward rear section when viewed from the side. However, the tailgate was a work of art, and the car will always stand as an important piece of automotive history.

Daimler-Benz itself was also looking into the possibility of a fastback version of the W113. In fact, several design sketches and scale models exist, most created in the spring of 1963 – some drawings are even dated the same week as the 230SL was launched in Geneva! However, this was to be a stillborn line of development.

MORE CHANGES

In August 1965, a few minor changes to the hood and trim mix were applied against one or two coachwork options. In addition, Dark Olive paint was added, replacing Dark Bordeaux Red on the colour palette, and there were two new red hues that came with matching hardtops.

This also marked the introduction of new inner door handles and window winder cranks, along with heavier seatbacks on the SL, although it appears that not all cars gained this latter feature. The author had a theory that maybe the backrest width was linked to whether a rear seat was fitted or not, but even this doesn't work out on all vehicles examined. It literally seems a case of pot luck with regard to this, although it's fair to say the vast majority of vehicles will have the deeper seatback from this date onward, and all cars gained stronger seat frames on the driver's side.

A luggage compartment light became standard, while at the other end of the vehicle, the under-bonnet view changed

World Champion Juan-Manuel Fangio with a travel-stained 230SL. Britain's favourite racing driver, Stirling Moss, bought a right-hand drive example for himself, picking it up personally at the factory.

(Above and right) Three stunning publicity pictures of 1965 home market vehicles, captured on film in contemporary colour.

(This page and opposite) These studio shots taken in the summer of 1965 were later converted to artwork for the catalogue released in time for the 1965 Frankfurt Show. This car is shod with Phoenix tyres, by the way, which had a heavy rubber band on the sidewall to protect not only the tyres, but also the wheels and hubcaps if a kerb was hit.

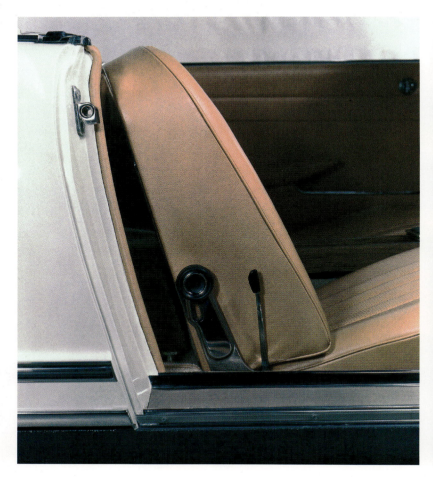

(This page and opposite) These detail shots were also used in the catalogue, even though, generally speaking, the window winder crank and grab handle on the passenger side were trimmed in the same colour as the door panel rather than black on 1966 MY cars. As far as the woodwork was concerned, dark-stained walnut was the official description, although perhaps more with regard to colouring than grain.

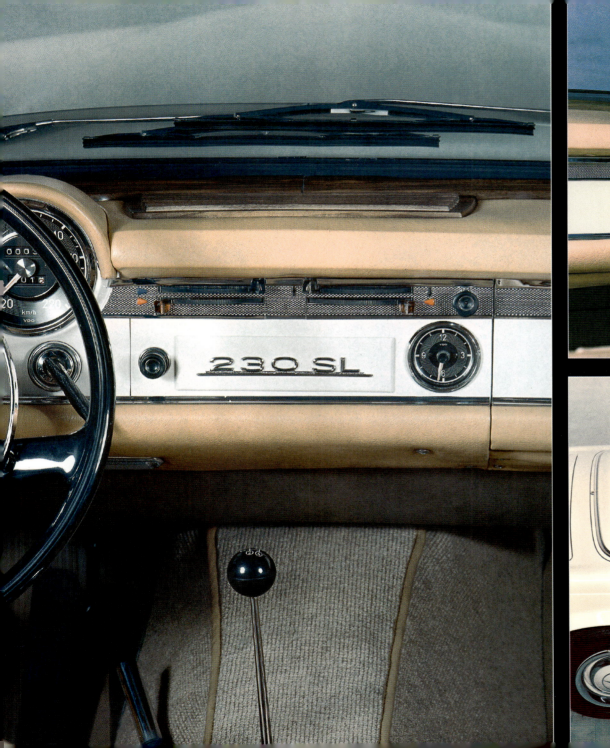

(Above and right) Cover and a couple of stunning images from the catalogue printed in August 1965, in readiness for the Frankfurt Show.

at this time, too, after separate brake and clutch reservoirs were abandoned in favour of a single reservoir to hold the fluid. Then, in the following month, it was acknowledged that the four-speed manual transmission's gearing was perhaps too widely spaced, with its low first and high top, and 1966 model year cars were supplied with a revised set of cogs in the gearbox and back axle.

There was still a big jump from first to second, but third was revised to 1.40. At the same time, the shorter 4.08:1 final-drive that would be adopted on ROW five-speed models was added to the spec sheet for all US cars, as getting the car off the line quicker was considered more important that top speed, and fuel costs were certainly not an issue. As it happens, the five-speed transmission was announced in November 1965, but there was

(This page and opposite) Three shots from a series of publicity photographs taken of the 230SL in the Alps, mainly to promote the new W108 series saloons (seen in the background in one of the pictures), which were introduced to the public in September 1965. Note the hubcap colour – usually these were supplied in body colour, but could be painted to match the hardtop instead.

no price listed against it until March of the following year.

Meanwhile, as part of a programme of constant development, in September 1965, the engine was given all-new camshaft gear, a fresh oil sump (and dipstick), and then in the first few days of October, a new crankcase, camshaft cover, water pump, ignition lead set, and revised rocker arms for the camshaft.

At the end of October 1965, a pair of cast-iron three-into-one exhaust manifolds from the M129 engine had

been adopted to replace the earlier fabricated steel versions, a new distributor followed at the start of November (new distributor caps duly came with them), and the gear linkage was modified on the 4MT unit.

A larger fuel tank (up from 65 litres/14.3 Imperial gallons to 82 litres/18.1 gallons) was fitted to the W113 series a few weeks later, from the end of November; naturally, a number of body-in-white modifications were required to allow this to happen.

Other than mention of a 5MT gearbox, there were no major changes in the November 1965 price list, although the cost of several options increased: The automatic aerial went up from DM 180 to DM 210, or DM 240 without a radio, the cost of radio preparation went from DM 35 to DM 60 without a radio (a move doubtless prompted by the end of fitting suppressors as standard from early 1965), the price of spotlights shot up from DM 50 to DM 60, the ski-rack from DM 130 to DM 135, the 'D' symbol from DM 8 to DM 10, and coconut floormats from DM 35 to DM 40. A tinted front screen was added as separate item at DM 75 at this time.

Interestingly, new wheels were fitted to the 230SL from this time. Borrowed from the W108 series, they differ mainly in the way the hubcap was secured, and are otherwise very similar to earlier versions.

In December 1965, the price of the 'D' shield was reduced from DM 10 to DM 3, although the basic design remained the same. There was a huge change in the personnel roster that month, though, as Professor Fritz Nallinger decided to take his retirement after 43 years with Daimler-Benz AG, 25 of them having been

(Above and opposite) Fascinating contrasts in German architecture, old and new. Note the registration number on the car – it was first seen on one of the pre-production prototypes, but even in monochrome, one can spot the black steering wheel on the later vehicle (the earlier car had a white wheel).

spent on the Board of Management. His successor as Technical Director of the company was Professor Hans Scherenberg, who took over responsibility for all areas of product development with immediate effect.

During March 1966, the cost of the basic car increased for the first time in Germany, rising to DM 21,100. The five-speed gearbox was marked as new on the March list (priced at

DM 1200, whereas earlier option lists had 'TBA' in the cost column alongside it). Coming with better gear spacing and an overdriven top, internal ratios were 3.92 on first, 2.21 on second, 1.42 on third, 1.00 on fourth and 0.85 on fifth; a 4.08:1 final-drive was specified with this gearbox, although its high price made the ZF S-5-20 unit something of a rarity (only 882 cars are said to have been built with the ZF five-speed during the W113 run). On saying that, of course, the automatic transmission cost slightly more, yet that was extremely popular in all markets – two in every five cars built left the factory with a 4AT unit! Incidentally, both the propshaft and transmission tunnel had to be modified to accommodate this new gearbox.

The 118 Light Grey MB-Tex vinyl trim changed to a slightly darker hue at the same time, as the factory was supplied with 2137 material instead of the earlier 2101. The shade was officially known as Grey from then on, otherwise there were no real changes to the colour and trim charts through to the end of the 230SL run.

The cost of the uprated heater, fitted luggage, and roof-rack increased in May 1966. Spotlight prices were also up, from DM 60 to DM 75, although they were reduced back down to DM 60 five months later.

In June 1966, a viscous fan coupling was added to the option list, priced at DM 130. This energy saving device, which also reduced noise at cruising speeds, was duly fitted as standard to the later 2.5-litre cars, and had six blades rather than the four of the older, regular fan.

German advertising for the 1966 season.

Standard coachwork colours (August 1965 to end of 230SL run)
Black (040), White (050), White-Grey (158), Light Beige (181), Graphite Grey (190), Dark Green (268), Dark Olive (291), Dark Blue (332), Dark Red-Brown (460), Red (501), Dark Red (542), Signal Red (568), Light Ivory (670), and Papyrus White (717).

Metallic coachwork colours (August 1965 to end of 230SL run)
Anthracite Grey (172), Medium Grey (178), Silver-Grey (180), Blue (387), Medium Blue (396), Bronze-Brown (461), Beige (462), Copper (463), Varnish Red (567), Red (571), and Moss Green (834).

Hood colours (August 1965 to end of 230SL run)
Black, Green, Marine Blue, Cream, White-Grey, Brown-Beige, Beige, Grey, Light Grey or Brown.

Two-tone combinations (August 1965 to end of 230SL run)
Solid shades: White, White-Grey, Graphite Grey, Dark Green, Dark Blue, Signal Red, Light Ivory or Papyrus White with a Black hardtop; Graphite Grey, Dark Blue or Signal Red with a White-Grey hardtop; Papyrus White with a Blue-Grey hardtop; Black with a Light Beige hardtop; White-Grey or Papyrus White with a Graphite Grey hardtop; Papyrus White with a Dark Green hardtop; White or Papyrus White with a Dark Blue hardtop; White-Grey, Light Beige or Light Ivory with a Havanna Brown hardtop; White, White-Grey or Light Beige with a Dark Red-Brown hardtop, or Dark Blue with a Papyrus White hardtop. Metallic shades: Anthracite Grey, Silver-Grey, Copper, Varnish Red, Red or Moss Green with a Black hardtop; Varnish Red or Red with a White-Grey hardtop, or Silver-Grey with an Anthracite Grey hardtop.

Trim colours & materials (August 1965 to end of 230SL run)
Turquoise (112), Bronze (113), Light Natural (114), Dark Blue (115), Caviar (116), Red (117), Light Grey (118), White-Grey (119), Cognac (120), Cream (121), Light Red (122), Medium Blue (123) or Green (124) MB-Tex vinyl, or Black (201), Red (202), Red (203), Light Red (204), Blue (205), Medium Blue (206), Light Grey (207), Cream (209), Natural (210), Dark Green (211), Reseda Green (212), Antique Yellow (213), Rust Red (214), Cognac (216), Turquoise (217), Bronze (218), Light Natural (219), Dark Blue (220), White-Grey (221), Wine Red (222), Medium Grey (223), Light Olive (224), Eggshell (230), Anthracite Grey (231) or Brown (232) perforated leather.

Carpet (August 1965 to end of 230SL run)
Black, Cream, Anthracite Grey, Graphite Grey, Dark Grey, Blue, Turquoise, Green, Wine Red, Rust Red, Medium Red or Brown.

Note: Five shades (268, 463, 501, 542, and 568) were only available when selected with either a 040 Black or 158 White-Grey hardtop.

Meanwhile, a new head gasket had been fitted from late spring, and a new radiator assembly was adopted in June, along with a lightweight, pressed-steel pulley for the alternator. A new Bosch fuel filter was employed from July.

Only a handful of 1967 model year 230SLs were built, but it's worth noting that an alternative 3.69:1 final-drive ratio was listed as a no-cost option for European 4MT cars, and the tinted front windscreen option was dropped again.

THE EXPORT MARKETS

In America, west coast prices started at $6285 for the 1966 model year, with the coupé version listed at $6443, and the car supplied with both tops commanding $6687; east coast buyers were lucky in being able to secure their SL for $100 less, due to New York being the US port-of-entry for Mercedes vehicles.

Road & Track tried an automatic 230SL in the summer of 1965, which it felt to be "... individual, and not quite like anything else on the road." In its November 1965 issue, the famous monthly noted: "About the ride, handling and brakes, we have nothing but praise. When it comes to the engine-transmission department, things get more complicated." It went on to say that "... the engine is probably the ultimate development of this series of Mercedes sohc sixes," but the testers were less than happy with the sluggish response caused by the second-gear starts. While it was possible to get away in first, the *R&T* people wanted easier access to it. Doubtless the new US gearing helped anyway, although the test took place too early to prove the point.

Styling was also questioned, with opinions ranging from "... a turtle too big for its shell" and "... clumsy," through to "... elegantly understated and ultra-contemporary." This was interesting, as American tastes naturally differ to European ones. There was also a call for greater performance – it *was* the start of the 'Pony Car' era in the States after all!

American advertising for one of the last 230SLs. Note the US-spec headlights.

Incidentally, American-bound cars gained hazard warning lights for the 1966 season, but differences between US and ROW vehicles were still few and far between at this stage of the proceedings. For the 1967 model year, the uprated heater and a stronger battery were added to the specification list, although prices were carried over.

In the UK, *Car* did an interesting comparison test between the 230SL and Fiat 2300S. Whilst admiring the 'character' of the Italian machine, it concluded: "On purely technical grounds, one can only hand it to the Mercedes for its almost unique achievement in reaching that elusive blend of sheer capability and physical comfort which has haunted sports car designers for decades. It is a beautifully made car, glamorous and exciting. For ride and cornering, it is right in the front rank. All it lacks, in the book of the man whose concern is to travel effortlessly and really quickly from point to point, is power; indeed, in this respect, it is left far behind by a certain rival from this country. Oh, and it does suffer from a ridiculously old-fashioned greasing schedule."

Unbeknownst to the people at *Car*, of course, was that a more powerful SL was on the way, and the maintenance intervals were duly increased later in the W113 run, although the author would rather deal with a grease gun than replacement parts, which is often the present-day cost of modernising suspensions inherited by classic car owners.

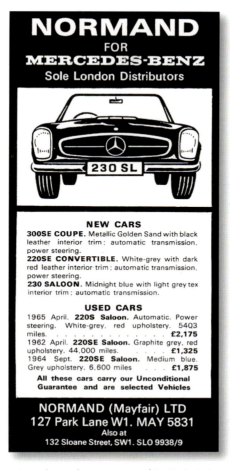

An advert that appeared in Britain's *Motor* in December 1965.

This French advert was actually a piece of deception, for the car is really a domestic German vehicle (registered S-WD 21) from the 1966 season; vehicles destined for France were given yellow headlight bulbs from July 1964 onwards, along with orange reversing light bulbs. Retouching artwork in catalogues and adverts was very common throughout the industry at the time.

Prices increased in mid-1966, with the Roadster now listed at £3527, the Coupé at £3588, and the Coupé/Convertible at £3717. However, there was roughly a £40 reduction on all SLs

Wonderful advertising from the National service station chain, this piece from the summer of 1966 featuring a UK-spec 230SL. Several variations were issued, using different cars, but each advert perfectly captured the mood of the Swinging Sixties.

later in the year after the import surcharge was abolished in November. Still, with the average UK wage at £17 a week at this time, this was of academic interest only for the vast majority, who were more likely to go for a house at the same kind of money as the Mercedes (the average house being £3840 in 1966). Notwithstanding, things then stayed the same until mid-1967, when the 250SL took over the reins.

In Japan, although the price had held steady for quite some time, by the start of 1967, the 230SL was up to 4,680,000 yen, which was twice what was being asked for a BMW 2000 saloon.

The last 230SL was built on 5 January 1967. Pilot production of the 250SL started in November 1966, with full-scale production beginning in the following month. As such, the 230 and 250 run overlapped for a short time before the 250SL made its official debut at the Geneva Show.

The final words in this chapter go to the ever-forthright LJK Setright, who wrote that the 230SL was "... the first of a new line of Mercedes-Benz sporting cars notable for combining superb proportions and handsome contours with ample comforts and higher performance than might have been expected.

"However one chose to drive it, the 230SL was delightful. The engine sang happily up to 6500rpm, the four-speed auto gearbox (with a simple fluid coupling, not a torque converter) was suave, the ride was stable, and the steering acceptable in everything but the excessive diameter of the steering wheel.

"According to the Stuttgart code, the letter 'S' might stand for either Sport or Super; the 'L' similarly hovers between Leicht, meaning lightweight, and Luxus – which, so long as the customer can pay, stands for everything imaginable and nothing that can hurt. Any and all of these terms would be fair when applied to the little 230SL, an enduringly impressive luxury sports car."

This is an Italian-specification vehicle, as distinguished by the small repeater indicators on the front wings, unique to the Italian market as far as the W113 model is concerned.

6

The 250SL

"Every driver who has more than a purely utilitarian interest in automobiles should drive a Mercedes-Benz 250SL at least once in his life. The car is an almost perfect yardstick against which to measure any other car. There are cars with better acceleration, cars with better brakes, cars with better roadholding. But there is no car we can think of that has such a remarkably good balance of performance, safety and comfort, and has them in such an absolutely civilized structure."
(***Car & Driver***, August 1967 issue)

The 250SL was unveiled to the press on 27 February 1967, with its official debut following a few days later at the Geneva Show in early March. The arrival of the 2.5-litre model didn't quite signal the end of the 230SL, though, as existing orders had to be fulfilled. While pilot production of the 250SL began in November 1966, with full-scale production beginning the following month, the final batch of 2.3-litre machines wasn't completed until the first week of January. Add in the lengthy shipping times to markets like the USA, Japan, and Australia, compared to 250s being delivered in Germany, not to mention the need to clear unsold stock in certain countries (UK price lists didn't mention the 250SL until the last days of May, for instance), and it can be seen there was actually a fair bit of overlap in the two model runs.

Poster from the 1967 Geneva Show, which attracted more than half-a-million visitors that year.

The 250SL was almost identical to the 230SL.

The only way to distinguish a 2.5-litre car from its 2.3-litre brethren from the outside was via the badge on the tail. Although the chrome strip between the rear bumpers is missing on this car, the general rule of thumb is that all vehicles fitted with an oblong number plate (which applied to most of Europe) had the trim, whereas US-bound machines, fitted with their squarer, deeper registration plates, didn't. Note that the

A NEW POWERTRAIN

The 1967 Geneva Show opened on 9 March, providing an ideal public launch location for the 250SL. In reality, there was little to differentiate between the 2.3- and 2.5-litre cars, as many of the running changes applied to the 230SL were carried over. It was under the bonnet, therefore, where one had to look for the biggest difference.

After two years development work under Andreas Weber, the 2.5-litre M129 six-cylinder engine had arrived with the W108 series saloons, introduced in the second half of 1965, and clearly based on 230SL technology rather than that of the old 2.2-litre saloons. The injected version of this unit (code 129.980), with a 9.3:1 compression ratio, gave 150bhp. This was the same output as that listed against the 2.3-litre six, despite the greater displacement. Furthermore, it wasn't as free-revving as the 230SL engine, but at least it delivered more torque, especially in the mid-range, and greater refinement, thanks to a seven-bearing bottom-end.

The power-unit used in the 250SL was given the M129 III (129.982) moniker, but was basically the same as that found in the SE sedans. The bore of the 2.3-litre engine was used, but with an increased stroke, the new dimensions of 82 x 78.8mm giving a cubic capacity of 2496cc. The Bosch fuel-injection was carried over, too, along with the 9.5:1 compression ratio that had been adopted on the saloons from September 1966.

Compared to the old 230SL lump, the use of seven rather than four main bearings was perhaps the greatest change, but the 2.5-litre engine also had a new cylinder head

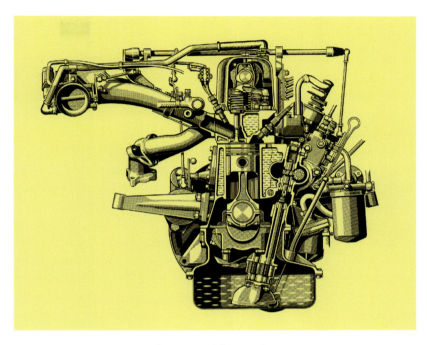

Cutaway drawing of the 2.5-litre engine.

The 2.5-litre engine with an automatic gearbox tacked onto the back. Note the fuel-injection pump and viscous cooling fan.

137

with bigger valves (41mm/1.61in diameter inlets, and exhaust valves that were 37mm/1.46in across), new cast-iron exhaust manifolds with square ports, an oil-water heat exchanger to keep the engine oil cool, and a viscous-coupled fan as standard.

Power output was officially the same, with 150bhp DIN developed at 5500rpm (thus meaning a reduction in specific output, down from 65bhp/litre to 60bhp/litre), but maximum torque output was improved by a worthwhile ten per cent, up to 159lbft at 4200rpm. This enhanced torque aided drivability in town, as well as safety when overtaking, and was also appreciated by those who specified the automatic gearbox.

As far as the transmissions were concerned, the three choices – 4MT, 4AT, and 5MT – were carried over, although the final-drive ratios were revised on four-speed units, now sitting somewhere between the old European specifications and those used in the US market. In European eyes, a shorter rear axle ratio was adopted to give a performance edge to the bigger-engined car, but to the Americans, it was a longer final-drive, reflecting the additional torque developed by the 2.5-litre engine.

Internal ratios were also revised, as the four-speed manual transmission was lifted straight from the 250SE. First was listed at 4.05, second at 2.23, third at 1.40, and fourth at 1.00. This was matched with a 3.92:1 final-drive, which was also being used on the contemporary saloons, although a 3.69:1 rear axle was offered as an option in Europe.

The four-speed automatic gearbox was carried over from the 230SL, with 3.98 on first, 2.52 on second, 1.58 on third, and a direct top, although the final-drive ratio was brought into line with the manual cars – 3.92:1, or 3.69:1 as an option.

The five-speed manual transmission was another carry-over, with 3.92 on first, 2.21 on second, 1.42 on third, a direct fourth, and an overdriven 0.85 on fifth; as before, a 4.08:1 final-drive was standard with this gearbox, with no alternative ratios offered.

CHASSIS UPGRADES

The other big mechanical change for the 250SL was in the uprated braking system, with discs now fitted all-round. While the 6J x 14 wheels continued unchanged, the diameter of the front discs was increased also, up to 273mm (10.7in) across, to better match the new 279mm (11.0in) items on the rear; both discs were sourced from the W108 series.

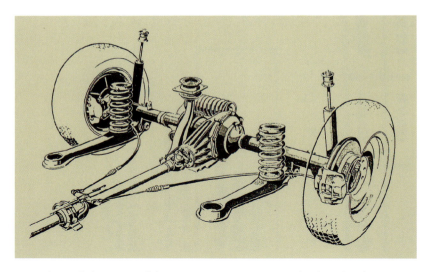

Technical drawing of the rear suspension. Disc brakes for the rear axle were a new addition for the 250SL, although small drums and shoes were fitted inside the 'top hat' of the disc to ensure an efficient handbrake.

As well as having a pressure regulator to prevent the rear wheels locking up, as per Porsche practice, and that of some other European sports car makers that found it difficult to produce an efficient parking brake, the rear discs had integrated drums for the handbrake only, giving the ultimate compromise between high-speed stopping power and holding ability once the car had come to a halt.

One contemporary magazine commented: "The new brakes are excellent in almost every case, but the old system was already damned good!"

Most of the other braking, suspension and steering details were carried over from the 230SL, although the anti-roll bar diameter was changed from 22mm (0.87in) to 20mm (0.79in) with the introduction of the 250SL.

Apart from the badging, there were very few body changes, such as the adoption of new bows in the soft-top frame, a different type of tinted glass (which absorbed heat but was optional anyway), and some subtle revisions to the spare wheel holding arrangements. Indeed, so few changes were made that some of the early press fleet was made up of 230SL factory hacks with engine and transmission transplants, suitably cleaned up and rebadged.

THE DOMESTIC MARKET

The first 250SL price list, issued in February 1967, noted that the basic four-speed manual car was DM 21,600. Automatic transmission added DM 1400, or there was the five-speed manual option, available for DM 1200. Alternative 3.69:1 final-drive ratios were a no-cost option on 4MT and 4AT vehicles.

The 250SL was supplied with a soft-top as part of the package. The distinctive hardtop was priced at DM 1180 (including the cloth hood), or DM 400 on its own, without the soft-top. It could also be ordered without the ragtop but combined with a bench seat in the rear, at DM 510 in MB-Tex, or DM 640 in leather.

This latter option, which was first seen with the introduction of the 250SL, was commonly known as the California Roadster model. In this format, the hood and its metal cover were deleted

One of the original press photographs announcing the arrival of the 250SL models.

to make way for a bench rear seat that could be used for children on shorter journeys. Alternatively, once folded, it provided a useful luggage shelf. The hood could not be retrofitted on this particular car, so the arrangement was only recommended for those living in areas with little rainfall, such as the US state that

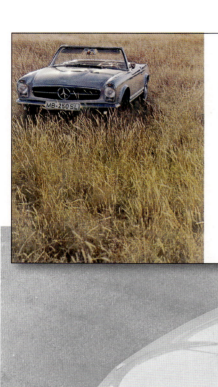

German advertising announcing the arrival of the 250SL.

The prototype California Roadster, built on a four-speed manual base car.

A couple of shots of the production 250SL in California Roadster guise, seen here making the most of the additional luggage space created when the rear seat was folded.

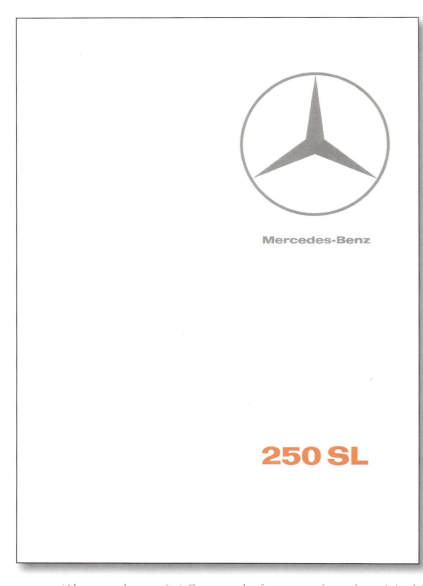
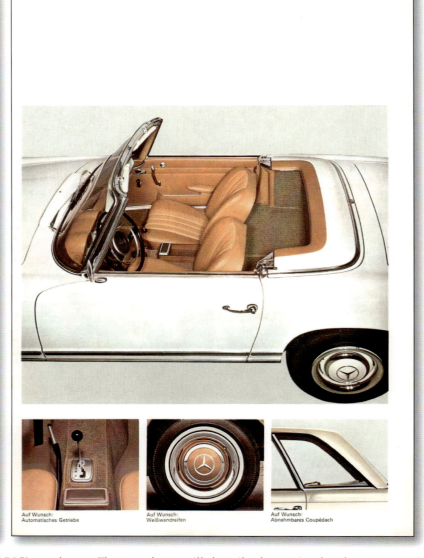

(Above and opposite) Cover and a few pages from the original 250SL catalogue. The wood was still described as stained walnut.

lent its name to the model, or one could leave the hardtop on during cold or rainy seasons.

For those less willing to give up the soft-top for whatever reason, the transverse seat option was still available, priced at DM 200 trimmed in the standard MB-Tex vinyl, or DM 250 in leather; leather upholstery for the other seats and trim sections was quoted at DM 800 by this time.

Tinted glass could be specified for the front and side windows for a DM 70 premium, or DM 105 if the hardtop window was included. Alternatively, DM 60 got the buyer tinted side and hardtop glass only; a hardtop carrier (useful given the weight and awkward shape/balance of the panel) was listed at DM 145, by the way.

Other options included metallic paint at DM 400 (plus an additional DM 170 for the hardtop), spotlights (DM 60), a passenger-side door mirror (DM 15), seatbelts (DM 110 a pair),

Große Lufteintrittsöffnungen, Luftstrom in alle Richtungen einstellbar

Fahrer- und Beifahrersitz in Längsrichtung und Lehnenneigung verstellbar

Roadsterverdeck vollständig versenkt und durch Metall-Blende geschützt

Scheibenbremse an allen vier Rädern

6-Stempel-Einspritzpumpe

Breite Spur

an uprated heater (DM 20), coconut floormats (DM 40), a first aid kit (DM 30), a fire extinguisher at DM 60, a 'D' country emblem at DM 3, and a selection of fitted suitcases and matching bags.

An ivory-coloured steering wheel was still available as an NCO, while power-assisted steering commanded DM 550. Whitewall tyres added DM 175 to the invoice, all-weather tyres were listed at DM 240, but for DM 12, uprated road springs were very reasonable.

As for audio options, there was the Becker Europa (DM 490), Mexico (DM 630), or Grand Prix (DM 650); these prices included preparation (DM 60 without a radio) and a manual aerial (DM 40 without a radio). An automatic aerial was available for DM 210, or DM 240 without a radio.

There was also a roof-rack (DM 290) or ski-rack (DM 135), although these required chrome trim pieces for the hardtop, sold separately at DM 40.

Standard coachwork colours (to March 1967)
Black (040), White (050), White-Grey (158), Light Beige (181), Graphite Grey (190), Dark Green (268), Dark Olive (291), Dark Blue (332), Dark Red-Brown (460), Red (501), Dark Red (542), Signal Red (568), Light Ivory (670), and Papyrus White (717).

Standard coachwork colours (March 1967 to end of 250SL run)
Black (040), White (050), White-Grey (158), Light Beige (181), Graphite Grey (190), Dark Green (268), Dark Olive (291), Dark Blue (332), Dark Red-Brown (460), Red (501), Dark Red (542), Signal Red (568), Light Ivory (670), Grey-Beige (716), and Papyrus White (717).

Metallic coachwork colours (for entire 250SL run)
Anthracite Grey (172), Medium Grey (178), Silver-Grey (180), Blue (387), Medium Blue (396), Bronze-Brown (461), Beige (462), Copper (463), Varnish Red (567), Red (571), and Moss Green (834).

Hood colours (to March 1967)
Black, Green, Marine Blue, Cream, White-Grey, Brown-Beige, Beige, Dark Grey, Light Grey or Brown.

Hood colours (March 1967 to end of 250SL run)
Black, Marine Blue, Cream, White-Grey, Beige, Dark Grey, Light Grey or Brown.

Two-tone combinations (to March 1967)
Solid shades: White, White-Grey, Graphite Grey, Dark Green, Dark Blue, Signal Red, Light Ivory or Papyrus White with a Black hardtop; Graphite Grey, Dark Blue or Signal Red with a White-Grey hardtop; Papyrus White with a Blue-Grey hardtop; Black with a Light Beige hardtop; White-Grey or Papyrus White with a Graphite Grey hardtop; Papyrus White with a Dark Green hardtop; White or Papyrus White with a Dark Blue hardtop; White-Grey, Light Beige or Light Ivory with a Havanna Brown hardtop; White, White-Grey or Light Beige with a Dark Red-Brown hardtop, or Dark Blue with a Papyrus White hardtop. Metallic shades: Anthracite Grey, Silver-Grey, Copper, Varnish Red, Red or Moss Green with a Black hardtop; Varnish Red or Red with a White-Grey hardtop, or Silver-Grey with an Anthracite Grey hardtop.

Two-tone combinations (March 1967 to end of 250SL run)
Solid shades: White, White-Grey, Graphite Grey, Dark Green, Dark Blue, Signal Red, Light Ivory or Papyrus White with a Black hardtop; Graphite Grey, Dark Blue or Signal Red with a White-Grey hardtop; Papyrus White with a Blue-Grey hardtop; White-Grey or Papyrus White with a Graphite Grey hardtop; Grey-Beige with a Dark Green hardtop; White or Papyrus White with a Dark Blue hardtop; White-Grey, Light Beige or Light Ivory with a Havanna Brown hardtop; White, White-Grey or Light Beige with a Dark Red-Brown hardtop, or Dark Blue with a Papyrus White hardtop. Metallic shades: Anthracite Grey, Silver-Grey, Copper, Varnish Red, Red or Moss Green with a Black hardtop; Varnish Red or Red with a White-Grey hardtop, or Silver-Grey with an Anthracite Grey hardtop.

Trim colours & materials (for entire 250SL run)
Turquoise (112), Bronze (113), Light Natural (114), Dark Blue (115), Caviar (116), Red (117), Light Grey (118), White-Grey (119), Cognac (120), Cream (121), Light Red (122), Medium Blue (123) or Green (124) MB-Tex vinyl, or Black (201), Red (202), Red (203), Light Red (204), Blue (205), Medium Blue (206), Light Grey (207), Cream (209), Natural (210), Dark Green (211), Reseda Green (212), Antique Yellow (213), Rust Red (214), Cognac (216), Turquoise (217), Bronze (218), Light Natural (219), Dark Blue (220), White-Grey (221), Wine Red (222), Medium Grey (223), Light Olive (224), Eggshell (230), Anthracite Grey (231) or Brown (232) perforated leather.

Carpet (for entire 250SL run)
Black, Cream, Anthracite Grey, Graphite Grey, Dark Grey, Blue, Turquoise, Green, Wine Red, Rust Red, Medium Red or Brown.

Note: Six shades (268, 463, 501, 542, 568, and 716) were only available when selected with either a Black, White-Grey or Dark Green hardtop.

Another German advert from the spring of 1967. It was at this time that the test facility for cars and commercial vehicles at Untertürkheim was unveiled. The site included a ten-mile (16km) high-speed section with steeply banked curves, a skidpan, a 'torture' track putting cars through outrageous driving conditions, and a series of artificial inclines.

Sie können Ihren 250 SL als Roadster oder als Roadster mit Coupé-Aufsatz bestellen.

Mit dem Fahrwerk und dem Motor eines Sportwagens, aber mit dem Komfort einer Reiselimousine

Der neue Mercedes-Benz 250 SL

Warum ändern wir jetzt den Mercedes-Benz 230 SL, obwohl er in einem einzigen Jahr mehr gekauft worden ist als der berühmte 190 SL in 6 Jahren?

Weil wir in der Entwicklung unserer Fahrzeuge nicht stehenbleiben.

Hier die wichtigsten Änderungen
Der Motorhubraum ist größer. 2,5 Liter. Die Kurbelwelle läuft jetzt in 7 wertvollen Lagern. Der Effekt? Noch weit ruhigerer Lauf als bisher. Der Motor verhält sich außerordentlich elastisch. In Verbindung mit dem hohen Drehmoment ermöglicht das ein kraftvolleres Beschleunigen in den einzelnen Gängen aus niedrigen Drehzahlen heraus. Im Stadtverkehr fahren Sie den 250 SL jetzt in ruhigeren, motorschonenden Drehzahlen.

Neu sind auch die groß bemessenen Scheibenbremsen an allen 4 Rädern und der Bremskraftregler. Zweikreis-Bremssystem und Servobremsanlage sind ja für einen Mercedes-Benz ohnehin Selbstverständlichkeiten.

Der 250 SL ist selbstverständlich auch mit Mercedes-Benz Automatischem Getriebe und Servolenkung lieferbar.

Damit ist der neue 250 SL mehr als bisher ein Automobil mit der Kraft eines echten Sportwagens, dem Komfort einer Reiselimousine und der Sicherheit eines Mercedes-Benz.

Mit dem neuen Mercedes-Benz 250 SL ist das Mercedes-Benz Personenkraftwagen-Programm für 1967 vollständig.

Weitere Änderungen in unserem Pkw-Programm wird es in diesem Jahr entgegen anderslautenden Gerüchten nicht geben!

Mercedes-Benz

(This page and opposite) Cover and selected pages from the 250SL driver's manual describing the dashboard and instruments. The red-line on the tachometer is wrong for a 250, as the artwork was carried over from the 230SL handbook; it started at 6300rpm on 2.5-litre cars.

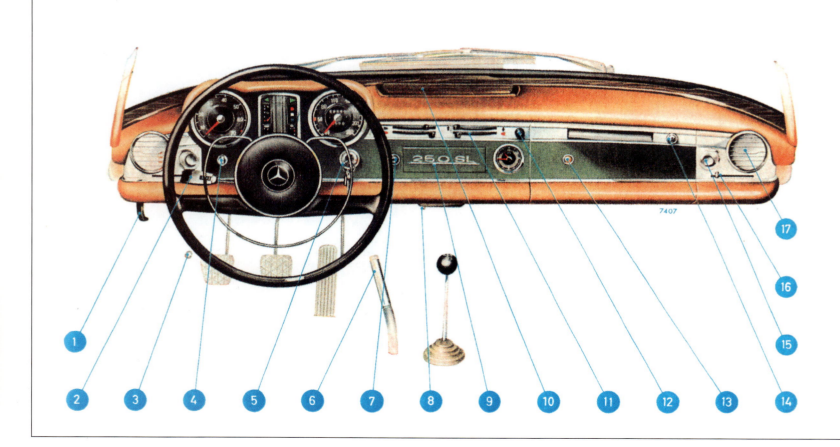

Armaturenanlage

Dashboard

Fahrersitz und Armaturenanlage	Driver's Seat and Dashboard	Siège du conducteur et tableau d'instruments	Asiento del conductor y tablero de instrumentos	Lugar do condutor e quadro de instrumentos	Posto di guida e cruscotto
1 Griff für Motorhaubenverschluß	1 Handle for Engine Hood Lock	1 Poignée pour fermeture du capot-moteur	1 Manilla para cierre del capó	1 Manípulo do fecho da capota do motor	1 Leva per chiusura cofano motore
2 Kombischalter	2 Combination Switch	2 Commutateur combiné	2 Interruptor combinado	2 Comutador combinado	2 Gruppo interruttori
3 Fußabblendschalter	3 Dimming Switch Pedal	3 Inverseur code au pied	3 Conmutador de pie de la luz de cruce	3 Comutador de pé da luz de cruzamento	3 Commutatore a pedale anabbagliamento fari
4 Lichtschalter	4 Light Switch	4 Commutateur d'éclairage	4 Conmutador de luces	4 Comutador das luzes	4 Interruttore fari
5 Lenkschloß mit Zündanlaßschalter	5 Steering Lock with Ignition and Starter Switch	5 Verrou de direction avec contacteur de démarrage	5 Cerrojo de la dirección con interruptor de encendido y arranque	5 Fechadura da direcção com comutador de ignição e arranque	5 Interruttore d'accensione ed avviamento combinato al dispositivo bloccasterzo
6 Handbremshebel	6 Handbrake Lever	6 Levier de frein à main	6 Palanca del freno de mano	6 Alavanca do freio de mão	6 Leva freno a mano
7 Automatischer, elektrischer Anzünder	7 Automatic Electric Lighter	7 Allume-cigares électrique, automatique	7 Encendedor électro — automático	7 Acendedor eléctrico e automático de cigarros	7 Accendisigari elettrico automatico
8 Einstiegleuchte	8 Entrance Light	8 Eclairage d'entrée	8 Luz de entrada	8 Luz de entrada	8 Luce di cortesia
9 Zierdeckel (Sonderwunsch Autoradio)	9 Ornamental Cover (Radio optional)	9 Couvercle enjoliveur (sur demande, radio)	9 Tapa decorativa (radio, a pedido)	9 Tampa postiça (lugar para rádio, extra opcional)	9 Cornicetta (a richiesta apparecchio radio)
10 Schallöffnung für Radio	10 Sound Aperture for Radio	10 Ouverture de résonance pour radio	10 Abertura de resonancia para la radio	10 Abertura de saída de som do rádio	10 Vano per altoparlante radio
11 Bedienungshebel für Heizung und Belüftung	11 Operating Lever for Heating and Ventilation	11 Leviers de commande pour chauffage et aération	11 Palanca de mando de la calefacción y ventilación	11 Manípulos para operar o aquecimento e a ventilação	11 Leva di comando per riscaldamento ed aerazione
12 Schalter für Belüftungsgebläse	12 Switch for Ventilating Fan	12 Commutateur pour soufflante de ventilation	12 Interruptor del soplador de ventilación	12 Interruptor do ventilador	12 Interruttore per ventilatore
13 Kombinierte Handschuhkasten- und Kartenlese-Leuchte	13 Combination Glove Compartment and Map Reading Light	13 Lampe combinée de lecture et d'éclairage du coffret à gants	13 Lámpara combinada de iluminación de la guantera y de lectura	13 Lâmpada combinada de leitura de mapas e iluminação do cofre guarda-luvas	13 Luce per vano porta-oggetti e di lettura
14 Verschließbarer Handschuhkasten	14 Lockable Glove Compartment	14 Coffret à gants verrouillable	14 Guantera cerradiza	14 Cofre guarda-luvas fechável a chave	14 Vano porta-oggetti con serratura
Jeweils rechts und links:	On the right and left:	Un de chacun de chaque côté	Lados derecho e izquierdo	A direita e à esquerda	Rispettivamente a destra e a sinistra:
15 Klappen zur Seitenscheibenbelüftung	15 Flaps for Side Pane Ventilation	15 Volets pour ventilation des glaces latérales	15 Portezuelas de salida de aire hacia los cristales laterales	15 Chapeletas de saída de ar para desembaciar os vidros laterais	15 Deflettore laterale
16 Betätigungshebel für Sommerbelüftung	16 Operating Lever for Summer Ventilation	16 Leviers de commande pour ventilation d'été	16 Palanca de mando de la ventilación adicional	16 Manípulo para operar a ventilação de verão	16 Leva per azionamento aerazione estiva
17 Drehbare Rosette für Sommerbelüftung	17 Louvre Plate for Summer Ventilation	17 Plaquette ronde rotative pour ventilation d'été	17 Roseta giratoria para la ventilación adicional	17 Roseta giratória para ventilação de verão	17 Rosetta girevole per aerazione estiva

Drehzahlmesser, Kombi-Instrument, Geschwindigkeitsmesser

Revolution Counter, Instrument Cluster, Speedometer

	Die Kontroll- und Warnleuchten können nur bei eingeschalteter Zündung in Funktion treten.	Controlling and warning lights will function only with the ignition switched on	Les lampes-témoin ne fonctionnent que lorsque l'allumage est enclenché	Las lámparas de control lucen sólo cuando el encendido está conectado.	As lâmpadas piloto e de controle só podem funcionar com a ignição ligada.	Le spie di controllo e di avvertimento non entrano in funzione che con accensione inserita.
1	Rote Markierung am Drehzahlmesser: Überdrehzahlbereich des Motors, nur kurzzeitig darin verbleiben keinesfalls nach oben überschreiten!	Red mark on revolution counter: overspeed range of engine, only for a short time, by no means to be exceeded	Repère rouge sur le compte-tours: plage de régimes excessifs; ne s'y maintenir que pendant un temps court; ne jamais dépasser	Marcación roja en el cuentarrevoluciones: margen de sobrevelocidad del motor, mantenerla sólo durante breve tiempo, de ninguna manera sobrepasarla	Marcação vermelha no conta-rotações: margem de rotação excessiva do motor; não permanecer nela senão muito pouco tempo, de nenhum modo aumentar ainda mais	Segno rosso sul contagiri: zona del No./giri superato, rimanerci soltanto di breve durata, nient'affatto accelerare di più!
2	Blinker-Kontrolleuchten — grün, rechts und links	Blinker control lights — green, right and left	Témoin vert des clignoteurs, à droite et à gauche	Lámparas verdes de control de las luces direccionales derechas e izquierdas	Lâmpadas piloto verdes dos pisca-pisca direitos e esquerdos	Spie di controllo indicatori di direzione — verdi, destra e sinistra
3	Ladestrom-Kontrolleuchte — rot	Charging current light — red	Témoin rouge de charge	Luz roja de control de carga de la batería	Lâmpada vermelha de controle de carga	Spia di controllo carica batteria — rossa
4	Weiß-rote Markierung am Geschwindigkeitsmesser: Bereich 50—60 km/h	White-red mark on speedometer: 31—37 miles/h (50—60 km/h) range	Repère blanc-rouge sur le tachymètre: plage de 50 à 60 km/h	Marcación blanca y roja en el velocímetro: margen 50 a 60 km/h	Marcação branca-vermelha no velocímetro: margem dos 50—60 km/h.	Segno bianco e rosso sul tachimetro: velocità 50—60 km/h
5	Gesamt-Kilometerzähler	Total mileage counter	Totalisateur kilométrique	Cuentakilómetros totalizador	Conta-quilómetros totalizador	Contachilometrie totalizzatore
6	Rückstellknopf für Tages-Kilometerzähler	Return button for daily mileage counter	Bouton de remise à zéro du compteur kilométrique journalier	Botón para volver el cuentakilómetros diario a cero	Botão para retroceder a zero o conta-quilómetros diários	Azzeratore per contachilometri giornaliere
7	Kraftstoffmesser. R und rote Warnleuchte: Reservemenge für ca. 35 bis 40 km	Fuel gauge, reserve and red warning light: reserve capacity for approx. 21—25 miles (35—40 km)	Jauge de carburant. R et lampe signalisatrice rouge: réserve pour environ 35 à 40 km	Indicador del nivel de combustible. R y lámpara roja de control: reserva para aprox. 35 a 40 km	Indicador de combustivel. R e luz vermelha de aviso: reserva suficiente para uns 35—40 km	Indicatore di livello carburante. R e spia rossa di avvertimento: riserva bastante per ca. 35—40 km
8	Öldruckmesser	Oil pressure gauge	Manomètre d'huile	Manómetro de aceite	Manómetro do óleo	Manometro olio
9	Regulierknopf für Instrumentenbeleuchtung; stufenlos	Control button for instrument light; continuous	Bouton de réglage de l'éclairage des instruments (progressif)	Botón regulador de la iluminación de los instrumentos; sin escalones	Botão de regular a iluminação dos instrumentos (regulação contínua)	Bottone di regolazione illuminazione strumenti; progressivo
10	Fernthermometer für Kühlwasser; roter Punkt: Höchstzulässige Temperatur	Telethermometer for cooling water; red mark: maximum permissible temperature	Téléthermomètre de l'eau de refroidissement; repère rouge: température maximum admise	Teletermómetro para agua refrigerante; punto rojo: temperatura máxima admisible	Teletermómetro da água refrigerante; segno vermelho: temperatura máxima consentita	Teletermometro acqua raffreddamento; segno rosso: temperatura massima consentita
11	Fernlicht-Kontrolleuchte — blau	High beam control light — blue	Témoin bleu des pharescute	Lámpara azul de control de la luz de carretera	Lâmpada piloto azul da luz de longo alcance	Spia di controllo luci abbaglianti — azzura
12	Tages-Kilometerzähler (rot: 100-Meter-Anzeige)	Daily mileage counter (red: 328 ft. [100 meters] indication)	Compteur kilométrique journalier (rouge: indication des hectomètres)	Cuentakilómetros diario (rojo: centenas de metros)	Conta-quilómetros diários (números vermelhos: hectómetros)	Contachilometri giornaliero (rosso: indicazione 100 m)

A factory hack called up for PR duty, pictured with the hood down and hardtop in place.

There were a few minor changes to the trim mix in March 1967, with a couple of hood options dropped, and some fresh two-tone combinations, some including a new colour – 716 Grey-Beige.

A limited-slip differential became available in the same month, priced at DM 160, and there were some changes to the fitted luggage. Otherwise, as far as options were concerned, there were no other revisions through to the end of the 250SL run.

Early American advertising for the 250SL, highlighting what was new and, just as importantly, what wasn't, compared to the 230SL. Interestingly, the advert, and US press releases, noted that the 230SL would "... continue being sold for an indefinite period," although production of the 2.3-litre car was limited to just 185 units in 1967. It's fair to say that there was therefore little intention of running the two SL grades alongside each other for long.

THE US MARKET

The 250SL was introduced to the US market at $6897 with both hoods on the east coast (a $100 premium was required for west coast customers to cover additional shipping costs), compared with $6587 for the last of the 230SLs in similar guise.

The coupé format was that of the 2+2 California Roadster for America with the arrival of the 250SL. The five-speed transmission was a $464 extra, while PAS commanded $200. Amongst those options often specified by US buyers, but not usually considered in Europe, were air conditioning and bumpers guards – the latter made available as a dealer-fitted accessory from around this time.

Even before options, though, the SL was an expensive car. *Road Test* posed the question: "Does the Mercedes-Benz 250SL justify its $7000 price tag? It depends upon the driver/buyer. If he seeks satisfaction in owning a precisely-created, extremely high quality, mechanically-sophisticated automobile, he'll love the car at any price."

In its August 1967 issue, *Car & Driver* noted: "Last month we tested a Ferrari 330GTC, and the comparison of the two cars is interesting. At roughly $16,000, the Ferrari is just about as far as you can go in automobile sophistication. It has a rear-mounted five-speed transmission, fully independent rear suspension, a sohc V12 with gobs of horsepower, and on and on.

"The only thing remotely 'far out' in the 250SL's specifications, by contrast, is its fuel-injection. The rest (in-line water-cooled six, albeit overhead cam; swing-axle rear suspension, albeit low-pivot; four-speed manual or optional automatic transmission, et cetera) are conventional if not old-fashioned. Yet it is difficult to appraise the 250SL in terms of its mechanical components – the matching and blending of them is done too well. Whereas the Ferrari is designed, rightly so, for all-out, hair-raising performance, surrounded by a kind of rough-hewn, brutal luxury, the 250SL is infinitely subtler. Its performance is in no way startling, yet it is capable of over-the-road averages that are limited in most cases only by the law.

"Similarly, the luxuriousness of the car is in total effect. Detail work is very good, with leather in obscure places, chrome plates on thresholds, everything operational and heavy, solid, bank-vaultish. The test car had the removable hardtop, and the fit was so good that it was hard to believe that it was actually removable. Everything fits. Everything works. The 'orthopedic' design of Mercedes-Benz seats is an unyielding Procrustean bed, [but the excellent shape makes the apparent hardness of the first impression quickly disappear], and there is a similar stern quality about the rest of the interior. There's no nonsense about German luxury, no sir.

"Fangio could never win a Mille Miglia in a car like this. But the average inbred aristocrat could drive it from Brescia to Rome and back to Brescia, pass just about everything in sight, post a remarkably high average speed for the trip, and never hear a murmur of complaint from the lady in the passenger seat. As a matter of fact, she'd probably never even lift her nose out of her latest copy of *Paris Match*. And that's what we mean by civilised."

Sports Car Graphic summed up its test with the following words: "It's an excellent car in every respect. It's pretty much alone in its price range, but there are a handful of fine sports cars about $500 below it. Yet, the 250SL offers enough extra quality to make it more than worth spending the extra money."

A couple of Italian-specification SLs from the time. The snowy shot is quite useful, as pictures of the 'Pagoda' roof cars with the hood up are very rare.

Interestingly, the cars shipped to America were not fitted with 'AUTOMATIC' badges from this time, although it continued to be used in other markets. Also, US cars with air conditioning and PAS had a different anti-roll bar to allow for the difference in weight distribution.

As it happens, it was during this period that US-spec cars started to pick up all manner of detail differences, minor changes that would only increase in number as the years went by. Some of the last 230s sold in the States had blue tyre pressure information stickers applied to the boot lip of the closing panel, although with the introduction of the 250SL, a new version (in red, with written data only) was being stuck to the inside of the bootlid. In addition, US-bound 250s had a unique VIN plate, attached to the nearside A-post (inside the door jamb) rather than on the bulkhead, where it remained on ROW machines. Also, a small yellow (later white) sticker further up on the A-post reminded owners of the service intervals.

In the first week of June 1967, all US cars inherited a 4.08:1 final-drive, but bigger changes were around the corner, not only for America-bound cars, but all SLs, although most of the modifications were introduced to satisfy Federal law.

For the record, a total of 20,691 Mercedes cars were sold Stateside in 1967, including 334 230SLs and 1753 250SLs. SL exports, expressed as a percentage of production, had risen from 48 per cent in 1964, to 76 per cent in 1967, with the US accounting for exactly half of the cars built for export. Needless to say, the American market had become a very important outlet for Mercedes-Benz sports cars.

SAFETY BECOMES AN ISSUE FOR ALL

Daimler-Benz already had a reputation for enhanced safety features, introducing one thing after another in the fields of active and passive safety, and whether it was required by law or not. There was no building down to a price and keeping just ahead of the rules by the bare minimum in Stuttgart – safety was an integrated part of car design.

Meanwhile, Ralph Nader's infamous book, *Unsafe At Any Speed*, highlighted a number of safety issues in the States, helping to prompt the 1966 National Traffic and Motor Vehicle Safety Act.

The US-specification 250SL after July 1967 – the most obvious distinguishing point compared to earlier examples of the breed being the addition of side reflectors. (Courtesy M-B USA)

With the formation of the DOT (active from 1 April 1967), this led to a snowstorm of paper listing new Federal regulations – some an excellent step forward in promoting safety (such as mandatory seatbelts), although many had little or no meaning whatsoever in real life, simply causing a great deal of trouble for makers.

There was even talk of banning open cars altogether in the States at one point, although the bill was thankfully never passed. Notwithstanding, the threat was very real, and had a dramatic effect on car design for almost a decade after the ban was first mooted. The Triumph TR7 is a perfect example of the uncertainty, with the open version following many years after the coupé, and tons of extra bracing needed to stiffen the convertible, as the engineering was carried out for a closed car to avoid the risk of having a vehicle that may not be able to be sold in the US – the biggest market for sports cars. The Jaguar XJ-S was another casualty, while Porsche went down the 'Targa' route to avoid problems.

(Above and opposite) An American catalogue produced after the July 1967 changes, thus including all the interior and exterior modifications. Note details like the padded windscreen frame, the new steering wheel boss and horn ring, the revised door furniture, and symbols having been added on the steering column stalk and heater controls.

Why all the panic? Well, granted, America was only one country, but it was by far the largest outlet for European sports cars. Therefore, the manufacturers of Britain (still a stronghold for LWS models, most of them finding their way to American shores), Italy, Germany and France had to take all moves by the Federal regulators seriously. It was a case of complying with the rules put before them or potentially lose their biggest market overnight. Therefore, in response to new rules laid down by the US DOT in readiness for the 1968 season, Daimler-Benz put through its first batch of changes for the 250SL on 12 July 1967.

For all cars there were new door mirrors, a new energy-absorbing steering column was fitted (readily identified by the revised centre boss with less chrome and a different-shaped horn ring on the wheel), the door furniture (including the locks and handles, armrests, and window winder cranks) was completely revised, foam padding was added to the windscreen frame, much of the switchgear was given flexible end caps to make it friendlier to those coming into contact with it in an accident situation, and likewise, the soft-top and hardtop locking catches for the header rail were changed to accept removable handles to reduce the risk of passengers being skewered.

It was also at this time that three-point seatbelts were introduced (the mounts had actually been in place from March 1966), with the old diagonal only – or shoulder – belts replaced by Kangol three-point seatbelts. They were still classed as an option in Europe, though.

Of the smaller revisions, a thin film was added to the windscreen to reduce fracturing, the finish on the wiper arms was toned down, the finish on the interior's rearview mirror went from chrome to black, a pad was added to the top of the steering column, just ahead of the central combination meter, the ignition barrel was set into the dash a fraction deeper, and given a soft outer edge and plastic-tipped key, a red brake warning light was added to the instrument panel, brake hoses were given a 'tested' symbol, and items like the top roll, clock bezel, centre console and ashtray were given softer edge profiles.

Basic Equipment

Windshield
Electric windshield washer system
Windshield wiper with two speed steps, butterfly model

Lighting System
Sealed beam type headlight
Fog lights
Blinker lights
Brake lights
Parking lights
Back-up lights
Rheostat controlled instrument lights
Dome lamp with door switch
Map reading lamp and hand switch
Lights for glove box and boot
Socket connection for hand lamp in engine compartment

Instruments
Instrument panel padded, yielding
Speedometer
Tachometer
Oil pressure gauge
Fuel gauge
Cooling water temperature gauge
Control lights for battery charging current, blinker, high beam, and gasoline reserve
Electric clock
Total mileage counter
Daily mileage counter

Signalling System
2 super-tone horns
Blinker with automatic return
Signal lever for blinker, and windshield wiper
Foot dimmer switch

Locks
Safety tap locks on doors
Trunk lid lock
Steering wheel lock, combined with ignition lock, starter and starter repeat lock
Glove box lockable
Tank lock

Heating and Ventilation
Dust and draft-free with additional blower for windshield and front legroom.
Air volume and air distribution variably adjustable towards top and bottom.
Heating separately controlled for right and left side.
Temperature regulation through mixing of warm and cold air, independent of vehicle speed.
Blower coupled to adjusting lever
Nozzles for side window defrosting.
Adjusting rosettes for summer ventilation, left and right.

Miscellaneous
Receptacle between front seats
Day-night rear view mirror
Padded sun vizors
Armrests on doors, padded
Cigar lighter
Ashtray mounted in front of receptacle
Steering wheel with padding
Seats adjustable lengthwise with adjustable backrest
Pockets on doors

Optional

MB automatic transmission
MB power steering
Limited slip differential
Radio with mechanical or automatic aerial
Harder springs
Leather upholstery
Transverse seat, rear for roadster/coupé
Ski holding brackets
Luggage set
Special paintwork in one or two colors

Further details are contained in the Mercedes-Benz catalogue for special equipment.

American-spec cars received some additional modifications, including side reflectors attached to the front and rear wings of US-bound cars for the 1968 season, subtle tuning revisions for lower exhaust emissions, seatbelts fitted as standard, ruffled bags underneath the armrests for map pockets rather than hard bins, a small plaque showing the heater controls, symbols on the steering column's multi-function wand, an illuminated AT quadrant with the 'O' position marked with 'N' instead, and a matt finish on the horn ring.

Continuing its development programme, as well as cutting costs through standardisation, Daimler-Benz introduced new steel wheels in September 1967. Although these were still 6J x 14 rims, they had more cooling vents integrated into the design, and were duly carried over to the 280SL. A symbol was added on the hazard warning light switch at the same time, and shortly after, a harder setting on the steering damper was adopted. Finally, in November, new shock absorbers were employed, both front and rear.

Enthusiasts had only just got used to the idea of the 250SL when it was resigned to the history books. This picture shows some of the last 250SLs rolling down the lines at Sindelfingen with some of the first W114 saloons. All the SLs in clear view were destined for US shores, by the way.

THE RHD MARKETS

In the UK, the 250SL finally took the place of the 230SL as spring gave way to summer. The Roadster was listed at £3611, the Coupé at £3672, and the Coupé/Convertible at £3806, meaning an increase of around £90 on the 2.3-litre cars. To put this into perspective, a Porsche 911S cost £3556 at the time, and an Aston Martin DB6 could be secured for £4068 (or £4578 in drophead guise); the Jaguar E-type started at just £1967, continuing William Lyons' policy of offering unbeatable value-for-money.

As far as Britain was concerned, the 250SL had a remarkably short run, being listed only until the middle of January 1968, with last cars having been imported in December 1967.

It was a similar story in the other right-hand drive markets. In Japan, the 250SL was listed at 4,880,000 yen (200,000 yen more than 230SL). At this time, a VW 1200 was available for just 788,000 yen, while the price of a Mazda Carol was half that! Perhaps a more realistic comparison from the Hiroshima maker, though, was the rotary-engined Cosmo, priced at 1,590,000 yen.

A sports car was a sprinter, not a slugger, which explains why the men in Stuttgart felt it was better to hold on to the spunky 2.3-litre engine for the SL long after the 2.5-litre six went into production, but with so many customers choosing automatic gearboxes, the extra mid-range punch was much appreciated. The problem, of course, is that things moved quickly in the automotive world in the latter part of the sixties.

No sooner had the 250SL found its niche than it was time to bring out another, larger-engined SL. The last 2.5-litre SL was manufactured in January 1968, which is when 280SL production officially began (two months after an initial pilot run). The 250SL was therefore destined to be a rare model, with only 5196 built.

7
End of the line

"Our experience of the original 230SL (same car, smaller engine), and the interim 250SL, made us feel that the engines had to work very hard to give the expected performance. With this latest version (which has 11 per cent more torque) all these criticisms go, and there seems to be a much greater reserve of power than the engine size, which is still small by absolute standards, would suggest." – Geoffrey Howard on the new 280SL, *Autocar*, May 1968.

In retrospect, it's fair to say the 250SL was simply a stop-gap model released to bridge the divide between the 230SL and 280SL – the two extremes of W113 SL motoring that ultimately come from very different eras, despite their closeness in looks and vintage. The 230SL made its debut at a time when few cared about safety to any great extent, and even less about the environment. The 280SL was brought into a new world, with green issues reaching the top of the agenda, and nanny states putting too much emphasis on safety – after all, why make a car into a padded tank, when it was considered perfectly okay

The first official picture of the 280SL, which looked virtually identical to a 230 or 250! Only after 45 cars had rolled down the line did the 280SL adopt the one-piece wheel trims that would help distinguish the 2.8-litre car from its smaller-engined brethren.

(This page and opposite) Studio shots of the 280SL. From the front and rear angles, only the badge on the tail would enable the bystander to tell this was a 2.8-litre machine, although small items like the black rearview mirror and door mirror help date the car as being a 1968 model or later, while from the side, the W114-style wheelcovers are the telltale clue.

to ride a motorcycle without any protection, or even a bicycle without a helmet? And did no-one see the irony that in making cars heavier and strangling engines by trying to make them run on almost pure air, larger power-units were required to keep performance levels on a par with those of yore, with more fuel being used in the process? Still, for better or worse, times had changed, and the engineers had to move with them ...

ENGINE TRANSPLANT

One of the key elements in the creation of the 280SL was its new engine capacity – the six-cylinder unit's displacement being upped from 2.5 litres to 2.8 litres in a bid to increase power and torque output.

The 2.8-litre engine was a development of the M130 series, its production overseen by Adolf Wente. Its main application was in the "New Generation" of Mercedes-Benz saloons – the W108 280S, 280SE and 280SEL, which had their press launch at Hockenheim on 9 January 1968 along with a new mid-range of smaller-engined W114 and W115 models, although some would find their way into the W111 280SE coupés and cabriolets, while the Type 130.983 was reserved for the 280SL.

It is interesting to note that the Type 130.983, with 170bhp DIN on tap, had ten more horses under the bonnet compared to the regular injected 130.980 lump, although the 170bhp six was also used in 130.981 form in the re-engined 300 S-Class from this time, with the 2.8-litre six replacing the old three-litre unit that had been expensive to build, yet only gave the same power as the latest M130 engine.

The larger displacement was achieved by leaving the stroke at 78.8mm, but increasing the bore by 4.5mm, giving 86.5mm pots. This gave a cubic capacity of 2778cc (2748cc for German tax purposes), although the bigger bore meant getting rid of some of the water jackets in the block (those around the two-three and four-five cylinders), which in turn led to a new bottom-end being required, but at least the latest design gave equal cylinder spacing, thus delivering more even cooling than the previous siamesed arrangement. In fact, the cooling system capacity went down from 12.9 litres (2.84 Imperial gallons) to 12.5 litres (2.75 gallons); oil capacity stayed the same as that of the 250SL, listed at 5.5 litres (1.21 gallons).

There were also major revisions to the cylinder head and combustion chamber shape to give a cleaner burn, as well as new piston rings. While the valve sizes were carried over from the 250SL unit, the camshaft profiles were changed with the aim of making the 2.8-litre six more free-revving than its predecessor, and indeed, more sporting than its M130 counterpart used in the saloons.

With a 9.5:1 compression ratio, 170bhp DIN was delivered at 5750rpm, along with 177lbft of torque at 4500rpm. As

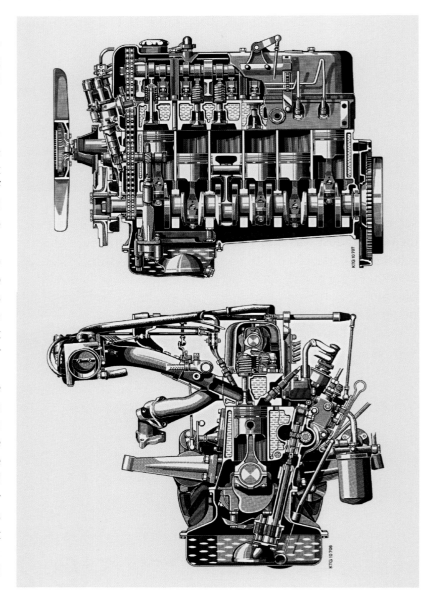

Cutaway drawings of the 2.8-litre engine. Early US 280s had a small sticker on the leading edge of the cam cover on the oil filter side, with another on the nearside of the bulkhead. There were quickly replaced by a single, large white sticker, positioned slightly farther back than the original cam cover one, and containing information on tick-over, timing, and valve clearance settings.

mentioned earlier, the SL had more power than the contemporary saloon, but it peaked 250rpm further up the rev-range compared to the 280SE; torque output was the same, but again, the peak figure was recorded 250rpm higher on the tachometer.

Specific output was now 61bhp per litre – a very slight improvement on the 250SL, but the power delivery was guaranteed, as each engine was bench-tested for two hours prior to being fitted.

There was mention of a lower compression ratio for North American-spec cars to get around emissions regulations in early magazine articles, but this train of thought was not carried through. Although an 8.7:1 c/r version of the engine was available for countries with poor fuel quality, US-bound cars had the same 9.5:1 pistons as ROW models – the necessary tuning for a cleaner exhaust was done via a few tweaks to the fuel-injection settings, the use of an '09' camshaft instead of the regular '01' item that gave significantly more valve overlap, and a fuel shut-off valve that kicked in when the driver backed off the throttle under low-speed deceleration.

US engines were rated at 180bhp SAE at 5700rpm, with maximum torque put at 193lbft at 4500rpm. In effect, in comparison with the 250SL's SAE figures of 170bhp and 173lbft, the specific output fell on US power-units from 68bhp/litre to 65bhp/litre. For makers exporting to the States, it was a similar situation throughout the industry, but at least the additional torque was appreciated, especially by owners who'd specified an automatic gearbox.

On the subject of transmissions, as before, 4MT, 5MT and 4AT gearboxes were offered. The four-speed manual gearbox continued with the same internal ratios (4.05, 2.23, 1.40 and 1.00); a 3.92:1 final-drive was the norm, with a 3.69:1 back axle available as a no-cost option.

The five-speed unit was also carried over, with 3.92 on first, 2.21 on second, 1.42 on third, 1.00 on fourth and 0.85 on fifth. A 4.08:1 final-drive was fitted as standard with this gearbox.

Interestingly, although a new automatic gearbox was specified for the W114 series, the SL continued with the old K4A025 four-speed unit with its fluid coupling, but no torque convertor; the only change was on the selector plate, with 'N' taking the place of 'O' for neutral on ROW cars, as per America-bound machines since the 1968 season. Internal ratios were 3.98, 2.52, 1.58 and 1.00, while the axle ratios were the same as those specified for the four-speed manual cars.

It's worth noting at this point, however, the US-spec cars had different final-drive ratios to ROW cars, with 4.08:1 specified for all three gearboxes, and alternative ratios of 3.92:1 and 3.69:1 on four-speed vehicles. This went some way towards making up for the eight per cent drop in power American owners had to swallow.

OTHER CHANGES

While the new W114 saloons introduced a fresh semi-trailing arm rear suspension into the Daimler-Benz armoury, the SL series continued with its tried and trusted setup, duly inherited from the 250SL.

However, with the aim of cutting servicing time and costs (finicky maintenance schedules and the cost involved had been a common source of complaint with owners, especially in the US), a number of suspension and steering parts were changed to sealed units without grease nipples, and more rubber bushes were introduced to eliminate greasing in other areas where replacement wasn't as straightforward. Without doubt, this move helped extend service intervals (from 2000 miles, or around 3000km, to 6000 miles, which is close to 10,000km), but allied to the use of regular radials instead of the bias-ply items that had been used on the earliest cars (improving high-speed handling characteristics at the cost of low-speed feel), sensitive drivers were able to tell the difference in the chassis' feedback.

After the first 45 280SLs had rolled down the line, the one-piece wheelcovers that became one of the only true distinguishing features of the 2.8-litre models – other than the badge on the tail, that is – were introduced. This change, from the original-style wheel trims to the W114 version (usually colour-keyed to match the body, or the hardtop if 'two-tone' paint was specified), took place in the first week of December 1967, so it's fair to say that 'all' 280SLs came with these hubcaps.

Apart from the return to a 6500rpm red-line on the tachometer and a different blanking plate for the radio slot (now sporting a '280SL' badge), that was about the extent of the differences between the 280SL and its immediate predecessor, as so many changes had been instigated at the end of the 250SL run.

For the record, the 2.8-litre car's weight was officially listed at 1360kg (2992lb), which was 65kg (143lb) up on the original 230SL.

THE DOMESTIC MARKET

Following the Hockenheim presentation with the other new Mercedes models, the 280SL was then given its public debut at the Brussels Show shortly after (the event opened on 17 January that month), thus leaving the limelight for the V8-engined 300SEL 6.3 model at Geneva a couple of months later.

The first price list was dated February 1968, with the basic car commanding DM 23,045. Options were generally cheaper, although, as of January 1968, all domestic prices had a newly-introduced purchase tax of 11 per cent to be added – there had been no VAT in Germany before this date.

The hardtop was listed at DM 1120 (including the soft-top), or DM 380 without the rag-top. It could also be ordered without the soft-top, but combined with a bench seat in the rear, which added DM 485 to the invoice (or DM 605 if the seat was trimmed in leather instead of MB-Tex vinyl).

Automatic transmission was available for a DM 1300 premium, and, like the standard four-speed manual gearbox,

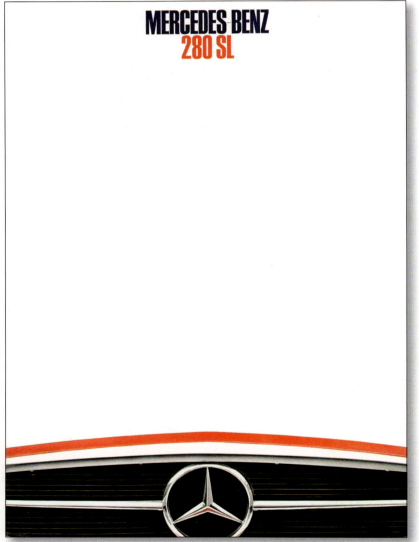

Cover and a couple of pages from the first catalogue, dated December 1967. The English-language version had different internal artwork.

Two shots from a series taken in early 1968, showing an automatic 280SL pictured with horses sharing the limelight.

came with a no-cost option of a taller 3.69:1 final-drive. The five-speed manual transmission was listed at DM 1120, while a limited-slip differential was priced at just DM 150.

Metallic paint was listed at DM 375 (plus an additional DM 160 for the hardtop, in matching or contrasting shade), while tinted glass was DM 79 for the front and side windows, or DM 98 if the hardtop window was included. The side window and hardtop glass only came in at DM 56, or DM 19 for the hardtop only.

MB-Tex vinyl upholstery was standard, with leather trim

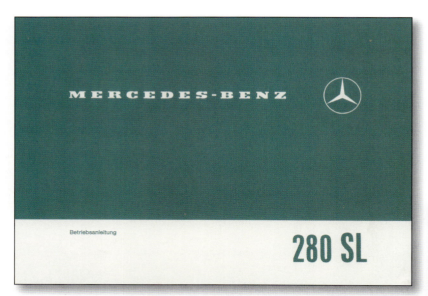

Cover of the domestic 280SL owner's handbook. The content was much the same as in the 230SL and 250SL versions.

Two more pictures of the 280SL used extensively in early catalogue artwork. As before, the soft-top dropped underneath a hinged metal tonneau panel, like that found on the 300SL roadsters and earlier W113 variants.

costing DM 700. A transverse rear seat was still available, priced at DM 190 in vinyl, or DM 235 when trimmed in leather.

Other options included PAS (DM 510), whitewall tyres (DM 165), all-season tyres (DM 35), uprated road springs (DM 11), spotlights (DM 55), a passenger-side door mirror (DM 14), an ivory steering wheel and gearknob (NCO), seatbelts (DM 100 a pair), hazard warning lights (DM 28), an uprated heater (DM 19), coconut floormats to protect the standard carpeting (DM 37), a first aid kit (DM 30), a fire extinguisher at DM 55, a 'D' country emblem at DM 3, a selection of fitted suitcases and matching bags (different to those offered for the 250SL), and a hardtop carrier, priced at DM 138.

There was also a roof-rack (DM 265) or ski-rack (DM 125), although these required chrome trim pieces for the hardtop, sold separately at DM 85 fitted.

As for audio options, there were the Becker Europa (DM 455), Mexico (DM 585) and Grand Prix (DM 600) units on offer. An automatic aerial was available (from DM 195) to replace the manual one, although DM 38 was required for a manual aerial if it was ordered without a radio. Likewise, radio preparation without a radio came in at DM 55.

The 280SL brought with it a whole new colour palette for both paint and trim, although there were fewer options per colour compared with earlier W113 SL offerings:

Standard coachwork colours (to September 1969)
Black (040), White (050), White-Grey (158), Anthracite Grey (173), Light Beige (181), Dark Green (268), Dark Olive (291), Horizon Blue (304), Medium Blue (350), Tobacco Brown (423), Dark Red-Brown (460), Dark Red (542), Signal Red (568), Red (576), Light Ivory (670), Papyrus White (717), Beige-Grey (726), Blue (903), and Dark Blue (904).

Metallic coachwork colours (to September 1969)
Anthracite Grey (172), Silver-Grey (180), Blue (387), Bronze-Brown (461), Beige (462), Whisky (467), Red (571), Beige-Grey (728), Moss Green (834), and Blue (906).

Hood colours (to September 1969)
Black, Dark Grey, Light Grey, Parchment, Dark Blue, Beige, Dark Brown or Dark Green.

Two-tone combinations (to September 1969)
Solid shades: White, White-Grey, Dark Green, Dark Red, Signal Red, Red, Light Ivory, Papyrus White or Beige-Grey with a Black hardtop; Black, White-Grey, Light Beige or Light Ivory with a Tobacco Brown hardtop, or Papyrus White with a Dark Blue hardtop. Metallic shades: Anthracite Grey or Red with a Black hardtop.

Trim colours & materials (to September 1969)
Black (131), Red (132), Light Red (133), Green (134), Blue (135), Grey (136-137), Dark Brown (138), Bamboo (139), Cognac (140), Beige (141) or Parchment (144-147) MB-Tex vinyl, or Black (241), Red (242), Light Red (243), Green (244), Blue (245), Grey (246-247), Dark Brown (248), Bamboo (249), Cognac (250), Beige (251) or Parchment (254-257) perforated leather.

Carpet (to September 1969)
Dark Grey, Blue, Dark Green, Light Red, Red, Beige, Brown or Dark Brown.

Note: Four shades (181, 268, 568 and 576) were only available when selected with either a Black or Tobacco Brown hardtop.

Technical Data   Mercedes-Benz 280 SL

Engine	
Number of cylinders	6
Bore/Stroke	3.41/3.1 ins.
Total displacement	169.5 cu. ins.
Engine output acc. to SAE	195 gr. HP at 5,900 rpm
Engine output acc. to DIN[1]	170 net BHP at 5,750 rpm
Max. torque acc. to SAE	195 ft. lbs. at 4,700 rpm
Max. torque acc. to DIN[1]	177 ft. lbs. at 4,500 rpm
Max. engine speed	6,500 rpm
Compression	9.5
Oil capacity crankcase max./min.	9.7/6.2 Imp. pts.
Capacity of cooling system	22 Imp. pts.
Generator	14 V/35 A
Battery	12 V/55 Ah
Max. speed	124 mph.
Tyres	185 HR 14
Fuel	
Fuel consumption acc. to DIN 70030[2]	25 m. p. Imp. gal.
Tank capacity	18 Imp. gal.
incl. reserve	1.5 Imp. gal.
Fuel	Premium
Weights	
Kerb weight	3,000 lbs.
Permissible total weight	3,780 lbs.
Trailer load with brake[3]	2,645 lbs.
Trailer load without brake[3]	1,575 lbs.

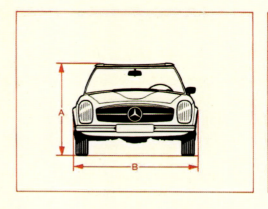
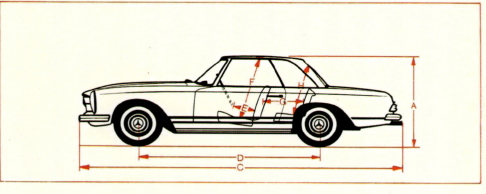

Supplementary pages from the English-language version of the original catalogue, showing technical specifications, and the 280SL with a bench rear seat fitted. Note also that the 280SL catalogues still list luggage capacity at 0.34m³ (12 cubic feet), which was correct with the car in its original form. After the spare wheel was moved and larger fuel tank adopted, the luggage space dropped to 0.26m³, or 9.1 cubic feet.

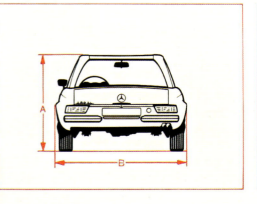
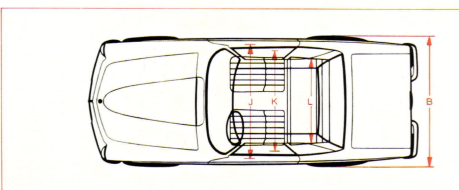

¹) The output given in net BHP/DIN is effectively available at the clutch for driving the vehicle, as any other power consumption has already been deducted. Output data given in gr. HP/SAE include the power required for operating auxiliary units not required to operate the engine.

²) Technical data acc. to DIN 70020 and 70030.

³) The weights quoted are maximum weights. By reason of legal stipulations in various countries outside the Federal Republic of Germany other figures will apply.

⁴) Dimensions vary acc. to sitting position.

The contents are not binding and the right is reserved for modifications.

A	Overall height, unloaded	51.4 ins. Coupé 52 ins. Roadster
B	Overall width	70 ins.
C	Overall length	168.8 ins.
D	Wheelbase	94.5 ins.
E	Steering wheel – driver's seat backrest⁴⁾	13.4 ins.
F	Seat height, unloaded front	36 ins. Coupé 36.6 ins. Roadster
G	Driver's backrest – rear seat backrest⁴⁾	22.8 ins.
H	Seat height at rear	28.3 ins.
J	Width at centre of upholstery front	55.5 ins.
K	Width at shoulder height front	52.5 ins.
L	Width at centre of upholstery rear	44 ins.
	Track width front	58.34 ins.
	Track width rear	58.46 ins.
	Boot space	12 cu. ft.

May 1968 witnessed the two-millionth post-war Mercedes-Benz car produced – a 220/8 saloon – as well as the use of a new distributor cap and ignition leads for the 280SL. The two-seater also inherited a revised steering column, first adopted on left-hand drive vehicles, but finding its way onto rhd cars shortly after.

In the following month, the price of the base car increased to DM 23,254, and while the structure had been in place since 230SL days, a substantial towbar with a fixed ball was added to the option list, priced at DM 270 and approved for pulling trailers of up to 1200kg (2640lb).

Halogen headlights and separate halogen foglights were announced at this time, along with a heated rear screen for the hardtop. However, the foglights and heated rear screen didn't

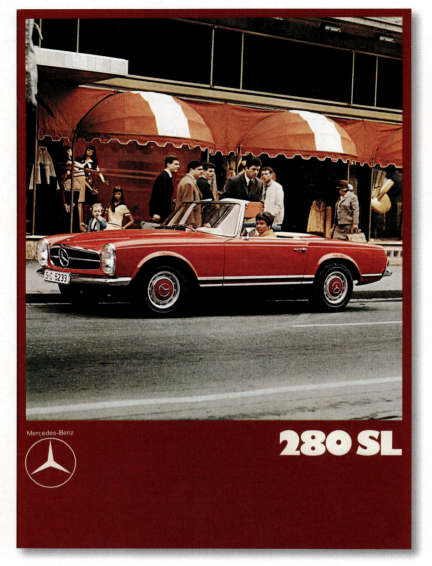

A German catalogue for the 1969 season, and an interior that was illustrated in the same brochure. The latter is particularly interesting in that it shows the transverse rear seat.

become available until the spring of 1969, and halogen light units wouldn't arrive until a year after that. Incidentally, the heated rear screen switch was like the hazard warning one, except it had a white dot in its centre instead of a red one, and was located in a small box section built into the central oddments tray, aft of the ashtray.

By July, new seals were being fitted to the hardtop supplied with cars with a rear seat, while vehicles shipped to the USA had a starter relay added to the specification sheet. All cars had a modified air filter from mid-August, designed to separate water from the intake more efficiently, and oil pressure hoses were given greater reinforcement.

In October 1968, the cost of whitewall tyres increased to DM 170 a set, but Daimler-Benz's commitment to safety was confirmed by reducing the price of seatbelts by almost half, down to DM 60 a pair. This was combined with the introduction of detachable headrests, which helped reduce whiplash neck injuries. These were priced at DM 88 per side in MB-Tex, DM 110 in leather, DM 80 in velour, or DM 78 in cloth.

The thermostatically-controlled cooling fan was set to cut in at a slightly higher temperature than before from mid-November, and a larger brake servo was fitted on left-hand drive cars from the end of that month. The brake regulator also came in for attention in December.

Early February saw European and ROW cars adopt a new rear combination lamp with an amber indicator section, although it wasn't used on US-spec cars until much later in the year.

The April 1969 price list stated that the five-speed manual transmission had become a POA item. This is because the ZF gearbox was supposed to have been dropped from this time, with Daimler-Benz now building its own G76 transmission in conjunction with Getrag. However, the G76 was too tight a fit in the W113 bodyshell, and the ZF unit was continued for the 280SL.

A 280SL on the Daimler-Benz test track.

One of a series of shots of an automatic 280SL. The pictures, taken at the Untertürkheim testing facility, were recycled on many occasions.

A 280SL in front of some of the imposing office buildings in Stuttgart.

The heated rear screen for the hardtop was available by now (priced at DM 190), along with circular halogen foglights, listed at DM 110. One could also buy a rear foglamp for DM 70 at this time.

Not surprisingly, the arrival of the heated rear screen further complicated the tinted glass options. When combined with front, side and rear glass, it cost DM 384, DM 342 with the side and rear windows, and DM 305 if only the rear glass was tinted. Naturally, the basic cost of the hardtop had to be added, too.

However, by far the most remarkable option was a Becker mobile telephone, its advanced technology status commanding a hefty DM 7400. A 15-channel TeKaDe version was listed from September, with the same lofty price tag applied. Perhaps one shouldn't be surprised to see technology like this in 1969, for the first Moon landing happened that July, but a carphone does seem way ahead of its time – a thing that must have seemed more science-fiction than fact to the majority of people.

Meanwhile, a new fuel pump was adopted in May 1969, and the brake pressure regulator was changed again soon after to fine-tune the front/rear brake balance. It's also worth noting that after a new key was required for America, Daimler-Benz finally opted for a single key to operate the ignition and all locks in the summer – the courtesy key idea with limited functions was thus abandoned.

Fuchs alloy wheels from the W108 series (6J x 14 – the same as the standard steel rims, but 35 per cent lighter) were available as a dealer option from the summer of 1969, although, oddly, they weren't offered as a factory-fitted option until August 1970.

THE AMERICAN SCENE

The American's classed the 280SL as a 1968½ model year car, with the basic roadster priced at $6485 and the coupé (hardtop only) at $6647, while a vehicle supplied with both tops commanded $6897. Automatic transmission was a $342 extra, with the five-speed manual option coming in at $464. Other items included PAS at $200, tinted glass at $43, whitewall tyres at $46, and a selection of radios, such as the $174 Becker Europa.

The weight on US 280SLs was listed at 1418kg (3120lb), so the difference in the power-to-weight ratio compared with the 230SL wasn't all that much (less than five per cent), despite the 472cc increase in displacement – a 20 per cent jump in cubic capacity. Of course, efficiency is relative, and if one thinks of a car like the AMC Rambler American weighing in at about the same as an SL in its lightest form, but having a 3.3-litre six developing just 128bhp SAE, perhaps the Mercedes buyer wasn't so hard done by after all.

Indeed, Road & Track seemed pleased enough: "No question about it, the 2.8-litre engine comes on strong. [It] is mechanically smooth and has a nice exhaust note that, while a bit obtrusive at 45-55mph in fourth, can be enjoyed to the hilt when revving up through the gears with the top down."

The famous monthly continued: "In matters of handling, brakes and ride, the SL is still one of the outstanding cars of the day," although it was noted that the suspension system (with uprated front springs on US cars) was at last starting to show its age, especially when having to deal with the extra torque of the 2.8-litre six.

Notwithstanding, the ride was described as "fantastic," despite the 'freeway hop' that a number of shorter wheelbase sports cars experience on concrete Interstate roads, brought on by waves in the road surface interacting with the suspension – at certain speeds, the frequency of the small humps and the movement of the shock absorbers is a bad match, causing the vehicle to vibrate or bob up and down.

With an automatic gearbox and a 4.08:1 back-end, the people at Road & Track recorded a 0-60 time of 10.3 seconds (reduced to 9.9 with manual holding on the gears until the redline), while the standing-quarter was dismissed in 17.3 seconds at a speed of 79mph (126kph); top speed was 114mph (182kph) with this gearing.

Road & Track summed up the latest SL with the following words: "The 280SL is a complex car, especially in the engine

A couple of US-spec 280SLs, as they looked during the 1968 and 1969 seasons, before the headlight units were changed. (Courtesy M-B USA)

compartment with the mechanical fuel-injection system looking like a graduate project at the Institute of Plumbing Engineers. But it is a well-proven, reliable car and the quality of its execution is a delight to the connoisseur of fine automotive machinery. It is somewhat paradoxical that this car does not offer the latest engineering developments of Mercedes-Benz – the improved automatic transmission, the anti-dive front suspension or the new semi-trailing rear suspension. In any case, it is still a unique and desirable car; for those who have less than $10,000 to spend and value finesse, pure quality and drivability more than jazzy looks, it is alone in the field."

It's fair to say that the 280SL was not quite as sporting as the original 230SL, but a good all-rounder for everyday use.

Motor Trend observed: "Probably the only features that could possibly fall into a minus category would be the fact that only two seats are available and the lack of space in the small jump compartment behind the seats make it impossible for anyone to ride in there. Even a petite five-foot gal was uncomfortable for a short trip of several blocks. The high price tag an the 280SL is also against this remarkable machine.

"Everything else is a plus, including quality, craftsmanship, ride, handling and performance. It's interesting to speculate on how the 280SL will perform with the new, big V8 and altered suspension it will get sometime in the near future."

Of course, the V8 SL was a long way off, and came with a completely different body. At the time, though, a facelifted W113 shell looked like the way to go…

Meanwhile, the 1969 model year cars, built from the first day of October 1968, were given new headlights – the 'AC' enclosures becoming the 'AN' type after the foglights were removed, although they look much the same at first glance, with the amber section restricted to a narrow segment at the very bottom of the light unit.

With Richard Nixon settled in the White House, *Road & Track* did a comparison test involving the 280SL in the spring of 1969, bringing together the two-seater Benz in hardtop guise, a 4.2-litre Jaguar E-type coupé, a 5.7-litre Chevrolet Corvette Stingray, and a two-litre Porsche 911T coupé – a varied bunch, with very different technical characteristics, but all very much in the same market segment.

The Mercedes was the most expensive car in the test, with its base price exceeding the cost of each of the other three vehicles when fully loaded with options. The biggest gap was about $2000, as the US car was the cheapest by far, but various extras on both machines reduced the difference to $1440.

Ultimately, the Porsche won the fight, scoring top marks 25 times, against 20 for the Mercedes, nine for the Jaguar, and seven for the Corvette. The SL was the weakest around the skidpan (0.67g), the slowest in top speed (114mph/182kph), the slowest through the standing-quarter (17.1 seconds), and only marginally worse than the gas-guzzling Chevy on fuel consumption, but it still had its fans.

At *Road Test*, it was noted: "The Mercedes-Benz 280SL is the ultimate in the conservative sports car. It is precise in every detail, from the impeccable interior/exterior finish to the 180bhp fuel-injected engine. It is the proud new standard bearer of a dynasty whose lineage goes back to 1894, when a Daimler car won the first automobile race."

Actually, the 1894 Paris-Rouen event was more of a demonstration run than a proper race (it wasn't until the following year that a full-blooded city-to-city race took place), and the car that won was a Daimler-engined Peugeot. But still, one gets the sentiment of the statement.

The *Road Test* article concluded: "The car lacks some 'go' power for the high price range. But it has extra 'stop' power which makes it secure. The price makes it a prestige item to be owned by the successful, conservative enthusiast who can afford luxury and quality."

An important change took place on the production cars at the end of June – the adoption of European-style rear combination lights, complete with their amber indicator lenses. In addition, American SLs had their VIN plate moved from the bulkhead to a more visible spot inside the door-jamb area on the driver's-side A-post close to the start of the 250SL run, but in June 1969, it was moved to a similar position on the B-post. Then, on the first day of July 1969, the US-spec cars gained new final-drive ratios, with the 4.08:1 rear axle being replaced by a 3.92:1 one, with no other options.

Despite the $6802 starting price, SL sales were still increasing steadily alongside the rest of the Mercedes-Benz range. Indeed, 26,193 Mercedes models found new owners in the States in 1969, of which 4102 were 280SLs.

International advertising from the August 1968 issue of *National Geographic*.

BRITAIN, JAPAN & AUSTRALIA

In Britain, the 280SL replaced the 2.5-litre model on 27 January 1968, introduced at £3850. The cheapest Mercedes-Benz at this time was the 220 saloon, priced at £2297, while the other end of the scale was occupied by the 280SE Convertible at £5435; the SL sat in-between.

By the summer of 1968, prices had increased across the board, leaving the 280SL Roadster at £4003, the 280SL Coupé at £4096, the 280SL Coupé 2+2 at £4129, and the 280SL Coupé/Convertible at £4155. As far as the competition was concerned, there were cars like the Triumph TR5 at £1261, the 4.2-litre Jaguar E-type drophead coupé at £2117, the Alfa Romeo 1750 Spider Veloce at £2198, and Porsche 911s ranging from £3228 to £4122.

Interestingly, it was around this time that *Motor* brought together the 280SL, TR5, and E-type, comparing them with the Lotus Elan, Marcos 1600, and AC 428 Fastback in a fascinating six-way battle.

The SL was a fully-loaded automatic version with PAS and both tops, and while it was over twice the price of the Lotus and Marcos (both with glassfibre bodies), the seven-litre AC was the most expensive model, listed at a hefty £5426 – something that goes a long way toward explaining the rarity of this Frua-styled beauty.

Anyway, the test highlighted the exceptionally low gearing of the Mercedes, restricting speed at the top-end, and giving the engine a "busy character, underlined by the excited scream it makes – albeit a very smooth one – at high revs." The ratios also resulted in poor fuel consumption (17mpg for the test, against 19.5 for the Jaguar and 31 for the Lotus), but the in-gear performance, moving up from 30-50 in top was quite stunning, with only the AC being quicker.

The Marcos was the best of the bunch in the roadholding department, although "under power, the wide-track Mercedes squats almost as securely as the Marcos, but just a touch of brake, even on the approach to a corner, will change the rear wheel camber sufficiently to 'edge' the tyres with inevitable oversteering consequences."

As for the handling: "The large moulded plastic steering wheel, soft nose-dive under braking and other saloon car reminders segregated the Mercedes from the rest as a touring, rather than a sports car. Yet its steering is bettered in response only by the Elan's and in smoothness – that is kickback and vibration – by none. Up to its very high limit (on Continental radials) the Mercedes is a very easy, pleasant car to handle – venture beyond and it feels twitchy and confused although, even with experimental provocation, it is difficult to run out of adhesion."

The overall refinement, good heating and ventilation system, practical packaging and excellent ergonomics (apart from the light switch, which was in an awkward position) were ranked highly.

Sports car nut, Jim Tosen, made probably the most interesting summary comment: "I just don't think there is enough pleasure motoring in this confined, congested and police purged island to justify the expenditure of £5500 on the AC or £4000 on the Mercedes. I'd rather buy an aeroplane." I wonder what Tosen would have to say today, over 40 years later, with much worse congestion and cameras everywhere …

By the end of 1968, prices had risen to £4090 for the Roadster, £4185 for the Coupé, £4219 for the Coupé 2+2, and £4245 for the Coupé/Convertible. By the middle of 1969, they'd go up again, however, with even the cheapest grade commanding £4253.

In Japan, the 280SL was introduced at 4,720,000 yen, while a bit further south, the four-speed manual car was $10,235 Down Under; the drophead Jaguar E-type was $7352 at the time, while a Porsche 911 commanded $8990.

Regarding the 2.8-litre SL, Australia's *Wheels* magazine stated at the time of its debut: "Several firms make sportier machinery – but damn few do it with the same sure sense of high society."

A recent advert from a Japanese fashion magazine featuring a 280SL. Note the late-style rear lights, with amber indicator sections.

THE 1970 MODEL YEAR

The 1969 Frankfurt Show (which ran from 11-21 September) witnessed the launch of the 3.5-litre V8 engine in the 300SEL, and the debut of the hugely popular 280SE 3.5 in coupé and drophead guise. The rotary-engined C111 prototype, with its stunning body and three-rotor Wankel unit was also put on display.

As far as the 280SL was concerned, hazard warning lights became standard equipment at this time, while the price of metallic paint rose to DM 410, plus a further DM 170 for the hardtop. The cost of uprated road springs, all-weather tyres and the hardtop carrier also increased, although the rear foglight option was reduced to DM 45. Headrests were also reduced, now listed at DM 70 in vinyl, DM 90 in leather, or DM 60 in velour (the cloth version was gone, and velour disappeared the following month). In addition, glassfibre shields were added to insulate the body from the exhaust, and carpet was used to line the bottom of the central oddments tray.

There were also changes to the colour and trim guide at this time, even if not immediately obvious in all cases. For instance, the grey leather shade kept the same 246/247 codes, but the factory was now supplied with 7049 instead of 7000 hide. Also, the beige leather went from 8000 to 8081, although the main code was still 251. The woodwork, meanwhile, was still described as stained walnut.

Standard coachwork colours (September 1969 to end of 280SL run)
Black (040), White (050), White-Grey (158), Anthracite Grey (173), Light Beige (181), Dark Green (268), Dark Olive (291), Horizon Blue (304), Medium Blue (350), Tobacco Brown (423), Dark Red-Brown (460), Dark Red (542), Signal Red (568), Red (576), Light Ivory (670), Papyrus White (717), Beige-Grey (726), Blue (903), and Dark Blue (904).

Metallic coachwork colours (September 1969 to end of 280SL run)
Anthracite Grey (172), Silver-Grey (180), Blue (387), Bronze-Brown (461), Beige (462), Whisky (467), Red (571), Beige-Grey (728), Moss Green (834), and Blue (906).

Hood colours (September 1969 to end of 280SL run)
Black, Dark Grey, Light Grey, Parchment, Dark Blue, Beige, Dark Brown or Dark Green.

Two-tone combinations (September 1969 to end of 280SL run)
Solid shades: White, White-Grey, Dark Green, Dark Red, Signal Red, Red, Light Ivory, Papyrus White or Beige-Grey with a Black hardtop; Black, White-Grey, Light Beige or Light Ivory with a Tobacco Brown hardtop, or Papyrus White with a Dark Blue hardtop. Metallic shades: Anthracite Grey or Red with a Black hardtop.

Trim colours & materials (September 1969 to end of 280SL run)
Black (131), Red (132), Light Red (133), Green (134), Blue (135), Grey (136-137), Dark Brown (138), Bamboo (139), Cognac (140), Beige (141) or Parchment (144-147) MB-Tex vinyl, or Black (241), Red (242), Light Red (243), Green (244), Blue (245), Grey (246-247), Dark Brown (248), Bamboo (249), Cognac (250), Beige (251) or Parchment (254-257) perforated leather.

Carpet (September 1969 to end of 280SL run)
Dark Grey, Blue, Dark Green, Light Red, Red, Beige, Brown or Dark Brown.

Note: Four shades (181, 268, 568 and 576) were only available when selected with either a Black or Tobacco Brown hardtop.

The C111 and the new V8 models unveiled at the 1969 Frankfurt Show. Note the ornate 'Barock' alloy wheel design on the rotary-engined machine, similar to that used for the optional alloys made available for the 280SL

This evocative shot was used for the cover of the December 1969 brochure.

Willy Brandt became Germany's new Chancellor in October after the 1969 elections, but these were troubled times, marred by the activities of a number of high-profile terrorist groups.

Meanwhile, Daimler-Benz issued a new price list for the 280SL. The October list saw the cost of the base car go up to DM 24,253, and options generally increased pretty much across the board, while uprated road springs fell by the wayside.

Option 255 (the 3.69:1 final-drive) was gone, replaced by 212 (also a NCO), which was a 3.92:1 rear axle. This was because, as of late November 1969 production, the standard 4MT and 4AT final-drive ratios swapped places on ROW cars, with 3.69:1 becoming the norm, and 3.92:1 moving to the option list. Likewise, the 4.08:1 axle used on 5MT cars was changed to a 3.92:1 one.

For the record, automatic transmission was listed at DM 1300, with the five-speed manual being a POA item. Indeed, it stayed that way until April, when the price was set at DM 1190.

The hardtop was priced at DM 1190 including a soft-top, or DM 405 without. It could also be ordered without the soft-top but combined with a bench seat in the rear, at DM 515 in vinyl, or DM 640 in leather (the familiar transverse seat was listed at DM 200 in vinyl, or DM 250 in leather). The cost of tinted glass ranged from DM 20 (hardtop only) to DM 105 for all windows, including the hardtop, while a heated rear screen was DM 200.

175

Im Fond kann auf Wunsch
ein Quersitz eingebaut werden.
Unter der Abschlußblende
ist das Roadsterverdeck
unsichtbar zurückgeklappt.
Jetzt kann entweder
das auf Wunsch lieferbare Coupédach
aufgesetzt werden,
oder man fährt im offenen Wagen.
Das Roadsterverdeck
ist als unsichtbarer Begleiter
immer vorhanden.

Interior of an automatic car featured in the domestic catalogue of December 1969. Note the transverse rear seat, the carpet in the central tray between the seats, and the anti-freeze symbol in the corner of the windscreen, showing the car was ready to face the winter. Not visible, but important nonetheless, was the sticker on the inside of the hood well, just above the nearside wheel, which originally warned owners not to leave the hood folded if it was wet, but later (in the 280 era) included diagrams describing the hood operation as well.

Metallic paint was a DM 435 extra (an additional DM 180 was required for the hardtop, in a matching or contrasting shade). As for the upholstery, MB-Tex vinyl was standard, with leather trim priced at DM 745; headrests were available at DM 70 per side in vinyl, or DM 90 in leather.

Power-assisted steering was priced at DM 510, while an ivory steering wheel and matching gearknob could be specified free-of-charge, replacing the regular black versions. Whitewall tyres were listed at DM 180, with all-weather tyres commanding a DM 100 premium.

Dashboard of a 280SL for mainland Europe finished in the same colour scheme as the last interior shot, although the image appeared in earlier catalogues, too. Note the 6500rpm red-line on the 2.8-litre models.

Other options included spotlights (DM 58), front foglights (DM 115), a rear foglight (DM 45), a passenger-side door mirror (DM 14), seatbelts (DM 60 a pair), an uprated heater (DM 19), coconut floormats (DM 40), a first aid kit (DM 30), a fire extinguisher (DM 58), a roof-rack (DM 280) or ski-rack (DM 135), chrome rails for the hardtop to allow racks to be fitted (DM 90), a towbar (DM 285), a 'D' country emblem (DM 3), and a selection of fitted suitcases and matching bags, with prices ranging from DM 9 to DM 105 per piece. There was also a mobile telephone, but at DM 7850, it's doubtful whether it was a big seller!

As for audio options, the Becker Mexico radio was gone, but there were still the Europa (DM 480) and Grand Prix (DM 630) models. An automatic aerial was listed at DM 205 (or DM 240 without a radio), and one had to fork out DM 40 for a manual aerial if it was ordered without a radio. Likewise, radio preparation without a radio was DM 55.

The chrome mouldings on the hardtop were replaced by polished aluminium items at the end of the year, by which time

The Mercedes-Benz stand at the 1970 Geneva Show, which ran from 12-22 March. The C111 (in updated form, with sharper lines than the Frankfurt Show car) can be seen taking pride of place, but the pair of 280SLs also have a good position in the display, despite their age.

Golde and Webasto were offering a sunroof for the hardtop. Then, in January 1970, the coconut floormats became listed as 'front only' instead of a set of four (although they still sold at the same price!), and there were some changes to the window winding mechanism. More importantly, the alternative final-drive ratio for the two four-speed transmissions was deleted.

A fair bit of fresh 280SL photography was done for the 1970 season. This is part of a series of pictures taken with a beautiful horse, possibly a Hanoverian.

From April 1970, the cost of metallic paint went up to DM 485 for the lower body, although the hardtop section remained at DM 180. Whitewall tyres were now listed at DM 255, with coconut mats up to DM 45 the pair, but the first aid kit was reduced to DM 27. The cost of the mobile phones, meanwhile, went up to DM 8200 – crazy!

New items included a fresh headlight unit with halogen main beam, dipped beam and foglights combined in one housing at DM 150. A hazard warning triangle was also added at DM 12, along with a Europa stereo radio at DM 765, and a Mexico Olympia stereo radio/cassette at DM 1015.

A revised check valve was fitted to the brake servo at this time, as several road test reports had complained of the brake action being too light, and a warning triangle became standard on domestic cars from the end of June 1970.

American advertising from 1970.

US REVIEW

The 1970 season brought with it another series of changes for Stateside-bound cars. 280SLs built after the last day of July 1969 came with side markers rather than reflectors, revised intake manifolds, engine speed control switches to further improve exhaust emissions, new headlights (the so-called 'AJ' type, with a far heavier amber lower section), a 55A alternator instead of the regular 35A one, a new ignition barrel that would not allow the key to be removed with the ignition on, a headlight warning buzzer, improved fuel tank ventilation, and a plate to show the car had passed 1970 model year emissions regulations (which was duly updated in the following year).

The 1970 cars also came with a new engine oil level sticker (oddly, this small white decal was placed alongside the tyre pressure one on the inside of the bootlid) and capacitive-discharge (CD) ignition to stop the sparkplugs fouling – something that had become a problem in the States ever since the arrival of the lazier 2.5- and 2.8-litre sixes. Indeed, in a Road & Track survey, it was the most common fault by quite some margin – one in five owners had been plagued by fouled plugs, yet this was the only reliability item that affected more than one in ten SL drivers.

For 1970, the 280SL was listed at $6952 POE in Roadster guise, $7118 as a Coupé, or $7374 with both tops; the sticker price was about $100 more on the west coast to cover shipping costs.

In the following season, the 1971 models were introduced on 1 October 1970. In a Mercedes range that went from $5312 for a 220 saloon all the way up to $30,120 for a 600 limousine, the 280SL Roadster

One of the last US-spec 280SLs, complete with the final style of headlight enclosures. The W113 series had aged well, though. The January 1970 edition of *Road Test* noted: "In any form, [the W113 SL] is attractive in a distinguished fashion, and body lines are just as stylish today as when the car first arrived in the dealerships."

was priced at $7469, while the Coupé version was $7642, and the Coupé/Roadster (with both tops) $7909.

Popular options for the SL included automatic transmission ($392), whitewall tyres ($90), PAS ($198), tinted glass (from $44), leather trim ($299), air conditioning ($597), a Becker Europa radio ($172, or $289 in stereo guise), and a power aerial ($88).

Interestingly, while some magazines felt the W113 suspension was showing signs of its age, *Popular Imported Cars* noted: "The 280SL's suspension let us storm over rough, narrow roads with nary a thought to our safe conduct. We could safely and comfortably blast over roads that have had us white-knuckled in other cars. Roads that are a challenge in other cars become just another road in an SL. The suspension is that good. It has an amazing ability to absorb shocks and jolts, yet still deliver cornering power far above sane limits."

The power-assisted steering and brakes were also highly praised, the latter giving "a feeling of complete confidence in any situation." However, the interior styling was considered dated, and the efficiency of the 'clap hands' windscreen wipers (a signature piece of W113 design, as they were unique to this SL generation) was described as "poor" by the testers.

The 1971 models were virtually identical to the 1970 US cars, although a new, larger tyre pressure sticker was employed (purple in colour, with the outline of a Benz saloon on it), and placed alongside the oil level one on the inside of the bootlid. In addition, a rear axle oil change reminder decal joined the service schedule sticker on the A-post.

The 1972 model year cars were introduced in the US on 2 August 1971, marking the end of the W113 and the start of 107-series SL sales. The importance of the American sports car market during this period is readily illustrated if one takes US exports as a percentage of production. By 1970, the 4992 280SLs that made their way across the Atlantic was equivalent to 63 per cent of the W113 models built that year, and in the final batch, no less than 520 of the 830 cars produced were for US consumption.

Meanwhile, annual MBNA sales as a whole rose to nearly 30,000 units in 1970, and, despite the poor US economy, jumped to 35,192 in 1971. For Daimler-Benz, this was still a fairly small number compared with a total production figure of 284,230 vehicles, although many European makers relied on the Stateside market to survive.

THE LAST RHD CARS

Political unrest led to the formation of a Conservative government under Edward Heath, but the 280SL kept soldiering on almost unchanged apart from the sticker price. For 1970, the Roadster was priced at £4466, the Coupé at £4570, the Coupé 2+2 at £4607, and the Coupé/Convertible at £4655 – the latter a full £500 up on the original 280SL Coupé/Convertible price, while the automatic transmission option commanded £221 extra, and PAS was £110.

A still from one of the author's all-time favourite films, *The Long Good Friday*, starring Bob Hoskins. This 280SL was cast as the leading lady's car, its H-registration meaning it was sold between August 1969 and July 1970.

However, even after conversion to the decimal system (which was used by a number of unscrupulous makers to disguise hefty increases), the prices then stayed the same until the 280SL was phased out from the UK market in early July 1971.

The last cars had been imported to Britain in February, as it happens. All told, around 1150 W113 models were sold in the UK, generating about £5,000,000 worth of business. To put this in perspective, a gallon of petrol was 33p at the time, up from 12p in 1970, while the average house was around £5000!

Autocar tried an automatic 280SL for size in 1970, recording a 9.3 second 0-60 time and a top speed of 121mph (194kph). But these are just cold figures that mean little in the real world – it is often visceral feelings that are hard to quantify that make the difference between a good sports car and one that simply goes fast.

The control offered by the automatic gearbox was appreciated, with manual-style shifts for overtaking and good engine braking, but the lack of a torque converter made shift quality quite rough by the standards of the day, even though they'd been quite acceptable only a few years earlier.

En route to Italy, the *Autocar* team certainly warmed to the SL, though: "Now in good visibility it was superb motoring, chucking the 280SL round the splendid lacets of the pass, and we lost no time in stopping to put the hood down – a simple 30-second operation. As a motorway car the 280SL had been a bit disappointing, giving a lot of wind noise with hood up or down, and seeming far too low-geared with the standard axle ratio for automatic transmission, but as a two-seater for the mountains it is really fun.

"By the time the 280SL was back in our office car park it had added 2158 miles to the mileometer reading on setting out, and the overall fuel consumption was 17.2mpg. It was necessary to add a pint of oil to the sump on completion of the trip, otherwise the only service the car required throughout was to add fuel on ten occasions, and periodically clean off the dead insects.

"At just over £5000 it is far from cheap, and in a few ways it is beginning to show the age of the original concept. Yet from behind the wheel one somehow feels that in its engineering alone it is worth the money and at the top end of the two-seater market it has barely a single rival in the world."

In Japan, the list price had increased to 4,978,000 yen by 1970, although the last few 280SLs were actually reduced to 4,700,000 yen to make way for the R107. This was about the same price as a 911T Lux, but, in reality, one could buy almost ten Toyota Corollas for the same money!

In Australia, prices were held until mid-1970, when the cost of the basic 280SL went up to $11,163. By end of 1970, it had increased another $180, but the next change was not until August 1971. This is when the Roadster was listed at $11,958, the Hardtop at $12,146 and the HT 2+2 at $12,234, while a car with both tops commanded $12,553. October 1971 saw the new 350SL take over the SL mantle, introduced at $15,620.

W113 SWANSONG

In the domestic marketplace, the cost of the basic car increased to DM 25,363 in August 1970. Although the cost of an automatic transmission, PAS, the rear foglight, radios and headrests remained unchanged, almost everything else went up in price. Bigger jumps included leather trim (up from DM 745 to DM 900), or a limited-slip differential (from DM 160 to DM 185), but the increase was usually between three and ten per cent, which was quite acceptable; the cost of the first aid kit even dropped, down to DM 25.

The only addition to the option list at this time was alloy wheels, priced at DM 1200 a set of five. Available in the previous year as an accessory, these alloys would duly become a signature Mercedes-Benz wheel.

The old steel radiator header tank was replaced by a modern plastic item in November 1970, the ignition coil received a protection shroud, and there were some changes made to the door locks. Shortly after, improvements were made to the bootlid locks, too.

January 1971 witnessed another price increase, with the basic, four-speed manual car now put at DM 26,640. The cost of options generally increased pretty much across the board, but with so many changes, for the record, we may as well go through the complete listing.

Automatic transmission was available at DM 1300, while the five-speed manual gearbox was DM 1315; a limited-slip differential cost an extra DM 195. Alloy wheels were DM 1200 a set, whitewall tyres commanded a DM 270 premium, all-weather tyres DM 105, and power-assisted steering DM 540.

The hardtop was DM 1315 combined with a soft-top, or DM 450 on its own. It could also be ordered without the soft-top but with a bench seat in the rear compartment, priced at DM 570 with the seat trimmed in MB-Tex vinyl, or DM 725 in leather.

A hardtop carrier was available at DM 255.

Tinted glass for the front and side windows was DM 95, or DM 120 if the hardtop window was included. A heated rear screen for the hardtop was priced at DM 220, but when combined with tinted glass all-round, it cost DM 395. Naturally, the basic cost of the hardtop had to be added, too.

Metallic paint was DM 535, plus an additional DM 200 for the hardtop (if specified) in either a matching or contrasting shade. MB-Tex vinyl trim was standard, with leather priced at DM 945. Headrests were DM 70 per side in vinyl, or DM 90 in leather, while a rear transverse seat was DM 220 in vinyl, or DM 275 in leather.

Other options included halogen headlight units with integral foglights (DM 170), spotlights (DM 65), a rear foglight (DM 45), a passenger-side door mirror (DM 18), a ski-rack (DM 155, although this required chrome trim pieces for the hardtop, sold separately at DM 100), a towbar (DM 310), seatbelts (DM 70 a pair), an ivory steering wheel and gearknob (NCO), an uprated heater (DM 25), coconut floormats (DM 50 a pair), a first aid kit (DM 25), a fire extinguisher at DM 40, and a selection of fitted suitcases and matching bags, with prices ranging from DM 10 to DM 115 per piece.

The mobile telephone option (Becker or TeKaDe), now came with automatic signal selection, and was priced at a whopping DM 8950. Audio equipment included the Becker Europa (DM 510), Europa Stereo (DM 780), Mexico Olympia

After a successful eight-year run, it was finally time to say goodbye to the W113 series ...

Stereo with cassette (DM 1045), and Grand Prix (DM 665), with all prices including preparation (usually DM 65) and a manual aerial. An automatic aerial was listed (DM 225, or DM 275 without a radio), and the same DM 50 difference was required for a manual aerial if ordered without a radio.

The last 280SL (chassis # 023885) was built on 23 February 1971, and the model was discontinued in Germany during the following month, thus bringing the 'Pagoda Roof' generation to an end. Including the 23,885 280SLs produced, the total W113 run came to 48,912 units. The next generation was destined to be even more successful ...

8

An SL for the Seventies

The W113 series had been in the showrooms for eight years, and was as popular as ever. However, times had changed politically, and demands for cleaner and safer cars – not to mention calls for cheaper and easier repairs from insurance companies – meant that the 'Pagoda Roof' models had reached the limit of their development. Some were shocked by the sheer size of their replacement, with a few even stating it was a mockery of the 'Sport Licht' moniker, but the 107-series would go on to be the longest-running model line in Daimler-Benz history, nonetheless.

Design work on the W113's replacement – the R107 – began in earnest in 1965. Initial design proposals were radically different to the established SL lines, with flowing curves eliminated and a distinctly boxy character.

Ironically, due to the uncertainty regarding the long-term future of the open sports car, running parallel with the new concept, a simple facelift programme was kept in place until mid-1968, when attention turned completely toward a full model change situation, with all-new running gear in a brand new body.

The W113 SL had a very glamorous image from the off, which it has managed to hold onto for decades (this Japanese advert dates from 1985, for instance), but work on a facelift was deemed necessary as early as the mid-1960s.

THE FIRST 107-SERIES MODELS

The R107 roadster took shape under Chief Designer Friedrich Geiger, with all manner of proposals finding their way to his desk before he settled on a Joseph Gallitzendörfer styling sketch as the basis for the final design.

Three full-size styling bucks (labelled Model I, II, and III) were reviewed on 18 June 1968, alongside a mildly facelifted W113 model, and the new generation was born after the Board gave the nod to the Model III mock-up, which displayed strikingly modern and bold lines, yet still managed to incorporate enough of the earlier SL DNA to make it recognisable as a continuation of the bloodline.

Things progressed quickly thereafter, and with the powertrain already entering production in the V8 models to be launched at the 1969 Frankfurt Show, there were even thoughts of releasing the new two-seater in the spring of 1970. However, Hans Scherenberg was still jumpy about the constant changes to US regulations, and recommended not only delaying production, but putting a back-up plan into action that gave rise to the long-wheelbase C107 – a close-coupled coupé based on the structure of the open car, known as the SLC.

Ultimately, the 107-series models (soft-top as standard with a removable hardtop for the SL roadster, and a fixed-head coupé configuration for the SLC) would provide the basis for a whole new generation of passenger cars, with various styling cues being duly adopted for the W116 S-Class to give a 'family' look to the Mercedes range.

Compared to the W113, the R107 was bigger all-round – it was important to think ahead on the safety front with the increasing importance of the US marker for the German maker, and the extra bulk allowed more engineering options, as well as added comfort for passengers. Indeed, with its completely modernised interior, the SL was destined to move even further away from pure sports than its predecessor, the Grand Touring car being infinitely more appealing to a wider audience.

The wheelbase on the new open car was 55mm (2.2in) longer than that of the W113 models, leading to an overall length increase of 95mm (3.7in), and the width was 30mm (1.2in) up. Despite the track being slightly narrower, due to the all-steel construction of the body and more luxury features, there

One of the prototypes displayed at a Sindelfingen review in June 1968. This car (Model IV) has a bolder grille, a simpler bonnet, deeper front valance, rubber-edged bumpers, less chrome down the sides, and the ribbed rear lights that would become a signature styling feature on the 107-series SLs sitting in flatter rear flanks. Ultimately, a full model change (FMC) was executed for the W113-series replacement.

Grille and headlight proposals for the 107-series SL.

was a weight gain of 200kg (440lb) compared to the 280SL, but computer-aided design made the shell stronger than ever before, to the point where a Targa bar (once thought a necessity to clear Federal regulations) was no longer needed.

The 350SL as it was first presented to the press, seen here with the hood down (hidden by the metal tonneau cover that was an SL styling signature), and with the soft-top erected.

The mighty V8 engine of the 350SL.

Motive power was provided by the 3.5-litre V8 introduced with the 280SE 3.5 and 300SEL 3.5 models – the M116 unit having a bore and stroke of 92 x 65.8mm to give a cubic capacity of 3499cc. With D-Jetronic fuel-injection and a 9.5:1 compression ratio, it developed a level 200bhp, along with 211lbft of torque.

However, soon after the launch of the new car, a long-stroke 4520cc version was introduced for the US market. Despite the additional displacement, this M117 engine developed 5bhp DIN less than its European counterpart, which shows how strict Federal regulations on emissions had become by this time.

A four-speed manual gearbox was the norm, with a four-speed automatic as an alternative in most countries until mid-1972,

The 450SL (front left), 450SLC (front right), 450SE, and 450SEL pictured in 1973. The new S-Class (W116-series) had first been presented to the

One of the first 280SL press pictures. Note the hardtop profile, which paid homage to earlier SLs. The 2.8-litre six under the bonnet had almost as much power as a Federal-spec 4.5-litre V8, and was quite different to the earlier 280SL unit, having twin-overhead camshafts. The 280SL was available with 4MT, 5MT, and 4AT gearboxes.

The 450SLC. Note the elegant roofline of the coupé, and the front spoiler that identifies this as a 4.5-litre machine.

when the 3AT unit with torque convertor used in the States from day one was adopted as the automatic gearbox option.

The suspension and steering was based on W114 practice, with braking provided by discs all-round; there was actually talk of offering ABS on the new SL, but it wasn't ready in time. As for the footwear, low-profile 205/70 radials were mounted on 6.5J x 14 rims, either made from pressed steel or cast alloy – the latter wheels being of the cookie-cutter 'Barock' design offered as an option on the last of the W113s.

The 350SL was launched in April 1971 at a price of DM 29,970 in Germany. Exports began in the middle of the year, allowing the '350SL 4.5' to reach American showrooms in August. The 350SLC, meanwhile, made its debut at the 1971 Paris Salon, with sales starting four months later.

The 4.5-litre cars were added to the ROW line-up in the spring of 1973, by which time they were formally known as the 450SL and 450SLC. From August 1974, the European market also gained a 280SL and 280SLC, powered by a 2746cc M110 straight-six that developed 185bhp DIN.

All engines moved over from D-Jetronic to K-Jetronic fuel-injection in the mid-1970s, reducing horsepower, and lower compression ratios on certain units only served to drop output still further. At least the 2.8-litre engine had its power restored in 1978, but the V8s would not make a comeback – they were left in their weakened state until they were replaced by a new range of eight-cylinder powerplants in 1980.

An American-spec 450SL from the 1977 season. Note the US-style bumpers and headlights, as well as the 'Barock' alloy wheels.

NEW ENGINES

The 1977 Frankfurt Show witnessed the debut of the 5-litre 450SLC 5.0 prototype, which not only employed a great deal of aluminium body parts, it also had an aluminium alloy cylinder block. This signified the birth of a new line of all-alloy V8s that made their debut in the autumn of 1979, and were duly adopted on the SL and SLC models from March 1980.

The 450SLC 5.0 model, which entered production in the spring of 1978. Against the odds, the SLC actually made a fine rally car, winning two WRC events.

Interior of a 380SL. Wood trim had been added to the centre console in September 1977, but, other than the clock moving from the middle air vent position to the bottom of the tachometer, the cockpit was much the same as it had been in 1971.

A 1981 model year 500SL. Note the dark grey lower section, applied to 5-litre cars when finished in certain colours, and the rear spoiler. All cars received an aluminium bonnet at this time.

A Mercedes-Benz showroom in Paris, pictured in early 1981. A 280SL has been given prime position in the front window.

While the 2.8-litre six was carried over in the 280SL/SLC (albeit hooked up to a new automatic transmission), the 350SL/SLC became the 380SL/SLC, and the 4.5-litre cars became the 500SL/SLC grade, with the old 450SLC 5.0 falling by the wayside in the process. Only the 3.8-litre machines were sold in the States, with 160bhp DIN under the bonnet (as opposed to 218bhp in Europe), while the 4973cc unit sold in other parts of the world produced a healthy 240bhp, linked to a new 4AT gearbox.

The SLC variant was dropped at the end of the 1981 season, replaced by the gorgeous 380SEC and 500SEC coupés. Power dropped slightly on the V8s at the same time, as emission standards tightened up globally, and more luxury items were fitted as standard as the eighties progressed.

Well over 200,000 107-series cars had been sold by 1985, and even if one takes out the 62,888 SLCs from the figure, no-one could deny the SL was a good seller, especially given its high price. Indeed, even without the SLC's help, it had only taken to the end of 1976 to outsell the entire W113 run, despite a major fuel crisis and a dreadful world economy.

The 300SL was perhaps the most sporting of all the R107s, introduced at DM 63,441. Note the late-style alloy wheels, introduced for the 1986 season.

A LAST FLING

The SL just kept selling, so the management in Stuttgart decided to keep it going with a 1986 model year update that would allow it to remain in the Mercedes line-up until 1989, when the all-new R129 SL made its long-awaited debut.

The main changes were in the engine bay, with new 3.0-, 4.2- and 5.0-litre power-units adopted for most markets, along with a 5.6-litre V8 for the USA, Japan and Australia. Even the 2962cc six had 188bhp available, while the 5547cc eight gave 242bhp, thus giving the SL the performance it deserved, even in the States.

Also new was the 4AT with switchable 'Sport' and 'Economy' shift modes, whilst larger 15-inch alloy wheels covered uprated brakes, suspension settings were changed, and a redesigned rear axle was employed, simultaneously improving ride and reducing unwanted NVH. There were subtle bodywork modifications, too, such as a new front airdam and black door handles to replace the old-fashioned chrome ones.

Amazingly, there were still full order books for the SL, even at this time, and a long waiting list in certain countries – buyers in the UK were told to expect a two-year wait before getting their hands on a new car. All told, a total of 300,175 107-series models were built, including SLCs.

Tailpiece. An early R107 350SL photographed with a W113 280SL (right), and one of their illustrious predecessors.

Appendix I: Year-by-year range details

This appendix brings together the brief specifications for all W113-series models, arranged in chronological/engine size order. Column one shows the vehicle type, the second column shows the basic engine details (to be used in conjunction with Appendix II, as there are subtle differences depending on the year and destination), whilst the third contains any useful notes. Only production road cars are listed for each model year (MY):

1963
230SL (113.042)   M127.981   Pilot run March 1963.
                                Full production from July 1963.

1964
230SL (113.042)   M127.981

1965
230SL (113.042)   M127.981

1966
230SL (113.042)   M127.981

1967
230SL (113.042)   M127.981   To January 1967.
250SL (113.043)   M129.982   Pilot run November 1966.
                                Full production from December 1966.

1968
250SL (113.043)   M129.982   To January 1968.
280SL (113.044)   M130.983   Pilot run November 1967.
                                Full production from January 1968.

1969
280SL (113.044)   M130.983

1970
280SL (113.044)   M130.983

1971
280SL (113.044)   M130.983   Discontinued March 1971.

Appendix II: Engine specifications

The following is a survey of all the mainstream production engines employed in the W113-series models featured in this book, complete with the leading specifications and any other notes of interest.

Type 127.981 (M127 II)

Production (MY)	1963-1967
Cylinders	Straight-six, water-cooled
Main bearings	Four, in cast-iron block
Valve operation	Sohc, 12v, in alloy head
Bore & stroke	82 x 72.8mm
Cubic capacity	2306cc (141cid)
Compression ratio	9.3:1
Fuel delivery system	Bosch fuel-injection
Power @ rpm	150bhp DIN @ 5500
	170bhp SAE @ 5600
Torque @ rpm	144lbft DIN @ 4200
	159lbft SAE @ 4500
Engine numbers	127.981-*0-000001 onwards (MT)
	127.981-*2-000001 onwards (AT)

Notes: Used in the 230SL from March 1963 to January 1967. Some later catalogues (1966 onwards) and handbooks state a 9.5:1 c/r, although the author has been unable to identify a positive modification or date of change to verify this – one theory could be a mix-up with the contemporary saloons. Nonetheless, power and torque output was unchanged. The asterisk in the engine number should be either a '1' or '2' depending on the market.

Type 129.982 (M129 III)

Production (MY)	1967-1968
Cylinders	Straight-six, water-cooled
Main bearings	Seven, in cast-iron block
Valve operation	Sohc, 12v, in alloy head
Bore & stroke	82 x 78.8mm
Cubic capacity	2496cc (152cid)
Compression ratio	9.5:1
Fuel delivery system	Bosch fuel-injection
Power @ rpm	150bhp DIN @ 5500
	170bhp SAE @ 5600
Torque @ rpm	159lbft DIN @ 4200
	173lbft SAE @ 4500
Engine numbers	129.982-*0-000001 onwards (MT)
	129.982-*2-000001 onwards (AT)

Notes: Used in the 250SL from November 1966 to January 1968. The asterisk in the engine number should be either a '1' or '2' depending on the market.

Type 130.983 (M130)

Production (MY)	1968-1971
Cylinders	Straight-six, water-cooled
Main bearings	Seven, in cast-iron block
Valve operation	Sohc, 12v, in alloy head
Bore & stroke	86.5 x 78.8mm
Cubic capacity	2778cc (169cid)
Compression ratio	9.5:1
Fuel delivery system	Bosch fuel-injection
Power @ rpm	170bhp DIN @ 5750
	195bhp SAE @ 5900
Torque @ rpm	177lbft DIN @ 4500
	195lbft SAE @ 4700
Engine numbers	130.983-*0-000001 onwards (MT)
	130.983-*2-000001 onwards (AT)

Notes: Used in the 280SL from November 1967 to March 1971. US-spec versions produced 180bhp SAE at 5700rpm, and 193lbft of torque at 4500rpm. The asterisk in the engine number should be either a '1' or '2' depending on the market. Purely for information purposes, the later 107-series 280SL and 280SLC used a different engine (Type M110).

Appendix III: Colour & trim summary

A great deal of confusion exists with regard to standard paint colour names, and especially trim and upholstery designations, where the same moniker was often used for a different shade. Depending on the year, ordering material by name only could result in the wrong hue being supplied, and some countries used different names altogether, so this list should help those looking to restore a car to original specification.

Solid paint colours

No	Year info	German name	English name	Other names
040	1963-71	Schwarz	Black	-
050	1963-71	Weiss	White	-
158	1963-71	Weissgrau	White-Grey	-
173	1968-71	Anthrazitgrau	Anthracite Grey	-
181	1963-71	Hellbeige	Light Beige	-
190	1963-68	Graphitgrau	Graphite Grey	-
268	1963-71	Dunkelgrün	Dark Green	Blue-Green
291	1965-71	Dunkelolive	Dark Olive	Dark Olive Green
304	1968-71	Horizontblau	Horizon Blue	-
332	1963-68	Dunkelblau	Dark Blue	-
350	1968-71	Mittelblau	Medium Blue	-
423	1968-71	Tabakbraun	Tobacco Brown	Dark Tobacco Brown
460	1963-71	Dunkelrotbraun	Dark Red-Brown	Dark Maroon
501	1965-68	Rot	Red	Maroon
542	1965-71	Dunkelrot	Dark Red	-
568	1963-71	Signalrot	Signal Red	-
573	1963-65	Dunkelbordeauxrot	Dark Bordeaux Red	Dark Burgundy
576	1968-71	Rot	Red	-
658	1963-64	Elfenbein	Ivory	Radiant Ivory
670	1963-71	Hellelfenbein	Light Ivory	-
716	1967-68	Graubeige	Grey-Beige	Prairie Beige, Sand Beige
717	1963-71	Papyrusweiss	Papyrus White	Off-White
726	1968-71	Beigegrau	Beige-Grey	-
903	1968-71	Blau	Blue	-
904	1968-71	Dunkelblau	Dark Blue	Midnight Blue

Metallic paint colours

No	Year info	German name	English name	Other names
172	1963-71	Anthrazitgrau	Anthracite Grey	-
178	1964-68	Mittelgrau	Medium Grey	-
180	1963-71	Silbergrau	Silver-Grey	-
387	1963-71	Blau	Blue	-
396	1964-68	Mittelblau	Medium Blue	-
461	1964-71	Bronzebraun	Bronze-Brown	-
462	1963-71	Beige	Beige	Tunis Beige
463	1964-68	Kupfer	Copper	-
467	1968-71	Whisky	Whisky	Whisky Beige
567	1963-68	Lasurrot	Varnish Red	Blazing Maroon
571	1963-71	Rot	Red	Brilliant Red
728	1968-71	Beigegrau	Beige-Grey	-
834	1963-71	Moosgrün	Moss Green	-
906	1968-71	Blau (Graublau)	Blue	Grey-Blue

Additional hardtop colours

No	Year info	German name	English name	Other names
162	1963-68	Blaugrau	Blue-Grey	-
408	1963-68	Havanna-braun	Havanna Brown	-

Hood options

No	Year info	German name	English name	Other names
720	1963-68	Schwarz	Black	-
721	1965-67	Grün	Green	-
723	1963-68	Marineblau	Marine Blue	-
725	1963-68	Créme	Cream	-
727	1964-68	Weissgrau	White-Grey	-
728	1964-67	Braunbeige	Brown-Beige	-
730	1963-68	Beige	Beige	-
732	1963-68	Grau	Grey	Dark Grey
736	1963-68	Hellgrau	Light Grey	-
737	1963-68	Braun	Brown	-
740	1968-71	Schwarz	Black	-
741	1968-71	Dunkelgrau	Dark Grey	-
742	1968-71	Hellgrau	Light Grey	-
743	1968-71	Pergament	Parchment	-
744	1968-71	Dunkelblau	Dark Blue	Blue
745	1968-71	Beige	Beige	-
746	1968-71	Dunkelbraun	Dark Brown	Brown
747	1968-71	Dunkelgrün	Dark Green	-

Vinyl trim

No	Year info	German name	English name	Other names
112	1963-68	Türkis	Turquoise	-
113	1963-68	Bronze	Bronze	Bronze-Brown
114	1963-68	Naturfarben Hell	Natural (Light)	-
115	1963-68	Dunkelblau	Dark Blue	-
116	1963-68	Kaviar	Caviar	Black
117	1963-68	Rot	Red	-
118	1963-68	Hellgrau	Light Grey	Grey (1966 on)
119	1963-68	Weissgrau	White-Grey	-
120	1963-68	Cognac	Cognac	-
121	1963-68	Créme	Cream	Light Cream
122	1964-68	Hellrot	Light Red	-
123	1964-68	Mittelblau	Medium Blue	-
124	1964-68	Grün	Green	-
131	1968-71	Schwarz	Black	-
132	1968-71	Rot	Red	-
133	1968-71	Hellrot	Light Red	-
134	1968-71	Grün	Green	-
135	1968-71	Blau	Blue	-
136	1968-71	Grau (#7000)	Grey	-
137	1968-71	Grau (#7000)	Grey	-
138	1968-71	Dunkelbraun	Dark Brown	-
139	1968-71	Bambus	Bamboo	-
140	1968-71	Cognac	Cognac	-
141	1968-71	Beige	Beige	-
144	1968-71	Pergament (#8014)	Parchment	-
145	1968-71	Pergament (#8014)	Parchment	-
146	1968-71	Pergament (#8014)	Parchment	-
147	1968-71	Pergament (#8014)	Parchment	-

Leather trim

No	Year info	German name	English name	Other names
201	1963-68	Schwarz	Black	-
202	1963-68	Rot (#641)	Red	-
203	1963-68	Rot (#1079)	Red	-
204	1963-68	Hellrot	Light Red	-
205	1963-68	Blau	Blue	-
206	1963-68	Mittelblau	Medium Blue	-
207	1963-68	Hellgrau	Light Grey	-
209	1963-68	Créme	Cream	Light Cream
210	1963-68	Naturfarben	Natural	-
211	1963-68	Dunkelgrün	Dark Green	-
212	1963-68	Resedagrün	Reseda Green	-
213	1963-68	Hellgelb Antik	Antique Yellow	Antique Light Yellow
214	1963-68	Rostrot	Rust Red	Russet
216	1963-68	Cognac	Cognac	Light Cognac
217	1963-68	Türkis	Turquoise	Light Turquoise
218	1963-68	Bronze	Bronze	Light Bronze
219	1963-68	Naturfarben Hell	Natural (Light)	-
220	1963-68	Dunkelblau	Dark Blue	-
221	1963-68	Weissgrau	White-Grey	-
222	1963-68	Weinrot	Wine Red	-
223	1963-68	Mittelgrau	Medium Grey	-
224	1963-68	Hellolive	Light Olive	-
230	1963-68	Eierschalen	Eggshell	-
231	1963-68	Anthrazitgrau	Anthracite Grey	-
232	1963-68	Braun	Brown	-
241	1968-71	Schwarz	Black	-
242	1968-71	Rot	Red	-
243	1968-71	Hellrot	Light Red	-
244	1968-71	Grün	Green	-
245	1968-71	Blau	Blue	-
246	1968-71	Grau (#7000/7049)	Grey	-
247	1968-71	Grau (#7000/7049)	Grey	-
248	1968-71	Dunkelbraun	Dark Brown	-
249	1968-71	Bambus	Bamboo	-
250	1968-71	Cognac	Cognac	-
251	1968-71	Beige	Beige	-
254	1968-71	Pergament (#8014)	Parchment	-
255	1968-71	Pergament (#8014)	Parchment	-
256	1968-71	Pergament (#8014)	Parchment	-
257	1968-71	Pergament (#8014)	Parchment	-

Cockpit from one of the very first 280SLs.

Carpet

No	Year info	German name	English name	Other names
3004	1968-71	Rot	Red	-
3008	1968-71	Hellrot	Light Red	-
5003	1968-71	Blau	Blue	-
6002	1968-71	Dunkelgrün	Dark Green	-
6117	1963-68	Graphitgrau	Graphite Grey	-
6125	1963-68	Schwarz	Black	-
6131	1963-68	Anthrazitgrau	Anthracite Grey	-
6143	1963-68	Dunkelgrau	Dark Grey	-
6213	1963-68	Grün	Green	-
6218	1963-68	Türkis	Turquoise	-
6314	1963-68	Blau	Blue	-
6434	1963-68	Créme	Cream	-
6454	1963-68	Braun	Brown	-
6508	1963-68	Rostrot	Rust Red	-
6509	1963-68	Mittelrot	Medium Red	-
6510	1963-68	Weinrot	Wine Red	-
7006	1968-71	Dunkelgrau	Dark Grey	-
8003	1968-71	Beige	Beige	-
8008	1968-71	Braun	Brown	-
8015	1968-71	Dunkelbraun	Dark Brown	-

Appendix IV: Option codes

This is an overview of the codes used by the factory to describe optional equipment. In reality, there are many others, but those listed here cover the vast majority of those encountered on the W113-series cars. For ease of reference, they have been listed firstly in numerical order, and then broken down by category and/or purpose, with notes added for clarification whenever necessary.

Overview

No.	Option
212	Alternative rear axle ratio
215	Uprated springs
217	Mobile phone
222	First aid kit
224	Luggage compartment light
226	Tinted glass
227	Tinted glass
228	Tinted glass
229	Tinted glass
230	Five-speed manual gearbox
232	Alternative rear axle ratio
246	Heated rear screen
248	Heated rear screen
249	Heated rear screen
250	Mobile phone
254	Model designation removal
255	Alternative rear axle ratio
256	Limited-slip differential
260	Model designation removal
267	Mobile phone
269	Roof-rack
273	Mobile phone
279	Manual aerial
280	Fitted suitcases
281	Fitted suitcases
282	Fitted suitcases
283	Fitted suitcases
288	Tonneau cover
289	Ski-rack
291	Suitcase
292	Suitcase
293	Suitcase
294	Hat box
295	Vanity case
297	Luggage straps
298	Luggage straps
305	Viscous-coupled fan
315	Hazard warning lights
319	Hardtop (or soft-top) carrier
345	Foglamps
410	Sunroof
411	Sunroof
414	Hardtop
415	Hardtop
416	Hardtop
417	Hardtop
420	Automatic gearbox
422	Power-assisted steering
424	Four-speed manual gearbox
426	Automatic gearbox plus PAS
429	Five-speed manual gearbox plus PAS
431	Seatbelts
434	Seatbelts
440	Bumper guards
441	Bumper guards
451	Laminated front windscreen
462	Rear foglight
463	Hazard warning lights
472	Oil bath air filter assembly
473	Low-compression engine
482	Uprated suspension
492	Uprated heater
493	Uprated heater
502	Outside door mirror
503	Outside door mirror
506	Outside door mirrors
507	Outside door mirror
508	Outside door mirror
509	Outside door mirrors
510	Becker Mexico Olympia radio/cassette
511	Becker Mexico radio
513	Becker Europa Stereo radio
514	Becker Europa radio
515	Becker Europa radio
516	Becker Grand Prix radio
518	Becker Europa Stereo radio
519	Becker Grand Prix radio
531	Automatic aerial
532	Automatic aerial
533	Suppressor kit
534	Manual aerial
550	Tow-bar
551	Ivory-coloured steering wheel
565	Transverse rear seat
571	Headrest
572	Headrest
573	Headrests
582	Air conditioning
591	Foglamps
593	Tinted glass
594	Tinted glass
596	Tinted glass
597	Tinted glass
600	Chrome strips for hardtop
618	Halogen headlights
622	'D' emblem
630	Radial tyres
631	First aid kit
633	Warning triangle
640	Alloy wheels
640	Tyres with inner tubes
641	Whitewall tyres
642	Whitewall tyres on alloy rims
645	Winter tyres
680	'D' emblem
682	Fire extinguisher
835	Coconut floormats
836	Fire extinguisher
875	Spotlights
–	Metallic paint
–	Two-tone paint
–	Leather trim

199

And here are the same options, this time split by category for easy reference:

Drivetrain & chassis

No	Option	Notes
473	Low-compression engine	-
472	Oil bath air filter assembly	-
305	Viscous-coupled fan	-
424	Four-speed manual gearbox	-
230	Five-speed manual gearbox	-
420	Automatic gearbox	-
212	Alternative rear axle ratio	3.92:1 version
232	Alternative rear axle ratio	4.08:1 version
255	Alternative rear axle ratio	3.69:1 version
256	Limited-slip differential	-
422	Power-assisted steering	-
215	Uprated springs	Regular suspension upgrade
482	Uprated suspension	Earliest cars only
640	Alloy wheels	Code applied in 280SL era
630	Radial tyres	-
640	Tyres with inner tubes	Code applied in 230SL era
641	Whitewall tyres	-
642	Whitewall tyres on alloy rims	-
645	Winter tyres	-

Body

No	Option	Notes
-	Metallic paint	-
-	Two-tone paint	-
414	Hardtop	Supplied separately, with soft-top
415	Hardtop	Hardtop only, without a soft-top
416	Hardtop	Supplied fitted to car, with soft-top
417	Hardtop	'California Roadster' specification, complete with rear bench seat
246	Heated rear screen	Safety glass
248	Heated rear screen	Regular glass
249	Heated rear screen	Tinted glass
410	Sunroof	Electrical operation
411	Sunroof	Manual opration
600	Chrome strips for hardtop	To allow roof-racks to be fitted
319	Hardtop (or soft-top) carrier	-
288	Tonneau cover	For California Roadster
451	Laminated front windscreen	-
226	Tinted glass	Front screen and side panes (early)
227	Tinted glass	Hardtop glass (early)
228	Tinted glass	Side panes and hardtop glass (early)
229	Tinted glass	Front screen
593	Tinted glass	Hardtop glass (late)
594	Tinted glass.	Front screen and side panes (late)
596	Tinted glass.	Side panes and hardtop glass (late)
597	Tinted glass.	All glass (front, side and rear)
502	Outside door mirror	Right-hand side
503	Outside door mirror	Left-hand side
506	Outside door mirrors	Both sides
507	Outside door mirror	Right-hand side
508	Outside door mirror	Left-hand side
509	Outside door mirrors	Both sides
440	Bumper guards	ROW version
441	Bumper guards	US version
254	Model designation removal	Removal of 'Automatic' badge
260	Model designation removal	Removal of model type badge

Lighting

No	Option	Notes
618	Halogen headlights	European market
591	Foglamps	Early version, white lens
345	Foglamps	Halogen type, round units
875	Spotlights	-
462	Rear foglight	-
463	Hazard warning lights	ROW version
315	Hazard warning lights	US version
224	Luggage compartment light	-

Interior

No	Option	Notes
-	Leather trim	-
431	Seatbelts	ROW version
434	Seatbelts	US version
572	Headrest	Left-hand side
571	Headrest	Right-hand side
573	Headrests	Both sides
565	Transverse rear seat	-
551	Ivory-coloured steering wheel	-
582	Air conditioning	US market
492	Uprated heater	ROW version
493	Uprated heater	US version
835	Coconut floormats	-

Audio

No	Option	Notes
511	Becker Mexico radio	MU bands, later LMKU
510	Becker Mexico Olympia	Stereo radio/cassette
514	Becker Europa radio	LMU bands, later LMKU
515	Becker Europa radio	AM/FM bands for USA
518	Becker Europa Stereo	Radio with LMKU bands
513	Becker Europa Stereo	For US market
516	Becker Grand Prix radio	LMU bands, later LMKU
519	Becker Grand Prix radio	For US market
279	Manual aerial	Without radio supplied (early)
534	Manual aerial	Without radio supplied (late)
531	Automatic aerial	With radio supplied
532	Automatic aerial	Without radio supplied
533	Suppressor kit	Without radio supplied
-	Audio preparation	Without radio supplied

Luggage

No	Option	Notes
269	Roof-rack	Hardtop mounting
289	Ski-rack	Hardtop mounting
280	Fitted suitcases	Three pieces in set
281	Fitted suitcases	Four pieces in set
282	Fitted suitcases	Three pieces for California Roadster
283	Fitted suitcases	Four pieces for California Roadster
291	Suitcase	Large
292	Suitcase	Medium
293	Suitcase	Small
294	Hat box	-
295	Vanity case	-
297	Luggage straps	For luggage compartment
298	Luggage straps	For California Roadster rear seat.

Miscellaneous

No	Option	Notes
222	First aid kit	Early version
631	First aid kit	Late version
633	Warning triangle	-
622	'D' emblem	Early version
680	'D' emblem	Late version
836	Fire extinguisher	Early version
682	Fire extinguisher	Late version
550	Tow-bar	-
250	Mobile phone	Becker model (early)
217	Mobile phone	Becker model (late)
267	Mobile phone	TeKaDe model (early)
273	Mobile phone	TeKaDe model (late)

Appendix V:
Chassis numbers & production figures

Chassis numbers
Early body codes and chassis start numbers for each model:

Model	MY	Body Code	Chassis No.
230SL	1963-67	W113	113.042-**-000001 onwards
250SL	1967-68	W113A	113.043-**-000001 onwards
280SL	1968-71	W113.E28	113.044-**-000001 onwards

Note: Chassis numbers started with the six-figure chassis code to differentiate model types, and were followed by a '1' for left-hand drive steering or '2' for right-hand drive steering, a '0' for manual cars or '2' for automatics following this, then a six-figure serial number to tie-in with the build sequence.

Chassis numbers at year-end
A rough guide to when vehicles were built via their chassis numbers. The last chassis number allocated for each year is shown, along with the final chassis number for each model type:

230SL
End of 1963	001561
End of 1964	008498
End of 1965	014779
End of 1966	019737
Final number	019832

250SL
End of 1966	000024
Final number	005196

280SL
End of 1967	000256
End of 1968	007114
End of 1969	015169
End of 1970	023111
Final number	023885

Note: Although the build numbers and chassis numbers tie-up on 250SL and 280SL, they do not on the 230SL – the final chassis number is one higher than the official build figure.

Production figures

A table showing a summary of the annual production for the W113 SL models, followed by yearly totals and export numbers for all three types:

Year	230SL	250SL	280SL	Total	Exports
1963	1465	-	-	1465	693
1964	6911	-	-	6911	3326
1965	6325	-	-	6325	3663
1966	4945	17	-	4962	3675
1967	185	5177	143	5505	4187
1968	-	2	6930	6932	5302
1969	-	-	8047	8047	6249
1970	-	-	7935	7935	6462
1971	-	-	830	830	558

Total 230SL models built 19,831
Total 230SL models exported 11,726 (4752 of which, to the USA)
Total 250SL models built 5196
Total 250SL models exported 3808 (1761 of which, to the USA)
Total 280SL models built 23,885
Total 280SL models exported 18,581 (12,927 of which, to the USA)

Total W113-series models built 48,912
Total W113-series models exported 34,115 (19,440 of which, to the USA)

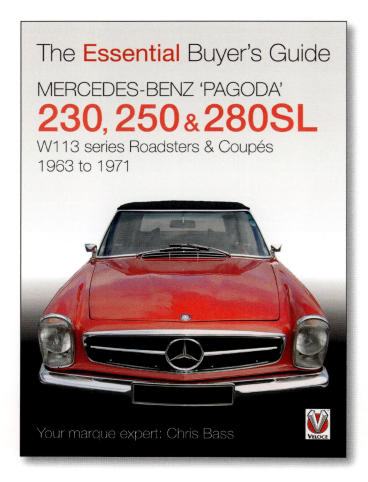
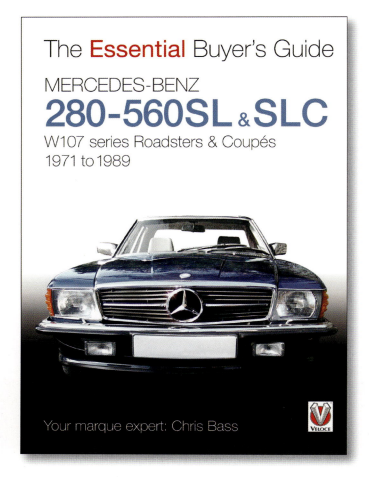

ISBN: 978-1-845841-13-3
Paperback • 19.5x13.9cm • £9.99* UK/$19.95* USA
• 64 pages • 122 colour pictures

ISBN: 978-1-845841-07-2
Paperback • 19.5x13.9cm • £9.99* UK/$19.95* USA
• 64 pages • 100 colour pictures

STOP! Don't buy a Mercedes-Benz 230-560SL or SLC without buying this book first! Having this book in your pocket is just like having a real marque expert by your side. Benefit from Chris Bass' years of Mercedes ownership: learn how to spot a bad car quickly and how to assess a promising one like a professional. Get the right car at the right price. Packed with good advice from running costs, through paperwork, vital statistics, valuation and the Mercedes community, to will it fit in your garage and with your lifestyle? This is the complete guide to choosing, assessing and buying your dream car.

For more info on Veloce titles, visit our website at www.veloce.co.uk • email: info@veloce.co.uk • Tel: +44(0)1305 260068
* prices subject to change, p&p extra

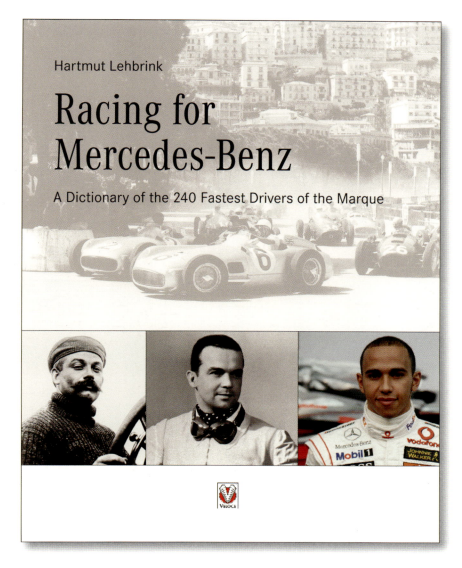

ISBN: 978-1-845840-44-0
Hardback • 27x21.5cm • £35.00* UK/$69.95* USA • 256 pages • 350 pictures

Of the vast number of drivers who have competed for Mercedes-Benz and its ancestors in the past 115 years, famous and obscure, the 240 fastest are examined in this volume. A unique insight into some of the quickest drivers the world has ever seen.

For more info on Veloce titles, visit our website at www.veloce.co.uk • email: info@veloce.co.uk • Tel: +44(0)1305 260068
* prices subject to change, p&p extra

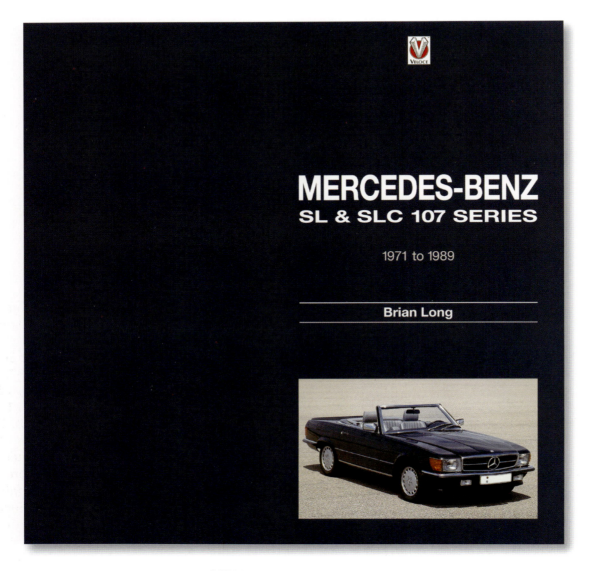

MERCEDES-BENZ
SL & SLC 107 SERIES

1971 to 1989

Brian Long

ISBN: 978-1-845842-99-4
Hardback • 25x25cm • £35.00* UK/$69.99* USA • 208 pages • 355 colour and b&w pictures

This detailed and beautifully illustrated book covers the Mercedes-Benz 107-series, which ran from 1971 to 1989. Written by a highly regarded motoring writer, with many years ownership of the Mercedes SL and SLC in question behind him, this is the definitive study of the subject.

For more info on Veloce titles, visit our website at www.veloce.co.uk • email: info@veloce.co.uk • Tel: +44(0)1305 260068
* prices subject to change, p&p extra

Index

Aaltonen, Rauno 111
AC 88, 171, 172
ACO 24
Acropolis Rally 111, 112
Adenauer, Konrad 95
Ahrens, Hermann 37
Alfa Romeo 78, 84, 101, 171
Algiers-Cape Rally 90
AMC 169
AMG 64
Aston Martin 106, 154
Audi 55
Austin-Healey 94, 111, 116
Australian Motor Sports 117
Austro-Daimler 13
Auto Union 24, 55
Autocar 46, 80, 88, 114, 116-117, 155, 181
Autosport 46, 61, 94

Barbarou, Marius 13
Barenyi, Bela 67-68, 74
Benz & Cie. 10, 14-16, 24
Benz & Co. 8, 10
Benz, Bertha 8
Benz, Carl 8-10, 13
Benz, Clara 8
Benz, Ellen 8

Benz, Eugen 8, 10
Benz, Richard 8, 10
Benz, Thilde 8
Berlin Motor Show 13
Berne GP 26
Bertone 84
BMW 55, 69, 134
Boddy, William 117
Böhringer, Eugen 90, 91, 94, 110-112
Bolster, John 46, 55
Bosch 69, 80
Bracq, Paul 69, 71
Brandt, Willy 175
Braungart, Martin 110, 111
Brussels Show 160

C Benz Söhne 10
Cahier, Bernard 88, 90
Car 133
Car & Driver 55, 88, 89, 135, 149
Car Graphic 106
Carlsson, Eric 94, 111
Carraciola, Rudolf 18, 25, 26
Carrera Panamericana 29-32
Castrol 46
Chevrolet 67, 170

Citroën 69, 94, 111, 112
Continental AG 82, 83

Daetwyler, Willie 26
Daimler (DMG) 8, 9, 11, 12, 16, 24, 170
Daimler (UK) 11
Daimler, Gottlieb 8-10
Daimler, Paul 9, 12
Dethleffs 106
Deutsche Bank 15
Deutz 9-10
DKW 55
Doehler, Bob 46
Douglas-Home, Alex 106
Dunlop 60

Earls Court Show 106
Erhard, Ludwig 95
Erle, Fritz 14
European GP 14

Fangio, Juan-Manuel 44, 119, 150
Ferrari 25, 26, 28, 45, 90, 149
Fiat 78, 84, 133
Firestone 83

Fitch, John 30, 32, 33, 44
Fleener, Lon 102
Ford 94
Frankfurt Show 22, 35, 51, 85-87, 90, 95, 97, 98, 120, 124, 173, 174, 177, 184, 190
Frua 118, 172

Gallitzendörfer, Joseph 184
Gasmotorenfabrik Mannheim 10
Geiger, Eugen 30, 32
Geiger, Friedrich 56, 67, 69, 71, 69, 184
Gendebien, Olivier 44
Geneva Show 47, 48, 56, 64, 78, 80, 84-87, 99, 105, 106, 134, 135, 137, 160, 177, 187
German GP 17, 18, 28, 30
Getrag 80, 166
Glemser, Dieter 110-112
Golde 177
Grupp, Erwin 25, 30
Gunzler, Rainer 90

Häcker, Walter 37, 47

207

Heath, Edward 180
Helfrich, Theo 28
Henry of Prussia, Prince 15
Hockenheim 158, 160
Hoffman, Max 20, 34, 56
Horch 55
Hoskins, Bob 180
Howard, Geoffrey 155
Huber, Guntram 67

Import Car Show 106
Inomoto, Yoshihiro 37
International Motor Sports Show 34, 36
Italian GP 66

Jaguar 21, 28, 67, 78, 84, 106, 116, 151, 154, 170-172
Jellinek, Emil 11, 12
Johnson, Lyndon 104

Kaiser, Klaus 90, 94, 110-112
Kennedy, John F 104
Klenk, Hans 25, 27, 28, 30, 31
Kling, Alfred 110
Kling, Karl 25-28, 30, 31, 44, 90, 92
Kobayashi, Shotaro 106
Kreder, Rolf 110
Kurrle, Ernst 25

Lancia 112
Lang, Hermann 18, 25, 28, 30
Le Mans 21, 24, 26-28, 30, 43
Levegh, Pierre 28
Liège-Rome-Liège Rally 45, 91
Lindner, Peter 95

Loren, Sophia 38
Lotus 171-172
Lyons, William 154

Macmillan, Harold 106
Mairesse, Willy 46
Marcos 171, 172
Masetti, Count Giulio 12
Maybach 9
Maybach, Wilhelm 9, 12
Mazda (Toyo Kogyo) 154
Mercédès 11-13, 16, 24
Michelotti 84
Mille Miglia 21, 25, 43, 150
MIRA 117
Moll, Rolf 46
Monthoux 88, 89
Monza 14
Morgan 106
Moss, Stirling 23, 44, 119
Motor 64, 80, 117, 133, 171
Motor Revue 88
Motor Trend 54, 170
MotorSport 105, 106, 117

Nader, Ralph 151
Nallinger, Fritz 34, 43, 66, 67, 71, 80, 87, 90, 128
National 134
National Geographic 108, 171
Neubauer, Alfred 18, 21, 23-25, 28, 43
Nibel, Hans 15
Niedermayr, Helmut 28
Nissan (Datsun) 67
Nixon, Richard 170
NSU 55
Nürburgring 17, 28, 30, 78

O'Shea, Paul 45, 60
Otto, N A 9

Packard 104, 114
Panhard & Levassor 9
Paris-Rouen Race 170
Paris Match 150
Paris Salon 20, 22, 30, 118, 188
Parkes, Mike 89
Peter Lindner Automobile 95
Peugeot 170
Phoenix AG 83
Pininfarina 84, 118
Pontiac 88
Porsche 20, 24, 55, 78, 89, 106, 138, 151, 154, 170-172, 181
Porsche, Ferdinand 13, 17, 24, 55
Prince Henry Trials 14

Rheims 43
Riess, Fritz 28
Road & Track 24, 44, 60, 88, 132, 169-170, 179
Road Test 149, 170, 180
Rolls-Royce 114
Rosquist, Ewy 110
Rumpler, Dr Edmund 14

Saab 94, 111-112
SCCA 45, 60
Scherenberg, Hans 38, 66, 128, 184
Schiek, Manfred 110
Schock, Walter 46
Seaman, Richard 18
Seiffert, Reinhard 66
Setright, L.J.K. 134
Simms, F.R. 9, 11
Spa 46
Spa-Sofia-Liege Rally 90-91, 94, 110-112
Sports Car Graphic 88, 150

Sports Car Illustrated 55
Springer, Axel 118
Steyr 67
Studebaker 46, 104, 114
Swedish GP 44

Talbot-Lago 28
Targa Florio 12, 21
Teves, Alfred 84
The Long Good Friday 180
Tjaarda, Tom 118
Tosen, Jim 172
Tour de France Automobile 45
Toyota 181
Tripoli GP 24
Triumph 116, 151, 171
Tuckey, Bill 117
Turin Show 118

Uhlenhaut, Rudy 22-24, 66, 68, 82, 87, 89-90
Unsafe At Any Speed 151

Volkswagen 24, 55, 154
Volvo 112
Von Brauchitsch, Manfred 18

Walker, Rob 38
Wanderer 55
Waxenberger, Erich 78, 86
Webasto 177
Weber, Andreas 78, 137
Wente, Adolf 158
Wheels 172
Whitten, John 24-25
Wilfert, Karl 67-68, 71, 73
Wilhelm II, Kaiser 15
Wilkins, Gordon 89
Wilson, Harold 114
Woron, Walt 54-55

Zeppelin 9

Mercedes-Benz and Daimler-Benz, along with its subsidiaries and products, are mentioned throughout the book.